Symbiotic Autoethnography

Also available from Bloomsbury

Embodied Inquiry, Jennifer Leigh and Nicole Brown
Narrative Inquiry, Vera Caine, D. Jean Clandinin and Sean Lessard
Diary Method, Ruth Bartlett and Christine Milligan
Community Studies, Graham Crow
Inclusive Research, Melanie Nind
Quantitative Longitudinal Data Analysis, Vernon Gayle and Paul Lambert
Rhythmanalysis, Dawn Lyon
Qualitative Longitudinal Research, Bren Neale

Symbiotic Autoethnography

Moving Beyond the Boundaries of Qualitative Methodologies

Liana Beattie

BLOOMSBURY ACADEMIC
LONDON • NEW YORK • OXFORD • NEW DELHI • SYDNEY

BLOOMSBURY ACADEMIC
Bloomsbury Publishing Plc
50 Bedford Square, London, WC1B 3DP, UK
1385 Broadway, New York, NY 10018, USA
29 Earlsfort Terrace, Dublin 2, Ireland

BLOOMSBURY, BLOOMSBURY ACADEMIC and the Diana logo are
trademarks of Bloomsbury Publishing Plc

First published in Great Britain 2022
Paperback edition published 2024

For legal purposes the Acknowledgements on p. xii constitute an
extension of this copyright page.

Cover design: Charlotte James
Cover image © Paper Boat Creative/Getty Images

A catalogue record for this book is available from the British Library.

A catalog record for this book is available from the Library of Congress.

ISBN: HB: 978-1-3502-0138-5
PB: 978-1-3502-0163-7
ePDF: 978-1-3502-0160-6
eBook: 978-1-3502-0161-3

Typeset by Newgen KnowledgeWorks Pvt. Ltd., Chennai, India

To find out more about our authors and books visit www.bloomsbury.com
and sign up for our newsletters.

To my partner Gary and my daughter Tammy
without whom this book would not have been possible.

Contents

Figures

Author's Biography

Liana Beattie is associate head of department at Edge Hill University, UK.

Liana.Beattie@edgehill.ac.uk

Liana gained her doctorate at the University of Chester for her autoethnographic research into how academics with Soviet background construct their perceptions of educational leadership at a contemporary UK university. Liana's research interests are, mainly, around the issues of educational leadership, autoethnography and creative approaches to qualitative inquiry, and she has a number of publications that reflect these key themes. She tweets as @LianaBeattie and @SymbioticAutoe1

Preface

In one of his greatest novels, 'War and Peace', Tolstoy (1869) inferred that history was not shaped by the actions of individual leaders but by the alignments of different forms of power, arising from shared ideology of groups of people coupled with specific historical circumstances of that epoch. In Tolstoy's view, Napoleon was merely engaging in the performance of power rather than leading the course of history, as events unfolded not as a sole result of his actions but as a product of multifaceted sociocultural and political contexts as well as the values, beliefs and aspirations of people under his command. Yet, Tolstoy's noteworthy ideas, essentially, congealed not from his descriptive historical chronicles of Napoleon's invasion of Russia but through his characters' individual narratives – the stories told by people from five Russian aristocratic families. It was that exploratory capacity of personal stories in amalgamation with the issues of power and sociopolitical structures that determined the original investigative direction of my doctoral study, which triggered my interest in autoethnographic approach. Specifically, the aim of my doctoral research was to use my autoethnographic story to make sense of how academics with Soviet background construct their perceptions of educational leadership at a contemporary UK university. And so, this book originated from my autoethnographic research focused on my experiences of transition from Soviet totalitarianism to the neoliberal condition of the UK. In particular, the diversities, contradictions and parallels of my encounters with various autoethnographic approaches piqued my ambition to find my own way through the density of theoretical perspectives on the subject. In this endeavour I allowed myself a degree of departure from the dominant autoethnographic perspectives towards, what I called, Symbiotic Autoethnography. Here, I used a biological concept of symbiosis in its broader sense as denoting a close, prolonged and mutually beneficial association between two or more different objects or notions based on widely varying types of interconnection (Miller, 1994; Dimijian, 2000). In constructing a symbiotic approach, I have resisted any temptation to offer another canonical framework, as I myself have been apprehensive of researchers' attempts to tidy up the disarray of autoethnographic approaches into one neat structure. Thus, my approach is based on the view of autoethnography as a fluid and adaptable amalgamation of multiple tumultuous features, which are not pressed into a bonding mortar like mosaic pieces but rather float like droplets of oil on a surface of water ready to be diffused, expanded, melded or dislocated at any moment in time.

Like air, stories are omnipresent. We make sense of the world around us by telling stories. The narratives created by these stories infiltrate our lives, our thoughts, our experiences, as well as the global systems of power, politics and education. They are an irreplaceable means of understanding our world. Every research study is also a story that goes beyond the parameters of its data to describe, explain and make sense of a phenomenon or an experience. Knowing the chemical levels of dopamine, serotonin and oxytocin in our brain does not help us understand what love is, and no naked data can explain why people cannot work together to build a better world. My autoethnographic research was also based on a story. Using a symbiotic approach in my autoethnographic story helped me to cope with complexities of autoethnographic data, allowing me to move beyond the conventional boundaries of qualitative methodologies, creating a new way of producing knowledge. I hope that this book on Symbiotic Autoethnography can also support fellow researchers in their future autoethnographic research projects across different disciplines and in different contexts. Nevertheless, I accept that the value of every book is defined by the judgements of its readers, and so, whilst I am hoping that this book can act as a stimulus to open new intellectual vistas, I am anxiously leaving it in the hands of the readers to let them have their final word.

Acknowledgements

I would like to thank the publisher's anonymous reviewers for their insightful comments on this manuscript as well as all those who contributed to the physical creation of this book. I am also grateful to Edge Hill University for providing me with time and space to complete this project. I would also like to express an immense gratitude to the members of the academic community, many of whom appear in the pages that follow. Without their wisdom and scholarly acumen, I would have been lost forever in this intellectual odyssey.

And finally, I owe a particular debt to my family and friends, who provided me with their continuous faithful support and encouragement.

Part 1

'De-mystifying' Autoethnography

1

What Is Autoethnography?

Introduction

From the day we are born, our worlds are filled with stories – stories that emerge from books, movies, pictures, photographs, conversations, fairy tales, legends, gossips and fables. Like air, these stories are omnipresent and indispensable, as they provide timeless connections between our histories, our cultures, our values and our knowledge about ourselves and the world around us. Our stories continuously merge, clash and intertwine with other stories, gradually fusing into narratives that invisibly infiltrate not just our thoughts, our experiences and our perceptions but the entire macro-fabrics of cultures, politics, economies and societal orders. In recent years, the paradoxes and controversies of such narratives exhibited themselves worldwide from the UK vote to leave the European Union to the election of Donald Trump as the president of the United States, from the rise of support for the right-wing parties in French, Italian and Hungarian elections to the establishment of authoritarian states, such as Putin's Russia and Erdoğan's Turkey. These events and developments bring the value of stories to the forefront of public inquiry, creating an opportunity for researchers to examine the impact of individual narratives on the context of current and emerging sociopolitical perspectives. Indeed, if we accept Reed-Danahay's (1997) widespread view that autoethnography is *a story* of the researcher's life and experiences, which combines auto- (self), -ethno- (the sociocultural connection) and -graphy (the process of writing the story), we can argue that autoethnography represents the most appropriate way of researching a social phenomenon through examining the researcher's personal experiences of that phenomenon. However, before going deeper into the debates about the existing definitions and purposes of autoethnography, I consider it useful to have a quick look at its origins.

A short historical overview

As the word 'autoethnography' suggests, this approach is closely associated with ethnography – a field of anthropology which focuses on exploring cultural practices and behaviours of the participants in their natural environments. Ethnographic studies spread their roots at the beginning of the twentieth century and were, mostly, associated with examining remote cultural groups and populations. The concept of ethnography presents an important aspect within the term 'autoethnography', linking the significance of cultural contexts back to traditions of early anthropological investigations. However, as the field evolved, these studies fell under increased scrutiny in terms of the Western researchers' prerogatives to make authoritative claims about 'exotic others'. These debates sparked a new interest within research circles towards the issues of researchers' subjectivity, motives and individual perceptions. Autoethnographic approach developed in response to these compulsions of social researchers to place more value onto the ethnographers' self-observations and self-reflections throughout their research studies. In the late 1950s, Mills (1959), convincingly, asserted that social scientists were not supposed to act as some autonomous beings, investigating the society from outside, but should place themselves at the centre of their intellectual work. Behar (1996) agrees that autoethnography emerged as a result of efforts by researchers to create an intermediate borderland between 'analysis and subjectivity, ethnography and autobiography, art and life' (p. 174). The outcome of that drive was twofold: first, it impelled the researchers to become full insiders within the communities and cultures being studied, and second, it added more rigour to the ways in which ethnographers interacted with the phenomena under investigation (Hayano, 1979; Holt, 2003; Bochner and Ellis, 2016). Thus, around the 1970s social scientists developed a stronger interest in exploring social phenomena from an insider researcher's perspective – that is, taken by a researcher who is a member of the community being studied – rather than an outsider perspective. Consequently, this has led social researchers towards the need to understand better the nature of their self-engagement with research topics, creating a fertile ground for incorporating their subjective self-reflective accounts into their research studies.

One of the first references to these kinds of subjective accounts as 'autoethnography' can be found in Heider's (1975) study of the Dani people of Western New Guinea, where he applied the term to the Dani schoolchildren's cultural accounts of themselves. Later on, Hayano (1979) also used the same term, when suggesting that ethnographers should research the cultures of their 'own people' as opposed to studying separate cultural groups 'as if they existed apart from other peoples or world economic and political forces' (p. 99). The next decade of the 1980s saw a general 'narrative turn' in the social sciences (Riessman, 2008), partially associated with the 'paradigm shift' that challenged existing established approaches to scientific research based on positivist quantitative traditions. This shift had a significant impact on further development of autoethnographic approach. Positivism was considered a prevailing research paradigm in social science from the beginning of the twentieth century with its main argument being that the world of experience was an objective world, and the role of the researchers was to find truth by eliminating any researchers' subjective judgements and interpretations. According to Sprague (2010, p. 79), 'positivism could be described as an epistemology of the fact'. Crotty (1998), helpfully, summarized the claims made by positivists as follows: 'Scientific knowledge is utterly objective and that only scientific knowledge is valid, certain and accurate' (p. 29). So, in simple terms, the ultimate aim of positivism was to adopt 'scientific' methods to uncover the laws that govern societies in the same way as scientists used those methods to discover the laws that govern the physical world. As these dominant positivist perceptions started to be gradually replaced by qualitative approaches, researchers began to prioritize 'the meanings people bring to situations and behaviour and which they use to understand their world' (O'Donoghue, 2007, p. 17). As Henn, Weinstein and Foard (2014) explain, social researchers had to acknowledge that they could only understand human behaviour if they were able to explore the subjective motives and intentions that underpinned human actions. Thus, ultimately, qualitative approaches to social research brought forward the idea that different individuals experienced and comprehended the same reality in very different ways and, in order to understand human action, researchers needed to see the world through the eyes of the actors doing the acting. This new-found emphasis of social sciences on personal and subjective perceptions and accounts resulted in renewed interest in personal narratives, autoethnographies and life histories, reaching worldwide popularity in the 1990s. As observed by Gannon (2017), during the late 1990s, autoethnography began to appear in its most recognizable form as a qualitative research methodology with its own established practices and principles. In 1996 Ellis and Bochner 'formalized' autoethnography as a new form of qualitative research, which contested traditional practices of ethnographic writing, bringing researchers' subjectivity to the forefront of their research inquiries.

Today, autoethnography has been widely acknowledged as an innovative, creative and rigorous approach that utilizes people's 'stories' to provide an epistemologically adequate template for reporting and assessing research within the context of a post-positivistic understanding of knowledge generation (Polkinghorne, 1997). Without any doubt, autoethnography has gained a firm position within the existing range of recognized approaches to qualitative studies. However, researchers' wide appreciation of this approach has also brought about a few controversies and disagreements about its definition and its purpose.

Defining autoethnography

Probably, the best way to start 'de-mystifying' autoethnography is to anchor its position within a wider spectrum of qualitative research. A brief look at the existing descriptions of 'autoethnography' reveals a general consensus amongst researchers (Denzin, 1989; Reed-Danahay, 1997; Ellis and Bochner, 2000; Chang, 2008; Trahar, 2009; Stanley and Vass, 2018; Grant, 2019; Sparkes, 2020) that autoethnography falls under a broad category of narrative research. Yet, this is as far as the conformity goes in relation to autoethnographic inquiry. Specifically, discussing definitional quandaries, Reed-Danahay (1997) warned us as early as in the 1990s that the term had already generated multiple meanings. Indeed, as a proof to that, Ellis and Bochner (2000), soon after, identified thirty-nine different types of research that indicated autoethnographic orientation and, thus, could, potentially, compete with each other in terms of their interpretation of the term. However, these early attempts to define autoethnography were not positioned within the 'omnibus spectrum' (Hayano, 1979, p. 103) of autoethnography as such, even though their studies contained specific autoethnographic features as we understand them today. An example of this can be found in Goldschmidt (1977), who did not use the term 'autoethnography', yet defining all types of ethnography as 'self-ethnography', arguing that all ethnographic representations privilege personal beliefs, perspectives and observations. This definition resonates convincingly with the very first 'official' reference to autoethnography by Hayano (1979), who described it as a type of research that involves researchers conducting and writing ethnographies of their 'own people' (p. 99). In terms of later definitions of autoethnography, Reed-Danahay (1997) defined it as a form of self-narrative that places the self within a social context, a point of view that was also supported by Denzin (1997), who emphasized that autoethnography involved the 'turning of the ethnographic gaze inward on the self (auto), while maintaining the outward gaze of ethnography, looking at the larger context wherein self-experiences occur' (p. 227). Scott-Hoy (2002) attempted to summarize these definitions by describing autoethnography as a genre of both writing and research, which emerged as a blend of ethnography and autobiographical writing that incorporated 'elements of one's own life experience when writing about others' (p. 276).

More recent definitions of autoethnography offer more variations to the earlier versions. For example, Denzin (2018) defines autoethnography as an account of one's life as an ethnographer, reflexively writing the self into and through the ethnographic text. O'Hara (2018) refers to autoethnographic writing as a method, which contextualizes experiences in cultural, social, political and personal history, whilst Griffin and Griffin (2019) add that autoethnography is a valuable and worthwhile research strategy that attempts to qualitatively and reflexively make sense of the self and society in an increasingly uncertain and precarious world. Adams and Herrmann (2020) reiterate the view of autoethnography as a fusion of three interrelated components: 'auto', 'ethno' and 'graphy', maintaining that 'autoethnographic projects use selfhood, subjectivity and personal experience ("auto") to describe, interpret and represent ("graphy") beliefs, practices and identities of a group or culture ("ethno")' (p. 2). Thus, we can see that the blend of personal, cultural and political represents the hallmark of autoethnography as an approach to a qualitative inquiry and yet, there is no one single definition that would bring unanimity into the ongoing definitional debates.

Multiplicity of autoethnographic approaches

Today, anybody who considers using autoethnography in their research is faced with a vast number of different approaches that could be both overwhelming and promising at the same time. Researchers' choice of any specific approach depends on the nature and purpose of their study as well as the researchers' view of the world and their personal preferences. Ellis and Bochner (2000) specify that these variations are determined by the level of emphasis on self and others in relation to the culture, as well as by the mode of analysis, the writing style and the type of relationships between researcher and participants. Thus, as noted by Denzin (2014), 'autoethnography can serve a different purpose across different projects and investigations' (p. 20). The emergence of various approaches to autoethnography can be traced in a number of recent publications.

Two of the most popular approaches that determined the direction of multiple contemporary studies include analytic (Anderson, 2006) and evocative (Ellis, 1997) autoethnographic practices, which will be discussed in more detail in Chapter 2. Richardson (2000a) suggested a Creative Analytical Practice (CAP) approach to autoethnography as defined by five criteria: (a) substantive contribution to our understanding of social life; (b) aesthetic merit of the text in terms of being artistically shaped and satisfyingly complex; (c) reflexivity as the author's subjectivity of both a producer and a product of the text; (d) impactfullness in terms of emotional and/or intellectual capacity of the text to generate new questions or move the reader to action; (e) expression of reality as a fleshed out lived experience. There are also critical autoethnographies (Holman Jones, 2016; Marx, Pennington and Chang, 2017; Stanley, 2020; Boylorn and Orbe, 2021), which focus on spotlighting powers behind social inequalities by situating researchers' personal experiences within the structures of wider political and sociocultural landscapes. Doloriert and Sambrook (2012) attempted to organize some of these approaches against three epistemological possibilities of autoethnography, creating three points of departure for autoethnographic studies to include: evocative interpretivist approach conveyed through the writing of emotional accounts, analytical approach where conceptual frameworks support autoethnographic process and, finally, a radical approach, where power relations presented the focus of the inquiry. Another popular strand within autoethnographic studies has been informed by performative approach. Within this range of studies, Denzin's (2018) concept of 'performance autoethnography' occupies a prominent place. According to Denzin (2018), it is a genre that blurs the meanings of ethnography, ethnographer and performance, obscuring separation between the writer, the ethnographer, the performer and the world and making the writer's self visible through performance writing. The same author also proposed an interpretive approach to autoethnography, which challenges autoethnographers to examine their personal experiences through interpreting them in the context of specific historical moments and cultures (Denzin, 2014). Sughrua (2019) offers us thirteen examples of autoethnographies as distinguished by the foci of their inquiry, amongst which are indigenous autoethnographies that rediscover an indigenous heritage as liberating (Houston, 2007; Whitinui, 2014; Parkes, 2015; Bhattacharya, 2020, 2021) and decolonial autoethnographies, where researchers write about their experiences of colonial powers (Diversi and Moreira, 2016; Sidhu, 2018; Osei, 2019). The range of research subjects also include autoethnographies, which explore researchers' experiences related to organizational issues (Doloriert and

Sambrook, 2012; Sambrook and Herrmann, 2018; Herrmann, 2020), racial and gender tensions (Goode, 2019; Orelus, 2020), as well as feminist perspectives (Ettorre, 2019; Peters, 2020; Chawla, 2021; Heath et al., 2022; Mackinlay, 2022) and Black feminist autoethnographies (Griffin 2012; Brown-Vincent, 2019; Williams, 2021).

In addition to the above-mentioned variations defined by the focus of the studies, autoethnographies also differ, depending on the number of researchers involved in their production. Chang, Nqunjiri and Hernandez (2013) specify a few of these varieties associated with multi-researcher autoethnographies to include duo-ethnography, co-ethnography, collective autoethnography and community autoethnography. Denzin (2018) explains that these approaches to autoethnographic writing move research projects into a dialogical space, where two or more autoethnographers merge their writing selves into multi-voiced performance autoethnographic texts. Collaborative autoethnographies, generally, involve several authors engaging in a joint process of writing and analysis (Allen-Collinson and Hockey, 2008; Bochner and Ellis, 2016; Roy and Uekusa, 2020; Martin and Garza, 2020). Chang, Nqunjiri and Hernandez (2013) explain that this type of autoethnographic research involves researchers sharing, in some manner, aspects of the research process, allowing through intersubjective processes, for example, communication and negotiation, the evaluation and challenging of views and assumptions. Duo-autoethnographies, as the name suggests, generally, involve two researchers, working alongside each other to write their individual stories and then joining their analytical accounts (Bochner and Ellis, 2016). Similarly to duo-autoethnography, a triple-autoethnographic performance evidences a process of three researchers collaboratively merging their stories into a performance text of collective sharing of experiences (Alexander, Moreira and Kumar, 2015). Within this range of approaches, we find a number of other innovative modes of performing autoethnography, some of which include exo-autoethnography (Denejkina, 2017), radiophonic autoethnography (Werner, 2017), speculative autoethno-satire (Heywood, 2020), visual autoethnography (Bleiker, 2019; Hunter, 2020), cyber or digital autoethnography (Atay, 2020) and, probably, a few other that are being written as I type these words.

All these diverse approaches and modes of writing do not, necessarily, form specific categories or fit any existing classifications. Every autoethnography is unique and can be perceived differently by the author and by its readers. Thus, any attempt to provide a rigid taxonomy of autoethnographic features and criteria is doomed to failure, since autoethnographies are like life itself, constantly moving, evolving and changing in its forms, purposes and contexts. As observed by Gannon (2017), these experimental modes of writing are important and particular to each project, as they demonstrate how autoethnography might be emboldened, politicized and shaken out of its habits.

Autoethnography within the narrative spectrum

The next question worth exploring is – how does autoethnography differ from similar genres of narrative research? Let us start this part of discussion with Denzin's (2018) observation that autoethnography can be easily confused with other terms, however, as he clarifies further:

> It is not: ethnography, autobiography, biography, personal narrative, personal history, life history, life story or personal experience story. It is not deeply theoretical. It is more than personal writing or cultural critique. It is more than performance. But it is performative. It is transgressive. It is resistance. It is dialogical. It is ethical. It is political, personal, embodied, collaborative, imaginative, artistic, creative, a form of intervention, a plea for social justice. (p. viii)

Though there are, certainly, multiple similarities between autoethnography and other types of narrative research, I focus here on only three approaches that seem to cause most confusion: ethnography, self-study and autobiography. Figure 1 provides a basic visual map of possible overlaps and differences between the three approaches.

Though the scope and purpose of this book would not allow a thorough engagement with all of the existing variations, I will attempt to 'de-mystify' a couple of potential uncertainties, starting with a differentiation between autoethnography and autobiography. Chang (2008) suggests that autobiography, as a type of narrative, along with autoethnography, memoirs and creative non-fiction, also involves storytelling; however, the main difference between autoethnography and autobiography is that the former is marked by the way it transcends mere narration of self to engage in cultural analysis and interpretation. Indeed, as pointed out by Ellis, Adams and Bochner (2010), what distinguishes autoethnography from autobiography is a purposeful focus on examining how these selected impactful moments 'stem from, or are made possible by, being part of a culture and/or by possessing a particular cultural identity' (p. 276). Both autobiographers and autoethnographers use

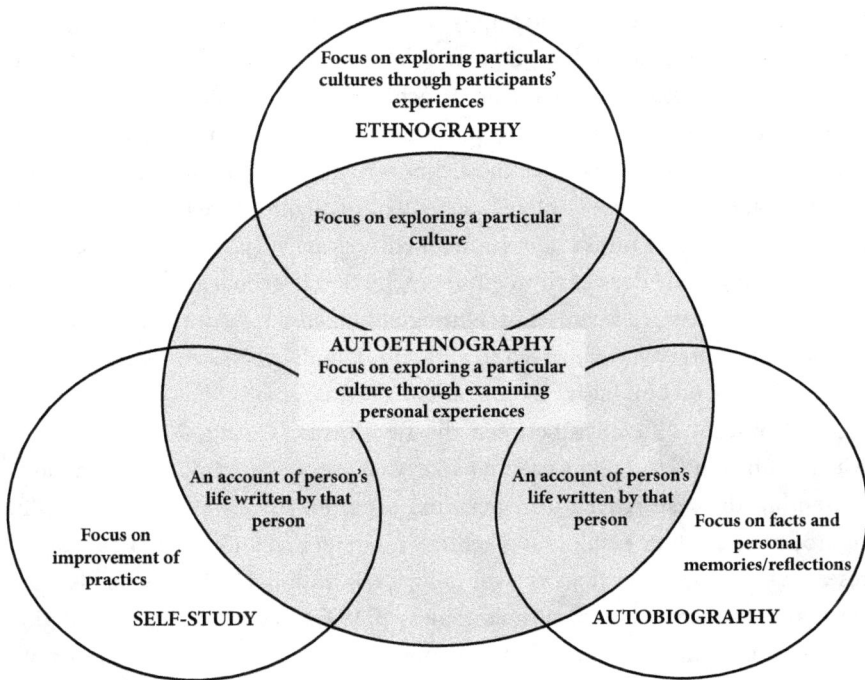

Figure 1 Autoethnography within the narrative spectrum.

first-person narration to tell a story based on their life experiences; however, autoethnographers engage with their stories in ways that broaden their (and their readers') understanding of specific cultures and societal groups they are embedded in, whereas autobiographers merely provide a retrospective account of their own life. So, similar to autoethnographies, autobiographies are a type of narrative written by the author about their life, where the author becomes the main character of the story. However, unlike autoethnography, autobiographers do not aim to examine and critique their social, cultural or political contexts through the lens of their personal experiences, which is the key characteristic feature of autoethnography. Yet, I have to acknowledge here that this is a somewhat simplified explication of the differences between the two genres, as in some examples, the actual demarcation line can become quite blurred and, at times, completely indetectable.

Let us move on now to the next area of potential confusion related to the differences between autoethnography and ethnography. In an attempt to identify a distinction here, I lean on Chang (2008), who provides a helpful analysis of the differences between ethnography and autoethnography, suggesting that, like ethnographers, autoethnographers follow a similar ethnographic research process of data collection and attempt to achieve cultural understanding through analysis and interpretation; however, autoethnographers use their personal experiences as primary data, so 'the richness of autobiographical narrative and autobiographical insights is valued and intentionally integrated in the research process and product unlike conventional ethnography' (p. 49). Thus, the genre of autoethnography derives from ethnography that is primarily concerned with studying the Other; however, whilst ethnography also emphasizes elements of the self, it is *the representations of self* in autoethnography versus the concentration *on the Other* (my emphasis) in conventional ethnography that epitomizes the most significant difference between the two forms (Chang, 2008). Similarly, Allen-Collinson (2012) suggests that a key feature of autoethnography involves presenting the researcher's own personal experiential narrative explicitly, 'in rigorous and analytic fashion as a central, fundamental and integral part of the research process, rather than as a subsidiary, confessional "aside", which is often the case with many "classic" ethnographies' (p. 194). As we can see, it is bringing the 'self' into the domain of ethnography that creates its distinction with autoethnography and whilst both ethnography and autoethnography reside in the domain of a narrative inquiry, in autoethnography, the individual's study of 'oneself' within a culture replaces the researcher-as-observer stance present in more traditional ethnographic forms (Patton, 2015). These deliberations resonate with Spry's (2001) standpoint that, in autoethnography, the researcher is the existential nexus upon which the research rotates, deviates and gyrates, presenting 'critical self-reflexive analysis of her own experiences of dissonance and discovery with others' (p. 726). Hence, though ethnographers and autoethnographers often share the same purpose of exploring and representing specific sociocultural contexts, autoethnographers also explicitly 'write in' (Tedlock, 1983) their own reflections, feelings, emotions, confessions and doubts.

Another difference in related to more various forms of representation associated with autoethnographic writing that might include poetry, drama, performance and a few other, which are not used in traditional ethnography. Ellis and Bochner (2000), specifically, note that these diverse ways of representation place autoethnography in stark contrast with more traditional forms of research on a whole series of dimensions, including 'the questioning or abandonment of the researcher/researched distinction, and attempts to write evocatively, emotionally and emotively' (p. 744). Similarly, Mizzi (2010) highlights that one of the core strengths of autoethnography is its capacity to move the researchers' reflections between their internal and external experiences of the phenomena under study, which can also be viewed as a critique of traditional ethnography, where the value of the researcher's life experiences is often overlooked through traditional ethnographic methods.

Now that we have, broadly, identified key differences between autoethnography and ethnography, I consider it useful to look at the distinctions between autoethnography and self-study, as charting demarcation lines between these two approaches can be particularly challenging. One of the first mentions of self-study as a distinct variety of qualitative methodologies can be found in Zeichner (1995, 1999), who acknowledged the development of the self-study movement as an important contribution of teacher educators to knowledge and understanding of teacher education for the larger community of researchers. These studies were focused, predominantly, on the roles of teachers in transforming educational practices as a result of their reflections on personal professional practice and engagement with relevant theoretical concepts. As noted by Hamilton and Pinnegar (1998), they involved the study of one's self as well as the 'not self', embracing autobiographical, historical, cultural and political, as well as considering literature, experiences and ideas. Later on, LaBoskey (2004) borrowed from Hamilton and Pinnegar (1998) to conceptualize self-study as a methodology for studying professional practice settings, whilst also suggesting a number of its defining characteristics, such as being:

- self-initiated and self-oriented, where the teacher educator decides on the focus of the inquiry;
- aimed at the improvement of teaching practice and its deeper understanding;
- interactive, involving other colleagues, pupils and friends;
- informed by multiple data sources;
- subject to a provisional validation through stimulating resonance with other educators in similar positions.

We can instantly spot here multiple lines of intersection with autoethnography and yet appreciate the nuances of distinction between the two. Hamilton, Smith and Worthington (2008) specify these distinctions by considering autoethnography as an approach where the researcher uses an ethnographic wide-angle lens with a focus on the social and cultural aspects of the personal, whilst in self-studies, researchers provide evidence and context for understanding their educational practice. Thus, according to Hamilton, Smith and Worthington (2008), the main distinction between the two approaches is that autoethnography focuses on looking at self within a larger context, whereas self-study aims to look at self in action, usually within educational contexts. Starr (2010) provides a slightly different view on these distinctions, suggesting that both autoethnography and self-study converge in the intersection of their relationship with and pertinence to the context of a time; however, autoethnography extends beyond solely literal study of self, extending its inquiry to include the space between the self and practice. More recent studies (Samaras, 2011; Hamilton and Pinnegar, 2014; Hordvik, MacPhail and Ronglan, 2020) that involve a self-study approach allow us to draw a brief summary of the main distinctions between autoethnography and self-study, accepting that the latter is, generally, focused on improvement of practice through examination of and reflection on teacher educators' professional practice, whilst autoethnographers draw on their experiences for the purposes of extending sociological understanding of their immediate cultural contexts.

However, as highlighted by Hamilton, Smith and Worthington (2008), even though a number of differences emerge within these research practices, there is a possibility of a potential overlap in their methodological approaches, as, for example, in the case where a self-study involves social or cultural issues, it could also fit the definition of autoethnography. Thus, it is important for the researchers to carefully consider the focus and the purpose of their study, so that they can delineate all aspects of their research in relation to the most appropriate positional stance.

Autoethnography as an interdisciplinary approach

In terms of the popularity of autoethnography, it seems to contest Keefer's (2010) assumption that 'autoethnography is not for everyone' (p. 208). Today autoethnography has become a widely adopted interdisciplinary approach that has been applied to a variety of domains, such as health (Chang, 2016; Grant, 2019; Schmidt and Leonardi, 2020; Racine, 2021), psychology (Kracen and Baird, 2018; Clarke and Wright, 2020; Parker, 2020), sociology (Hughes and Pennington, 2017; Bergfeld, 2018; Bochner and Adams, 2020), sports (Garratt, 2014; Sparkes, 2020) and education (Starr, 2010; Hamood, 2016; Beattie, 2018; Klevan and Grant, 2020). The reason behind such diversity of applications is that autoethnographic approach provides an opportunity for new forms of 'knowing' to emerge through deep and intimate engagement with personal experiences, reflections, feelings and thoughts. Moreover, autoethnographic studies offer researchers an opportunity to utilize many different formats of presentation, such as monologues, dialogues, polyvocal narratives, poetry, memoires, stories, theatrical performances and photo-collages. This richness of different genres and approaches draws attention to autoethnography from a wide range of disciplines, ranging, as noted by Chang, Nqunjiri and Hernandez (2013), 'from a more literary-artistic to a more scientific-analytical' (p. 118).

Given the diverse range of subjects, disciplines and researchers' backgrounds, autoethnography has firmly ascertained its capacity to sensitize researchers to the subjective nature of their experiences, enabling them to bring their insider perspective to the outside world. As I note elsewhere (Beattie, 2018a), autoethnographic writing and life are inextricably connected, as the former provides intellectual space for conscious exploration of diverse personal experiences through reflexive self-narratives. Similarly, Sambrook, Jones and Doloriert (2014) argue that autoethnography is particularly well suited to getting 'at the depth' of workplace practices, weaving together participant and researcher experiences and accounts to yield greater insights. In this sense, autoethnography goes beyond the boundaries of specific disciplines, as it permits researchers to combine personal and professional across a variety of contexts. Schmid (2019) confirms that autoethnography is a qualitative, interdisciplinary research methodology and method that helps researchers across disciplines to link their identity and culture, simultaneously contextualizing the research and the researcher.

Thus, autoethnography opens up for us a global inter- and multidisciplinary space, where, in Madison's (2012) words, 'a grand mix of intellectuals, activists, artists, scholars and all combinations of in between' (p. 207) engage in a diverse body of work that takes research away from the constraints of approved ways of knowing towards new academic vistas. It can be an intense and challenging task, but one that is worth embracing.

2

Contemporary Debates about Autoethnography

Introduction

As indicated in the previous chapter, autoethnographic research has been a subject of considerable debate, contestation and development in recent years. These debates spread across a wide range of subjects, including, but not limited to, the questions of credibility of autoethnographic research, its methodological integrity, diversity of approaches and forms of writing, ethical dilemmas, questions of representation and a few other. These debates have been discussed throughout the book in different chapters and with different levels of intensity as determined by the scope of this publication. In this chapter, I would like to focus, specifically, on three key aspects of these debates: perceiving autoethnography as method or methodology, disputes between evocative and analytic approaches and, finally, addressing the main criticisms of autoethnographic research.

Autoethnography: Methodology or method?

Multiplicity of definitions presented in the previous chapter prompted me to take a deeper dive into the literature to see whether such diversity of definitional variations can be, partially, due to the lack of agreement within the research community or whether autoethnography should be defined as a methodology or a method. Indeed, a number of researchers (Ellis, 2004; Denzin, 2014; Stahlke Wall, 2016; Dunn and Myers, 2020; Johnson and LeMaster, 2020) refer to autoethnography as research method, whilst others (Parry and Boyle, 2009; Wiley, 2019; Ramalho-de-Oliveira, 2020) define it as research methodology. A partial reconciliation of these dissonances has been suggested by Adams, Holman Jones and Ellis (2015), who argue that autoethnography can be seen as both research method and methodology, a point of view which resonates with Stanley and Vass (2017), who, similarly, refer to autoethnography as both the method and product of researching and writing about personal lived experiences.

These dissonances in the use of terms 'method' and 'methodology' as applied to autoethnographic research appear to be pertinent to the overall tensions related to methodology-versus-method debate in general, which continues to permeate autoethnographic landscape. Wall (2008) offers a radical solution to the matter, advising researchers to leave methodological associations unsettled and, instead, just accept that, regardless of assigned methodological alliances, autoethnography can be seen as an intriguing and promising qualitative approach. Nevertheless, some of us might feel that categorization can still be useful here for outlining our methodological affiliations, even if this outline remains obscure and fuzzy. And so for the purpose of 'de-mystifying' this aspect of autoethnographic approach, I turn to Crotty's (1998) relatively loose definition of methodology as 'the strategy, plan of action, process or design' (p. 3), as it allows us to assign autoethnography the status of methodology as opposed to methods, which Crotty (Crotty 1998) defines simply as the techniques or procedures used to gather and collect data. In simple terms, even though the two terms are often used interchangeably, they are not the same: methodology, generally, includes a discussion of methods, but it is not a method and neither is it a discussion of methods. Methodology provides explanation and justification for selected research design as underpinned by the researcher's view of the world; thus, it does not merely describe the techniques of collecting data (methods) but also incorporates more significant aspects of the study. In relation to autoethnography, Hughes and Pennington (2017) confirm that, when citing autoethnography as research methodology, we refer to the larger aspects of the study rather than just the methods of doing research.

Despite these prevailing arguments towards referring to autoethnography as research methodology, the ultimate choice will always depend on the specific nature of researchers' studies and their paradigmatic views of the world. So, whilst these suggestions might help autoethnographic researchers to, partially, resolve their doubts, other opportunities do not need to be immediately excluded from their considerations. As Punch and Oancea (2014) rightly point out, it can be very tempting for the beginning researcher to draw a neat line and 'position' oneself on one side of the debate, and yet, such neat positioning 'carries the risk of foreclosing creative opportunities for research and of freezing identities into an artificial landscape of paradigmatic and disciplinary crevasses' (p. 19).

Autoethnography: Evocative or analytic?

In attempts to identify and systematize distinct characteristic features of autoethnographic writing that would fit best the purpose of their studies, researchers almost certainly will come across several schools of thought related to autoethnographic research, which either compete with or complement each other. Current energetic debates in research circles point towards researchers' continuous attempts to identify set criteria that would apply to all existing autoethnographic praxes; yet the main attention of the ongoing deliberations seems to be focused on the two prevailing approaches to autoethnographic praxes: evocative (Ellis, 1997; Ellis and Bochner, 2017) and analytic (Lofland, 1995; Snow, Morrill and Anderson, 2003; Anderson, 2006).

Let us have a closer look at each of these approaches in terms of their similarities and differences. As noted by Ellis (2004), the main similarity between evocative and analytic approaches is that they both perceive the researcher as the object and the subject of a narrative inquiry. However, the first traces of differences can be detected in the aims associated with these two approaches. The main aim of evocative autoethnography is to elicit emotions by means of engaging in an emotionally charged subjective writing style that resonates with readers' feelings (Ellis, 2004) through the 'revelations of personal pain' (Muncey, 2010, p. 36) in the 'act of performing personal stories' (Spry, 2001, p. 718). In contrast, analytic autoethnographers try to distance themselves from the emotional aspects of their personal narratives, bringing autoethnography closer to more traditional ethnographic practices with a stronger focus on analytical examination of the studied cultural phenomena (Anderson, 2006). Thus, the main difference between these two approaches is that evocative autoethnographers aim to utilize their personal stories to evoke emotional responses to the issues under examination, using experimental research techniques to upset the traditional scientific narrative and to 'inspire imagination, give pause to new possibilities and meaning and open new questions and avenues for inquiry' (Ellis, 2004, p. 215); whereas analytic autoethnographers contest the evocative indulgencies of autoethnographic studies, stating their commitment to more traditional empirical research practices.

As suggested by Anderson (2006), analytic autoethnography is based on five key features: '(1) complete member researcher (CMR) status, (2) analytic reflexivity, (3) narrative visibility of the researcher's self, (4) dialogue with informants beyond the self and (5) commitment to theoretical analysis'

(Anderson, 2006, p. 378). The first three features require autoethnographers to be fully embedded into the culture under examination to enable them to engage in sustained reflexivity, which involves a deep awareness of reciprocal influence between ethnographer's self, their settings and their informants. The fourth feature of analytic autoethnography involves a requirement for autoethnographers to engage in a 'dialogue with informants beyond the self' (p. 385), highlighting that self-absorption and failure to adequately engage with others (as in evocative autoethnographies) might potentially lead researchers to lose sight of their ethnographic imperative of understanding the complexities of the social world around them. Anderson (2006) clarifies that 'no ethnographic work – not even autoethnography – is a warrant to generalize from an "N" of one' (p. 386). This feature is closely associated with the procedures and structure of research studies related to the two approaches. Duncan (2004) suggests that in analytic autoethnographies we are more likely to see conventional ways of systematic data collection followed by thematic analysis. The 'evocative' approach is more controversial and is, by no means, universally accepted. Here the expression is central, and less conventional styles (and mediums) than the traditional academic styles are employed. Closely linked to this feature is the final aspect of analytic autoethnography, which urges autoethnographers to use empirical data to gain insight into a broader context of the social phenomenon under study, strengthening further researchers' analytical focus.

Hence, we can see that the advocates of analytic autoethnography rely on more traditional ethnographic methodologies to produce research that, in their view, can withstand the tradition of rigour and scrutiny in the academy (Hughes and Pennington, 2017), whilst evocative autoethnographers focus on emotive narrative texts that dramatize researchers' emotional experiences, eschewing a disembodied academic voice. Chang (2008) summarizes these differences through her typology of autoethnographic writing, where two of such approaches are represented by confessional-emotive writing, which exposes confusions, problems and dilemmas in life but does not always enjoy favourable reviews; and analytical-interpretive writing, which is associated with conventional qualitative processes that aim to balance description, analysis and interpretation. Later on, Le Roux (2017) also attempted to summarize these differences, suggesting that

> analytic autoethnography is consequently directed towards objective writing and analysis, whereas evocative autoethnography leans towards researcher introspection from which readers are expected to make a connection with the researcher's emotions and experiences. (p. 199)

Another difference between the two approaches is related to the forms of writing itself, where evocative autoethnographers prefer to use a wide variety of tools, media and art-based techniques and performances, whilst analytic autoethnographers favour a more traditional structured approach. As I have mentioned in previous sections, evocative writing includes a variety of forms, from poetic texts to dance performances, from visual collages to radiophonic presentation. These variations are also reflected in the visual formatting of the text, where neat paragraphs of writing, generally associated with analytic autoethnography, are often disrupted and ruptured by irregular line breaks, empty spaces, unconventional fonts and random images in evocative narratives. As early as the 1980s, Tedlock (1983) called attention to the various transformations that a text undergoes moving from an oral presentation, a performance or a recording to its written format. The author suggested that written dialogue between researchers and participants is meditated and interpreted through visual formatting of the text, where researchers need to be constantly aware of the performative aspects of their writing and try to use the richness of expressive textual means to write as closely as possible to the spoken word. According to Tedlock (1983), researchers, who fail to seek graphic solutions to the problems of making a visible text, resemble 'an artist who sets out to work from life but discovers he has left his brush and paints at home and brought only his pens an india ink' (p. 9). Indeed, the choices of writing styles and visual representations of the text can, in most cases, indicate the researchers' alliances with either analytic or evocative autoethnographies, though this distinction is not always as obvious or consistent.

Yet, in their later work Anderson and Glass-Coffin (2013) step away from a clear-cut evocative–analytic differentiation, referring to autoethnography as positioned within a 'spectrum from "evocative" to "analytic"' (p. 64). Similarly, Grant (2019) advocates for a more careful balancing of intellectual rigour with emotive expression in autoethnographic writing practices that would demonstrate both researchers' ability to engage in novel methods of expression and their commitment to methodological coherence.

Defending autoethnography

Similar to any other type of innovative practice, the emergence of autoethnography from the landscape of qualitative research caused some disturbances, disgruntlements and, in a few cases, open condemnations. As

Sparkes (2000) notes in his early work, the emergence of autoethnography within the social sciences has not been trouble free and its status as proper research remains problematic. One of the early flows of criticism comes from Atkinson (1997), who questions the appropriateness of using narratives of suffering and illness as a way of offering the researchers privileged access to personal experience, as well as using autoethnography as a personal therapy rather than a critical analysis. Clough (2000) critiques autoethnography from a slightly different angle, describing this new experimental writing as a naive and overly self-conscious approach that lacks adequate level of responsiveness to political and cultural complexity. She urges ethnographers to stay close to theory, allowing their writing 'to be a vehicle for thinking new sociological subjects' (Clough, 2000, p. 290). Similarly, Walford (2004) suggests that autoethnography is self-indulgent and is sometimes more akin to therapy than social science. His specific target of criticism, however, is focused on the autoethnographers' efforts to produce texts that are open to multiple interpretations. As the author explains,

> The reports of social research, on the other hand, are surely fundamentally attempts to construct a readerly text – one where the attempt is made to restrict multiple meanings as far as possible. For me, research reports need to be logically constructed and clear about what empirical claims (factual and explanatory) are being made and what empirical data have been generated that support those claims. The text is one where attempts are made to reduce ambiguity and to exhibit precision. (Walford, 2004, p. 412)

Hammersley (2008) joins the same line of criticism, asserting that this new approach to ethnography licenses speculative, exaggerated conclusions and discourages careful attention to how well evidence supports the knowledge claims made. In consideration of these multiple critiques, Ellis (2020) suggests grouping them into three overlapping categories, based on the claims that autoethnography is (1) not sufficiently realist and tried to be too authentic, (2) too realist and (3) not sufficiently aesthetic. Yet, she admits not to be too bothered by these criticisms, as these 'critiques from outside autoethnography offer a sign that scholars from other areas are paying attention, that they find something of interest to push back against or something so irritating that they can't help but respond' (p. 210). Though in a general agreement with Ellis's (2020) broad categorization of critical views, I suggest that, essentially, these critiques group more tightly around the two key issues: too much emphasis on 'self' rather than 'ethno' and a lack of analytical grounding.

In relation to the first one, the presence of researcher's self in research reports, traditionally, has been considered awkward or, even, inappropriate, for that matter. Unsurprisingly, when autoethnography disturbed that established methodological terrain, making its appearance as an approach based on writing about the self, it was immediately attacked by the researchers, who questioned its methodological validity and academic rigour. As noted by Etherington (2004), a few critics argued that, as a methodology, writing about the self was self-indulgent, self-confessional and even narcissistic. Undeniably, a decision to engage in autoethnography and turn oneself into a 'research subject' is not always an easy one, as it seems to go against the grain of most orthodox forms of research, where, according to Freeman (2015), the researcher has been 'historically hidden, camouflaged in borrowed cloaks and behind the representation of other' (p. 918) and where the writer's self has traditionally been limited to the idea of observation from a distance, 'as though this act of disentanglement would somehow result in rigour; as though good research could only take place when the researcher stays firmly outside the frame' (Freeman, 2015).

We can trace similar arguments throughout the subsequent condemnations of autoethnography as a credible research approach. For example, Morse (2002) advised academics against using autoethnographic approach with students for fear of shifting the focus from their research question to themselves. Roth (2009) also warned against autoethnographies becoming 'of the woe-me kind, auto-graphies', adding that 'the difficulties self-ascribed auto/ethnographers face in academe derive from the frequently unprincipled, egoistical and egotistical, narcissistic preoccupation with and auto-affection of the Self' (p. 10), whilst Holt (2003) cited that such disregard of the standards of qualitative research made autoethnographies 'nothing more than journalism with a smattering of theory' (p. 10). A few authors went further in their animosity towards the autoethnographic approach, such as Delamont (2007), who described autoethnography as 'essentially lazy, literally lazy and also intellectually lazy', Atkinson (2015), who argued that autoethnography creates a danger of treating ourselves as being more interesting than the social worlds around us, and Madison (2006), who suggested that the rootedness and embellishments of the self 'diminish the thickness and complexities of the encompassing terrain, as when the gaze is on one's own navel one cannot see the ground upon which one stands or significant others standing nearby' (p. 321).

In addition to these relatively moderate oppositions, there were also those who openly ridiculed autoethnographic approach, going as far as seeing its 'indulgence in personal ratiocination' as a form of 'academic wanking'

(Marowitz, 1991, p. 72), similar to Morrison's (2015) perception of these confessional tales as 'public masturbation'. Before moving on to the responses related to these criticisms, I would like to pause here to dwell a bit longer on the last two associations, as the language expressions used, whether unintentionally or not, by these authors have created an interfering stratum within my discussion by inducing strong masculine overtones into the otherwise gender-neutral debate. These new overtones have generated an instinctive link to a different type of a discourse – a discourse based on the patriarchal mode of reasoning that privileges masculine in the construction of meaning, the style of thinking that was once defined by Derrida (1976, p. xix) as 'phallogocentric'. Grosz (1989) explains that within such phallogocentric discourses 'masculinity has taken upon itself the right to speculate about the world, about women and about itself: above all, it eschews the right to self-reflection, the right to self-speculation, self-critique and self-justification' (p. xxii). And so to Grosz's list of phallocentric speculations we can now add the above-mentioned perceptions of the autoethnographic writing, as its virile opponents deny its capacity of making valid contributions to knowledge by pushing it outside the methodological ghetto of male supremacy and 'the truth of the phallus' (Derrida et al., 1975, p. 60). Taking the same line of defence, a number of researchers (Lather, 1997; Griffin, 2012; Ettorre, 2017) used autoethnographic narratives, explicitly, as a vehicle for raising 'oppositional consciousness by exposing precarity' (Ettorre, 2017, p. 359) of women's present and future. Nevertheless, I have to admit at this point that this intellectual detour has taken us slightly off course in relation to the task at hand and so, going back to the main purpose of this chapter, I maintain that finding a way of 'defending' a methodological choice of autoethnography against such a widespread backdrop of critique and intolerance can be seen as both a necessity and an obligation.

To contest the first line of criticism related to autoethnographers' overvalued emphasis on self, I first turn to an earlier exploration of a researcher's self by Mooney (1957), who perceives research as 'a personal venture', where 'who a researcher is, is central to what the researcher does' (p. 155). Later on, this view is supported by Bochner and Ellis (1996), who confirm the prominence of researcher's self in research as a vehicle through which culture flows. Langellier (1998) offers a similar compelling assertion that the body needs a voice to resist the colonizing powers of discourse and personal narrative provides such a voice. Wall (2006) also confirms that using self as subject is a way of acknowledging the self that was always there anyway and of exploring personal connections to the culture under examination. Starr (2010) expands this discussion by adding that autoethnography revolves around the exploration of self in relation to other and the space created between them, thus providing ripe grounds for a social construction of knowledge that places emphasis on a transformative or emancipatory processes for both the researcher and the wider sociocultural domains of which the researcher is a part. Similarly, Grant and Zeeman (2012) argue that, with regard to the issue of solipsistic self-indulgence, it can only be the case if the researcher's self is assumed to be autonomous and culturally, dialogically and relationally disconnected from other people, whilst autoethnography is predicated on quite the opposite, that is, seeing researchers as inscribed within socially shared cultural and representational practices rather than unconnected phenomena. This endorsement towards the value of the researcher's self is also supported by Pelias (2019), who claims that putting researchers on display brings them forward in the belief that an emotionally vulnerable, linguistically evocative and sensuously poetic voice can place us closer to the subjects we wish to study.

These arguments help us to create a powerful line of defence against the claims related to self-indulgent and narcissistic nature of autoethnographic studies. Indeed, the actual contention here is, really, about how close the researchers can get to their participants and the data, as no qualitative research, or any type of research for that matter, can be 'sterile'. From this position, it seems impossible to argue against the fact that the closest proximity to the research data can be obtained through 'researching oneself' as both the subject and the object of one's study, positioning researcher's self at the centre of investigative inquiry about the culture under examination.

Moving next to defending autoethnography from the claims about its lack of analytic grounding, I turn here to a wide range of literature to support my view that autoethnographic approach can provide a sound epistemic platform upon which meaningful challenges to prevailing research conventions can be built. One such challenging argument can be found in Nietzsche (1910), who suggested, well before the appearance of autoethnography, that 'a man may stretch himself out ever so far with his knowledge; he may seem to himself ever so: objective, but eventually he realises nothing therefrom but his own biography' (p. 361). In the same way, contemporary authors (Denzin, 2018; Pelias, 2019; Griffin and Griffin, 2019; Bochner, 2020; Grant and Young, 2022) all seem to agree that ethnographic derivatives, such as autoethnography, emerged as a result of the crisis of representation that occurred in the 1980s, when previously agreed scientific or objectivist stances on the criteria of ethnographic research validity were challenged to emphasize the power and significance of the individual in creating new forms of knowledge, where the identity of the researcher advanced to being central. The questions of 'producing different knowledge and producing knowledge differently' (St. Pierre, 1997, p. 175) are not new to the field of qualitative research. Spry (2001), for example, suggests that knowledge production needs to include the process and production of knowledge in the context of the body from which it is generated, referring to autoethnography as 'embodied methodology' (p. 725), which resists objective research that decontextualizes subjects and searches for singular truth. Similarly, Wall (2006) sees autoethnography as a new epistemological opportunity for removing the risks of representation for previously silenced groups, allowing for the production of new knowledge by a unique and uniquely situated researcher. Along with the claims related to the general lack of analytical rigour in autoethnographic studies, their critics also refer to more specific aspects of research studies, such as validity, reliability and generalizability. These notions are discussed in detail in Chapter 6, so I intend to only briefly outline here the main lines of defence against such claims. First, it is important to mention that the debates associated with these aspects apply to the whole domain of qualitative research and not just autoethnography. The notions of validity, reliability and generalizability are rooted in positivist perspective and associated with statistical data and quantitative research.

Thus, any attempts to mechanically transfer the same concepts to qualitative studies cause difficulties and controversies. Starr (2010) confirms that using validity, reliability and generalizability generates a veil of ambiguity relating to conventional notions of methodological trustworthiness that needs to be resolved. Generally, autoethnographers dismiss these concepts altogether as associated with a positivist paradigm and traditional research and writing conventions, which 'create only the illusion that the knowledge produced is more legitimate' (Wall, 2006, p. 149). Hayes and Fulton (2015) add a valuable point to this debate, arguing that any qualitative research only has context specificity at the particular point in time of the experience being reported upon, which means that the ability to generalize from autoethnographers' narrative account of experience comes from a critical view of their own selves. Similarly, Starr (2010) suggests that autoethnographers provide a bridge between traditional conceptions of validity, reliability and generalizability and their autoethnographic counterparts through replacing rigid scientific structures with the criteria derived from researchers' reflexivity.

Thus, the relevant concepts are addressed in autoethnographic studies through the application of such notions as trustworthiness, authenticity, fairness, crystallization and a few other, which will be discussed further in this book. At this point, though, we have accumulated sufficient evidence to defend autoethnography against both flows of criticism, related to the issues of overemphasis on the self and scarcity of analytic theorization. Both of these lines of criticism are closely linked to researchers' commitments to positivist research traditions, whilst autoethnography falls outside this approach, creating new forms of knowledge that stand 'outside time, in a strange timeless space' (Denzin, 2018, p. 4). These new forms of knowledge cast a shadow of doubt on the privilege of any one method for obtaining authoritative knowledge about the social world or, in fact, on the existence of such authoritative knowledge. Such deliberations are strongly associated with the ideas of postmodernism, which problematize and politicize autoethnography, moving it beyond a world of harmonious social order into a political radical world where dissensus and power conflicts prevail (Stanley and Vass, 2018; Pelias, 2019; Sparkes, 2020; Walford, 2021). So in the next chapter I aim to discuss postmodernism as one of the world views that can, potentially, be adopted by autoethnographic researchers to help them cope with the challenges of justifying their methodological choices and commitments.

Autoethnography and postmodernism

When I was working on my doctoral thesis, I found it problematic, and at times impossible, to fit my autoethnographic study into the conventional formats of qualitative research, as seemingly straight linear trajectories of my chronologically neat narrative kept being disrupted by contradictory events, fuzzy boundaries, incompatible imperatives, self-doubts and an overall chaotic life experiences, in which the notion of uncertainty became a defining attribute. The need to somehow accommodate these fluid, elusive and disjointed experiences compelled me to look beyond the well-defined systematic epistemological and ontological alliances towards a more supple way of theorizing that would free me from the constraints of unyielding frameworks. A helpful contribution to the task at hand was found in Tarnas (1991), who suggested that the way of theorizing, which allows appreciation of the plasticity and the constant change of reality and knowledge, whilst subverting all existing epistemological taxonomies, is associated with a postmodern approach:

> Reality is not a solid, self-contained given, but a fluid, unfolding process, an 'open universe', continually affected and moulded by one's actions and beliefs. It is possibility rather than fact. One cannot regard reality as a removed spectator

against a fixed object; rather, one is always and necessarily engaged in reality, thereby at once transforming it while being transformed oneself. (p. 396)

And though a deeper engagement with postmodernism enabled me to disrupt familiar epistemological and ontological boundaries, positioning my work within the postmodern vista has not been straightforward, since postmodernism does not offer any specific frameworks for theorizing. It is also notoriously difficult to define postmodernism, as noted by Bell ([1978] 1996), who observes that 'everyone who has written a book or article on postmodernism begins with an apology for the inability to define the term. This is understandable, for if one could define it, it would not be postmodernism' (p. 297). To avoid going against the flow of this reasoning, rather than engaging in definitional experiments, I choose to lean on Natoli's (2001) view of postmodernism, as a 'journey off one map of both culture and self and toward another, toward what is yet unmapped, inconceivable to the present state of our imaginations. Beyond latitudes and longitudes, we already know' (p. 43). From this perspective, the intentions of autoethnographic researchers to seek meaning within their ambiguous and fragmented experiences align well with postmodernist unconventional practices of expression, which incorporate a variety of textual and visual means, multiple voices and fragmented forms with the purpose of breaking 'the boundaries of genres and to encourage the audience to see and see through, to participate in events and to interpret experiences gained at (almost) first hand' (Grbich, 2004, p. 18). Indeed, autoethnographers' gesture towards postmodern ways of thinking can, potentially, enable them to grapple with the complexities of their lived experience saturated with multifaceted relations of 'I' with themselves and the others. In the face of a crisis of authority and legitimization within positivist paradigmatic field, Lather (1998) argues for a research praxis that 'is about ontological stammering, concepts with a lower ontological weight, a praxis without guaranteed subjects or objects, oriented toward the as-yet-incompletely thinkable conditions and potentials of given arrangements' (p. 495), confirming later on that 'facing the problems of doing research in this historical time, between the no longer and the not yet, the task is to produce different knowledge and produce knowledge differently' (Lather, 2006, p. 52). A choice of the postmodern approach seems to be congruent with this aspiration, as it erases traditional system of 'static, ahistorical and decontextualized narratives of "Truth" and "Knowledge"' (Le Blanc, 2017, p. 790) in a manner that foregrounds 'narrative truth' (Ellis, Adams and Bochner, 2010) as 'the primary scheme by which human existence is rendered meaningful' (Polkinghorne, 1988, p. 11).

The association between autoethnography and postmodernism has been favoured by a number of authors (Reed-Danahay, 1997; Spry, 2001; Wall, 2006; Le Roux, 2017; Denzin, 2018), who endorsed postmodern exploration of autoethnographies as spatially, culturally and historically located narratives shaped by multiplicity of contexts, identities, experiences and powers. St. Pierre and Jackson (2014) express their surprise at the fact that, despite the presence of 'post-' approaches (e.g. post-positivism, post-subjective, posthumanism, postmodernism, post-structuralism, post-foundationalism, post-empiricism/materialism) in qualitative research for at least three decades, analysis in qualitative methodology continues to be mired in positivism. In line with this argument, Gannon (2017) reminds us that the first coupling of postmodernism with autoethnography appears in Françoise Lionnet's (1989 cited in Gannon, 2017) close reading of African American anthropologist Zora Neale Hurston's autobiography as an exemplary postmodern autoethnography, where 'ethnicity is mediated through language and history and the text draws attention to style through exaggeration, vivid imagery, poetic language, allegory, aesthetic sensibilities and textual performance of the self' (p. 2). Similarly, in her early work, Reed-Danahay (1997) refers to autoethnography as a synthesis of postmodern ethnography (where researchers' objectivity was called into question) and postmodern autobiography, in which 'the notion of the coherent, individual self has been similarly called into question' (p. 2), allowing a direct connection between the self and the social context to take place. In this sense, postmodern way of thinking aims to problematize positivist methodologies with their persistent dichotomies of 'researcher-researched, objectivity-subjectivity, process-product, self-others, art-science and personal-political' (Ellingson and Ellis, 2008, p. 450), nurturing new ways of knowing through subjective experiences. Nevertheless, an important point to remember here is that it is not the aim of postmodernism to completely discard scientific positivist notions and methodologies. Postmodern thinking compels researchers to question the appropriateness and legitimacy of these concepts in the context of their studies but does not endeavour to annihilate them. In contrast, autoethnographers problematize the application of these concepts to a narrative inquiry, seeking to destabilize positivist claims about the possibilities of discovering objective truth. Hayes and Fulton (2015) argue that the ideas of postmodernism are central to the development of autoethnographical approaches, where data is often presented in a storytelling fashion, in which the message is more important than the literal truth. Indeed, it is the absence of authoritative knowledge or 'truth' which brings autoethnographies in line with postmodernism, urging autoethnographers not to look harder or more closely but to examine the frame of their seeing, or the 'regime of truth' (Lather, 1993, p. 676) that would allow them to establish an acceptable dialogue with readers about how to go about reality construction. Denzin (2018) adds that these postmodern moments have been defined, in part, by a concern for composing ethnographies in new ways, as shaped by researchers' new perceptions and their refusal to privilege traditional, post-positivist values of objectivity, evidence and truth.

Since the notion of postmodern truth is central to these debates, I intend to dwell on this subject a little bit longer. As suggested in my previous discussion, autoethnographic researchers do not anticipate their studies to uncover one single truth but rather aim to provide a multifaceted story that contributes to the current insights into how a particular issue is experienced and can be understood in different ways by different individuals. These stories have an infinite potential of exploring reality, which becomes possible once researchers distance themselves from positivist conceptions of truth and validity. In addition, these emancipatory faculties of postmodern autoethnography also allow autoethnographers to deny a conventional image of *self* as a single existent entity, instead shattering it into multiple fragments with the purpose of examining their multiple Selves as 'a series of shifting construals of relationship among bodily experience, world and habitus' (Csordas, 1994, p. 15). As noted by Thomas (1993), critical potential of postmodernism lies in its subversion of conventional ways of thinking and its ability to force re-examination of what we thought was real. Thus, knowledge in a postmodern sense turns into the process of an active construction predicated on the social, historical, moral and political (Howe, 2001). At the centre of postmodernism is a rejection of the notion that truth itself can be objectively pursued, or that there even is any singular truth. As pointed out by Lee (1999), postmodernists claim that many truths may exist simultaneously and that no one version of truth or method of arriving at that knowledge should be considered superior.

These arguments, once again, highlight the nexus between autoethnography and the postmodern way of thinking, as the latter enables researchers to look beyond the actuality of one single truth towards the acceptance of alternative views on the same events and the existence of more than one view of the world (Zeeman et al., 2002). The same position is shared by Spry (2001), who argues that autoethnographic writing resists grand theorizing and the façade of objective research that decontextualized subjects and searches for singular truth. Instead, we can recognize that the task of a postmodern autoethnographer is to create *meaning* by weaving together a story from the fragments of data (Clough and Nutbrown, 2012). Patton (2015) summarizes that, whilst both ethnography and autoethnography reside in constructive qualitative inquiry, autoethnography is more firmly rooted in the postmodern paradigm, where individual's study of one's self within a culture replaces the researcher-as-observer stance present in more traditional ethnographic forms.

The issues related to interpreting life experiences in relation to the concept of truth are discussed in more detail in Chapter 4, so, at this point, I consider these ponderings as just another brick to our wall of defence related to critiques of autoethnography as lacking analytical foundations. In response, I argue that within postmodern philosophy, analytical intentions of autoethnographic research are not about hiding 'behind the illusion of objectivity' and allowing claims of single truth to 'triumph over compassion, try to crush alternative possibilities and try to silence minority voices' (Pelias, 2004, p. 1). Instead, it is about proffering stories rather than theories and offering self-consciously value-centred accounts rather than pretending to be value free (Bochner and Riggs, 1994).

Yet, I accept that my personal endorsement of postmodernism as the most suitable avenue for conducting an autoethnographic inquiry will not, necessarily, resonate with all autoethnographers. Every researcher's view of the world is subjective and based on individual principles of theoretical thinking, varied methods of cognition and diverse perspectives, all of which create unique research journeys and ways of obtaining knowledge. Sughrua (2019) makes a useful observation, linking the appearance of new paradigms and views of the world to specific 'historical moments' (Denzin, 2015, p. 33), which are all presently active, including

> (1) 1900–1950, traditional/positivist; (2) 1950–1970, modernist/postpositivist; (3) 1970–1980, blurred genres; (4) 1980–1985, paradigm wars; (5) 1986–1990, crisis of representation; (6) 1990–1995, the postmodern; (7) 1995–2000, postexperimental inquiry; (8) 2000–2004, the methodologically contested present; (9) 2005–2010, paradigm proliferation; (10) 2010-present, the fractured, posthumanist present; and (11) 2016 to present, uncertain and utopian future/ critical inquiry in the public domain. (p. 461)

There is no doubt that this 'uncertain and utopian' future will bring more paradigmatic possibilities and opportunities for all researchers; hence, it is unreasonable to expect every autoethnographic study to fit into a certain prescribed model. What is more important, however, is that we undertake research that is honest and consistent with our values and beliefs. As noted by Punch and Oancea (2014), 'in many cases, coherence and depth of thought, coupled with a degree of irreverence, may enable more fulfilling research experiences and more interesting contributions to research conversations than strict and deferential paradigmatic loyalty' (p. 19).

Part 2

Theorizing about Symbiotic Autoethnography

3

What Is Symbiotic Autoethnography?

Introduction

In previous chapters I provided a brief overview of autoethnography and the multiplicity of autoethnographic approaches to a qualitative inquiry. In these chapters I, predominantly, focus on highlighting key differences between the most popular of these approaches. Yet, several schools of thought related to autoethnographic research call attention to the commonalities in the existing autoethnographic praxes and attempt to demonstrate how they can or should complement each other. As observed by Doloriert and Sambrook (2012), different autoethnographic praxes are not necessarily discrete, as they may overlap and include more than one position. Thus, prior to presenting my approach of Symbiotic Autoethnography, I find it valuable to start with the acknowledgement of other researchers' efforts to work out a pliable format that fits the diverse nature of researchers' autoethnographic experiences.

Symbiotic Autoethnography in context

Researchers' efforts aimed at embracing the diversity of autoethnographic experiences seem to concentrate mainly on reconciling the differences between evocative and analytic approaches to autoethnography. Richardson (2000c) rightly points out that 'any dinosaurian beliefs that creative and analytical are contradictory and incompatible modes are standing in a path of a meteor. They are doomed for extinction' (p. 10), whilst Tedlock (2013) suggests that narratives can invoke emotions while being analytical, advising 'braiding evocative and analytic autoethnography' (p. 358). Comparably, Spry (2001) sees autoethnography as having the capacity to embrace the fragments of being critical, reflexive and performative at the same time, a point that resonates with

Burnier (2006), who thinks that autoethnographic writing is 'both personal and scholarly, both evocative and analytical and it is both descriptive and theoretical when it is done well' (p. 414). In addition, Winkler (2018a) also stresses the need to find the right balance between evocative and analytical approaches, arguing that putting too much emphasis on personal feelings, impressions, thoughts, attitudes and experiences can lead authors towards being accused of conducting autobiography not autoethnography, whilst too much emphasis on the 'ethno' may lead to the charge of slipping into more traditional forms of ethnography. One of the ways of embracing these opinions can be found in Stahlke Wall (2016), who suggests the notion of 'moderate autoethnography' as a way forward in taming these debates by finding a middle ground:

> Commentators on both sides of the methodological debate concerning autoethnography have valid points to make. A moderate autoethnography would reconcile the best of these ideas and combine the power of the personal perspective with the value of analysis and theory, so that sociological understanding is advanced in ways it might never have otherwise been. (p. 6)

A number of authors (Allen-Collinson and Hockey, 2008; Anderson and Glass-Coffin, 2013; Tullis, 2013; Stahlke Wall, 2016; Sparkes, 2020) address the gap between evocative and analytic approaches by suggesting a concept of *continuum*, alongside which autoethnographers' studies are positioned, depending on the degree of attention to analytical or emotive aspects of their narratives. Manning and Adams (2015) recognize these variations in autoethnographic practice as a 'writing continuum' (p. 191), identifying its four common orientations: social-scientific, interpretive-humanistic, critical and creative-artistic. Yet, the authors stress that autoethnographers are likely to blend the goals and techniques of these orientations, depending on the design of their individual projects. Denejkina (2017) refers to the gap between evocative and analytic autoethnographies as a *spectrum*, within which lie varied approaches to the method, including, but not limited to, meta-autoethnography; collaborative autoethnography; co-constructed decolonizing autoethnography; relational autoethnography and collaborative witnessing. Similarly, Hughes and Pennington (2017) mention autoethnographic spectrum, when discussing the presence of researchers' self in their inquiries.

In contrast to the *continuum*- and *spectrum*-based solutions, Chang (2008) offers another way of reconciling the existing debates around autoethnographic praxes, suggesting anchoring autoethnography in more conventional methodological approaches. In her textbook-style discussion she suggests four styles of autoethnographic writing, with each having its own advantages and risks: descriptive-realistic (that focuses on accurate depictions of places and events); confessional-emotive (which spotlights feelings and dilemmas in life); analytical-interpretive (aimed at balancing analysis with interpretation) and imaginative-creative (that blurs fiction and non-fiction, whilst dismissing academic or scientific methods). These styles of writing are offered by Chang (2008) as an opportunity for researchers to build their own approaches to writing, using the described four options. Sughrua (2019) takes a slightly more complex route in his attempt to reduce the gap between evocative, analytical and critical autoethnographies. To achieve this, he proposes to move evocative autoethnography from its current position of a co-type of autoethnography to a lead or superordinate type of evocative-like autoethnography, with the suggested name of *critically oriented evocative autoethnography as a methodology without methods and situated within critical qualitative inquiry* (CEAM-CQI). The author explains that this intention is not to antagonize or combat the analytical side, nor to reify divisionism, but rather to place evocative autoethnography into a 'unified, respectful and mediated position alongside that of analytical autoethnography' (p. 430), allowing the former to fully achieve its social justice agenda.

All these attempts to bring together varied autoethnographic praxes inspired me to engage in my own search for an alternative approach to autoethnography, encouraging me to craft 'a generative methodology that registers a possibility and marks a provisional space in which a different science might take form' (Lather, 1993, p. 673). In this endeavour I allowed myself a degree of departure from the dominant autoethnographic perspectives towards, what I call, a *Symbiotic Autoethnography*.

My attempt to pierce an already dense autoethnographic nomenclature with new terminology has not been without a risk. Palmer (2014) refers to the invention of such neologisms as a 'liberating force' (p. 81). Yet, the author warns us that, whilst the concept of 'neo' is fundamental to the entirety of the postmodernism, researchers need to avoid creating 'nonsense' words: the radical novelty of the word needs to be 'sufficient to uphold the proposed substantive material that is at the forefront of thought and creation' (Palmer, 2014, p. xxiv). Eisler (2004) also acknowledges that 'to create new realities, we need new words: social categories that describe new possibilities' (p. 44). With consideration of these points, I use a biological concept of *symbiosis* in its broader sense as denoting a close, prolonged and mutually beneficial association between two or more different elements based on widely varying types of interconnection (Miller,

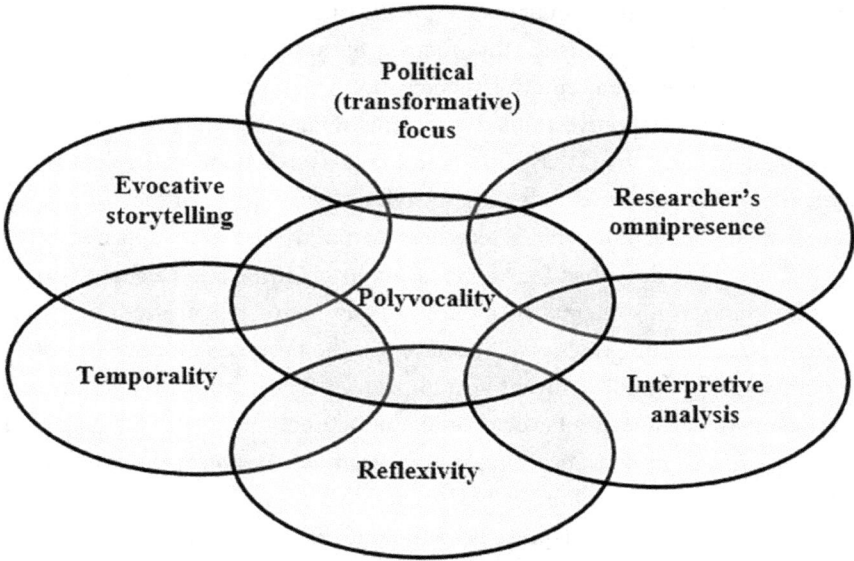

Figure 2 Seven features of Symbiotic Autoethnography.

1994; Dimijian, 2000). Constructed around that idea of interconnectedness, my interpretation of symbiosis as an interdisciplinary concept has been based on the view of autoethnography as a fluid amalgamation of multiple tumultuous features that represent a meeting point of *auto*, *ethno* and *graphy*. This lens served as a stimulus that helped me move away from the dichotomies of opposites, linearities of continuums and gradualities of spectrums. Instead, my aim was to combine heterogeneous elements of an autoethnographic inquiry into an adaptable arrangement, where its components are not pressed into a bonding mortar like mosaic pieces but rather float like droplets of oil on a surface of water ready to be diffused, expanded, melded or dislocated at any moment in time.

My interpretation of symbiosis, in some ways, resonates with its construals found in other qualitative studies. For example, Lewis (2011) suggests that the relationship between narrative and humans is akin to symbiotic relationship, where the narrative process is inseparable from the story product, as each gives form to the other. Elie (2013) discusses the existing symbiosis between ethnography and fieldwork, suggesting to delink them, since each represents a distinctive research practice. Blockmans, De Schauwer, Van Hove and Enzlin (2020) describe the concept of symbiosis as the connection of heterogeneous elements into new assemblages in their autoethnographic exploration of dance and meaning. Yet, these studies mention the notion of symbiosis, mostly, as a figure of speech rather than a foundation for a distinct methodological approach. In contrast, my interpretation of symbiosis aims to offer a more systematic example of an adaptable approach, capable of accommodating the diversity, the ambiguity and the dynamics of autoethnographers' subjective experiences across varied contexts and disciplines. The next chapter will introduce and discuss in detail the seven suggested features of Symbiotic Autoethnography, including (1) autoethnographic temporality, (2) researcher's omnipresence, (3) evocative storytelling, (4) interpretative analysis, (5) political (transformative) focus, (6) reflexivity and (7) polyvocality (Figure 2).

4

Key Features of Symbiotic Autoethnography

Introduction

Constructed around the idea of interconnectedness, my interpretation of 'symbiosis' as an interdisciplinary concept is presented in this chapter based on the view of autoethnography as an amalgamation of seven features as shown in Figure 2. These features combine, repel, intersect and fuse under the umbrella of Symbiotic Autoethnography as a way of exploring a particular phenomenon within a culture, in which the researcher is a part. Each feature is explained in this chapter in detail with consideration of current theoretical debates and with justification for each as essential components of the suggested approach.

Autoethnographic temporality

Time and time-related contexts are central to our understanding of any cultural phenomena and yet, despite a growing corpus of autoethnographic research, relatively small number of studies make the concept of time their investigative focus. In fact, a few autoethnographers seem to neglect altogether the temporal aspect of their experiences both theoretically and methodologically. This strikes me as a surprising lacuna, considering the significance of time in our life occurrences as well as in our autoethnographic narratives. In my endeavour to present the concept of temporality as an essential feature of Symbiotic Autoethnography and a way of theorizing about the dynamic nature of our experiences I lean on the Oxford Dictionary definition of temporality as the state of existing within or having some relationship with time. However, I argue that, when it comes to autoethnography, this definition sounds incomplete, as autoethnographic temporality not only includes more than just references to time but also incorporates the qualities of being subjective, locational and evanescent, as discussed further in this chapter. It is not my intention to offer a precise definition of autoethnographic temporality, as most definitional attempts tend to contain conjectural flaws. Hence, I propose here just a loose outline of the term as applicable to Symbiotic Autoethnography, suggesting that autoethnographic temporality can be understood as researchers' subjective perceptions of chronological times as experienced across different localities and captured in the moment of writing. In this sense, Symbiotic Autoethnography is a 'snapshot' of our temporal recollections of events, places, feelings and relations caught in their illusory stillness during one specific moment of writing – our 'present past'.

To further my discussion, I move to the acknowledgement that a number of authors (Spry, 2011a; Abrahao, 2012; Bochner and Ellis, 2016; Eguchi, 2020; Sparkes, 2020) have, to some extent, engaged with the concept of temporality in relation to autoethnography through mentioning various temporal aspects of researchers' trajectories. For example, Ellis and Bochner (2000) conceive autoethnography as a narrative that 'is always a story about the past and not the past itself' (p. 745). Duncan (2004) refers to the 'four facets of time, location, project type and point of view' (p. 8), when reflecting on her autoethnographic study. Spry (2011a) also asserts that 'autoethnography is place and space and time' (p. 15). Abrahao (2012) specifically highlights the temporal nature of researchers' personal and social journeys that create a correlation between time and narrative, where present, past and future mix in a three-dimensional perspective, explaining that 'narratives are linked both to the moment of the experience and to the moment of the utterance' (p. 31).

In addition, different authors use a number of terminological variations related to temporal experiences, depending on the main focus of their study, such as 'spatio-temporality' (Castree, 2009), 'event time' (Adkins, 2009), 'polytemporality' (Knight, 2014), 'tempo-locality' (Tlostanova, 2017), 'temporospatial' dimensions (Gill, Gill and Roulet, 2018) and 'tempography' (Scheller, 2020). Building on these works, I maintain that introducing temporality as an integral feature of Symbiotic Autoethnography offers researchers a better-defined opportunity to reflect on their subjective, locational and evanescent experiences of time. Nonetheless, my interpretation of autoethnographic temporality is not intended to be a single ultimate pathway towards understanding all time-related matters but rather just one possibility amongst others of theorizing about the dynamics of autoethnographic experiences.

Historically, the notion of time originated from the ancient Greeks, who began to measure time via tracing shadows of sundials. For them, time could be differentiated into three different forms: Chronos, Kairos and Aion. Chronos denoted a linear time as moving continuously in one direction, whilst Aion was used to recognize cyclical flow of some natural phenomena, such as change of seasons and a day–night reversal. In contrast, Kairos was perceived as neither linear nor measurable but as an indeterminate qualitative time that was associated with brief, decisive and significant moments in the life of human beings or in the universe (Miller, 2002, p. xii). Tracing here all philosophical developments related to the concept of time would be both impossible and futile, since these developments touch upon a number of fundamental questions that fall outside the scope of this book. Nevertheless, I do find it useful to mention a couple of these developments. The first one is related to one of the earliest theories of subjective time perception posed in 1897 by French philosopher Paul Janet. As Mazur (2020) explains in his book *The Clock Mirage: Our Myth of Measured Time*, Paul Janet's psychochronometry model of human temporal impressions of time passing suggested that these impressions were in direct proportion to the individuals' age: the more time one has lived, the shorter time felt. These deliberations led to other major discoveries about the physical world and thus the consequent new ways of theorizing about space and time not as absolute entities but as deeply subjective conceptions, which depended on the observers' value and meaning (Sartre, 1938; Heidegger, 1962; Merleau-Ponty, 1962; Husserl, 1991). These ideas advanced our thinking of time from a clock time towards 'perceived time', creating, what Zimbardo and Boyd (2008) described as, a 'time perspective' associated with a subjective modality of 'living the time' rather than measuring it chronologically. Van Manen (1990) refers to it as 'lived time' (p. 104) or subjective time as opposed to clock time. Yet, the debates related to different scientific and ethnographic positions on people's perceptions of time are ongoing, as researchers try to associate their theoretical alliances with either an objective model of clock time or a philosophical model, where notion of time is understood as a subjective and illusory process that is 'constantly produced in everyday practices' (Munn, 1992, p. 116). This view of time as a subjective experience has shaped my construct of autoethnographic temporality, where *autoethnographic time* is seen not as linear and measurable but as 'perceived' or 'imagined' according to the context (Lucas, 2005). This approach strongly resonates with Sharma's (2014) understanding of temporality as being different from time, since the former is centred around individuals' synchronization of their 'body clocks, their senses of the future or the present, to an exterior relation' (p. 18). Similarly, Dawson (2014) explains that a linear notion of time does not accommodate a view of the world, in which individuals make sense of fluidity, flux and movement:

> The recall of the past is rarely uncontentious with different groups and individuals reinterpreting key events in different ways (asynchronous subjective time) with the consequent emergence of competing accounts that often seek to gain purchase and dominance (this is the way it really happened). The past is relived in the present just as expected future scenarios can influence our current understanding and sense of the world around us. These subjectivities of human experience all highlight the non-linearity of lived time and the importance of context. (p. 131)

Thus, the issue of autoethnographers' subjective perceptions of time can be seen as an inherent and inescapable feature of autoethnographic temporality. To say that autoethnographers only refer to precise chronological units of time in their narratives is an absurdity, as the evidence from a wide assortment of autoethnographic studies against this positivist claim is quite convincing. Yet, resigning to a complete rejection of chronological time for many autoethnographers would be totally untenable. Hence, autoethnographic temporality serves here as a middle ground that allows autoethnographers to both anchor their stories within specific chronological times, whilst acknowledging and negotiating their subjective experiences of these times. It is worth mentioning at this point that the concept of subjectivity in autoethnographic writing extends well beyond the issues of temporality, penetrating the whole fabric of our narratives. These discussions will continue throughout the subsequent chapters to bring a deeper level of understanding related to autoethnographers' subjective insights into the 'objective reality' (whatever that might be).

In terms of the evanescent nature of autoethnographic temporality, I consider it useful to juxtapose it here with our traditional chronological perceptions of time. These traditional perceptions of time are, generally, associated with the notions of past, present and future as ultimate time referents; however, using these structural referents does not harmonize with autoethnographic writing, since all our experiences and memories are non-sequential and subject to different interpretations depending on specific localities in certain spaces and times. In this sense, 'past/present' becomes just another unhelpful dichotomy as we, actually, cannot separate our past from our present. Indeed, what is our past? Can we point at it or touch it? Is it just our memories of the past? But it cannot be, since our *past* only exists as our *present* memories of it, the memories that are experienced now, as we look back at our life experiences from this very moment. Massey (2005) calls this engagement with temporality as 'holding time still' (p. 28). Thus, engaging with the concept of temporality goes beyond just moving in time between the past and the present, but rather is about taking account of and acknowledging our subjective position in relation to chronological events in our attempts to 'hold them still' by the process of writing. We write our autoethnographic stories, looking back at the events that chronologically took place in the past, but what makes us apprehend the idea of the past is the fact that we have present memories of them – memories that exist in this instantaneous moment of our conscious life – our 'present past'. Tomorrow we might remember and interpret same events and feelings in a different way. As argued by Nielsen (2017), 'memories are always reconstructions in the present of what happened in the past and the narratives will therefore be characterised by selections, linking of memories, interpretations and chosen perspectives' (p. 53). From this standpoint, autoethnographic temporality is a symbiotic fusion of part–present–future, which denies a neat chronological arrangement of events, feelings and relations. Sartre ([1938] 2000) provides an insightful way of thinking about the concept of time, describing his feeling of time passing,

> when each instant leads to another, this one to another one and so on ... then you attribute this property to events which appear to you in the instants; what belongs to the form you carry over to the content. You talk a lot about this amazing flow of time, but you hardly see it. (p. 85)

This perception contributes to the view of our autoethnographic trajectories as ephemeral and evanescent, where our fragmented memories and past encounters intertwine with our current observations and thoughts in a fleeing, dynamic and chaotic 'back-and-forth movement between experiencing and examining a vulnerable self and observing and revealing the broader context of that experience' (Ellis, 2007, p. 14).

The idea of 'broader context' provides a helpful cognitive bridge to the subsequent discussion of the locational nature of autoethnographic temporality. Our autoethnographic narratives have an inseparable connection to various sociocultural localities as perceived by the researchers at specific temporal points. These localities, however, are different from locations, which are associated with specific geographical spaces or setting. Localities, in most cases, are not defined by any visible boundaries and can only exist in the imagination of researchers or their informants. Sometimes, researchers would perceive themselves as tied to static localities that are moving through time, and sometimes, they would feel that time is moving through them as integral parts of these localities. Thus, I define autoethnographic temporal locality here as a particular cultural phenomenon under study that is demarcated by commonly acknowledged or illusory boundaries, as they appear at the moment of writing. Van Manen (1990) discusses similar methodological strategy, referring to four types of, what he calls, 'lifeworlds' to include 'lived space (spatiality), lived body (corporeality), lived time (temporality) and lived human relations (relationality or communality)' (p. 101), which represent the different modalities of how human beings experience the world. Massey (2005) also emphasizes the integral connections of local spaces with temporality, arguing that these spaces are not just static or neutral surfaces torn by 'succession of slices through time' (p. 22) but are about dynamic juxtaposition of events and people, where 'the very concept of multiplicity entails spatiality' (p. 91). She further argues that if we accept time is the dimension of change, these 'spatial times' (p. 61) become the dimension of the local struggles that extend our politics beyond the personal in our autoethnographic narratives. Similarly, Pillow (2020) urges researchers to do their work to 'know histories of places, times, lands and bodies and begin to be able to see how colonial histories define epistemologies, ontologies and ethics' (p. 42).

These connotations bring a strong political accent into the debates about how times and localities are represented in autoethnographic research of cultural phenomena. Historically, the issues of representing local cultures in the context of specific temporal ways of thinking have a long record of vigorous debates in the fields of anthropology and ethnography. As observed by Geertz (1973), in the past, researchers attempted to solve these issues by either seeing local cultures as ideal microcosmic models of global spaces or as 'natural experiment' (p. 21) models for ethnographic investigations; nevertheless, they could not be resolved by 'regarding a remote locality as the world in a teacup or as the sociological equivalent of a cloud chamber' (p. 23). A significant contribution to the study of local cultures was made by Franz Boas (1894), who questioned evolutionary views on cultural development, arguing that new ideas that drove cultural progress were not born in a linear way but rather were diffused through people's communication with each other, and that neither race nor language nor distance limited that process of diffusion. Later on Boas (1904) concluded that local cultures did not advance in an evolutionary trajectory from 'low' savage stages to 'high' civilized forms of culture and we must 'consider all the ingenious attempts at constructions of a grand system of the evolution of society as of very doubtful value' (Boas, 1940, p. 276).

In this sense, the concept of autoethnographic temporality ties to a philosophical idea of 'historicity' that was, originally, defined by Jameson (1991) as our 'social, historical and existential present and the past' (p. 67). Yet, this perception of our past and present as ultimate referents has been challenged by later explorations of the notion (Trouillot, 1995; Hirsch and Stewart, 2005; Ringel, 2016). Hirsch and Stewart (2005), for example, depart from common understandings of human situation in a flow of time from the past to the present and into the future, developing the argument that such perceptions are based on standard Western concepts of history, where the past is separated from the present. In contrast, the authors suggest an interpretation of 'historicity' as a temporal amalgamation of 'past-present-future', which transcends any implicit assumptions that a Western way of doing history is the single 'true' version against the non-Western Other:

> 'Historicity' is analogous in that it draws attention to the connections between past, present and future without the assumption that events/time are a line between happenings 'adding up' to history. Whereas 'history' isolates the past, historicity focuses on the complex temporal nexus of past-present-future. Historicity, in our formulation, concerns the ongoing social production of accounts of pasts and futures. (Hirsch and Stewart, 2005, p. 262)

These contributions to the studies of local spaces and cultures as a hybrid of sociopolitical and temporal facets serve as a basis for our enhanced understanding of ethnographic and autoethnographic practices. Indeed, contemporary attempts to study local cultural phenomena are more fruitful when instigated not from a universal standpoint but from specific time-related social and political contexts informed by 'the diversity of the ways human beings construct their lives in the act of leading them' (Geertz, 1983, p. 16). For example, Fabian ([1983] 2006) offers a valuable perspective on the researchers' interpretation of time in relation to local cultures, arguing that all anthropological knowledge is affected by historically established relations of power and domination between the researchers and the researched cultures, where references to time are used to conceptualize relationships between us and our objects of study (the Other):

> Fabian regards allochronic discourse as a vehicle of Western domination, reproducing and legitimizing global inequities. In this context, Fabian's critique of anthropological allochronism emerges as an overtly political intervention, effectively identifying the rhetorical elements of temporal distancing – such as ethnographic depictions of the Other as 'primitive' or 'traditional' – as part and parcel of a (neo) colonial project. (Bunzl, 2006, p. xi)

Adkins (2009) suggests another way of looking at the fusion of times and locations, where time is not seen just as a standardized and decontextualized unit of measure but one that is intrinsically linked to the powers of social structures in, what she calls, 'event time'. According to Adkins (2009), this move from 'clock time' to 'event time' suggests 'not only that the hegemony of the mechanical clock is in decline, but also that the political economy of time is restructuring and certainly that it is not in the pull of devices measuring time in units of the clock in which protensive practical action is (or is not) actualised' (p. 90). Interestingly, this kind of deliberations can also reveal to contemporary autoethnographers potential pitfalls in how temporal categorizations of local cultures can divide researchers from the researched. Notably, a number of researchers (Fabian, [1983] 2006; Schulz, 2012; Scheller, 2020) problematize the use of past and present tense when writing about different cultures, arguing that researchers' choices of particular time determinants can 'freeze' their descriptions of these cultures in a specific time frame. Fabian ([1983] 2006) expresses particular concerns in terms of creating a discourse of 'allochronism' (p. 32), where researchers' choice of past tense is used to describe 'other men' as 'primitive', 'savage', 'tribal' or 'Third World' (p. 17) and, thus, not only different but also removed from us in a faraway space and time. Schulz (2012) explains that, even though researchers share a common temporal dimension with the culture they study, they tend to 'hide' the aspect of contemporarily in their narratives. Fabian calls this process a 'denial of coevalness' ([1983] 2006, p. 25), where researchers persistently and systematically place their subjects under study in a time other than the present of the producer of research. Eguchi (2020) problematizes temporal aspects of autoethnography through the lens of a transnational queer of colour critic, suggesting that the queer logics of time, with its undefined boundaries between past, present and future, are messy, never neat and unintelligible, thus 'impossible possibilities of queerness exist in the present-ness of a borderlands space, that is, a vague and undetermined place' (p. 310).

Placing these observations in connection with each other enables me to sketch the tensions that surround any autoethnographic project in relation to the way temporal aspects of the study are presented and justified. I suggest that in a symbiotic approach these discussions need to be made explicit, highlighting the limits and possibilities of thinking outside or beyond the logic of chronological time towards social dimensions of temporal understanding. Low (2017) agrees that both the production and the construction of spaces are mediated by social processes, especially being contested and fought over for economic and ideological reasons. She suggests a concept of 'spatializing culture', where cultures are studied simultaneously through the lens of space and place, providing a stimulus for 'uncovering material and representational injustice and forms of social exclusion' (p. 34). Sharma (2014) uses Foucauldian notion of biopolitics to locate subjects in culture and space/place, encouraging researchers to examine how individualized experiences of time intersect with others' experiences of time to create a grid of temporal power relations, which calibrate 'how individuals and groups synchronize their body clocks, their senses of the future or the present, to an exterior relation' (p. 18). For Sharma (2014), temporal does not imply a transcendent sense of time or a general sense of time in particular but denotes the specific experience of time that is fused with specific political and economic contexts, creating a

> social fabric composed of a chronography of power, where individuals' and social groups' sense of time and possibility are shaped by a differential economy, limited or expanded by the ways and means that they find themselves in and out of time. (p. 9)

Comparably, Matus (2019) also utilizes a post-structural lens for interpreting temporalities as entanglements of times, sites, experiences, subjects and objects that help researchers to explore the ways dominant notions of time allow for specific societal hierarchies and powers to persist as real and intelligible. We can make a connection here to Foucault's way of thinking about the discursive formation of historical knowledge and specifically, his concept of archaeology that is based on the presumption that systems of thought and knowledge are governed by the 'temporality of discursive formations' (Foucault, 1972b, p. 167), which define particular discourses as approved and accepted knowledge within particular historic periods, 'overturning all spatial orders in obedience to the onward thrust of time' (Foucault, 1972b, p. 152). Political (transformative) nature of Symbiotic Autoethnography is discussed in more depth further in this chapter, so I am going to curb my discussion here by, merely, highlighting the integral links between autoethnographic temporality and the sociopolitical nature of the cultural localities under study.

To conclude, I maintain that autoethnographic temporality presents an essential facet of a symbiotic approach to autoethnography, since the ways we write about our life experiences are inseparable from our perceptions of times and locations in the context of our studies and thus, these considerations are critical to the ways that contemporary autoethnographic practices produce knowledge. Engaging in discussions of temporality on both theoretical and methodological levels is a challenging task for autoethnographers and yet, as suggested by Butler (2005), even when autoethnographers do not place the questions of time at the centre of their inquiry, their autoethnographic narratives will be of a temporal nature, because 'when the "I" seeks to give an account of itself, it can start with itself, but will find that this self is already implicated in a social temporality that exceeds its own capacities for narration' (p. 8). Thus, considering temporality as an essential element of autoethnographic narratives holds potential for autoethnographers' deeper engagement with their understanding of autoethnographic time not as a linear chronological structure but 'as a matter of change, transformations and ruptures and as a matter of stability, continuity and inertia' (Hamann and Suckert, 2018, para. 3). In this sense, autoethnographic temporality decolonizes conventional ways of knowledge production, allowing autoethnographers to cross the boundaries of qualitative inquiry beyond its Eurocentric conventions, locating their subjective experiences in broader spatio-temporal rhythms of global cultural nuances. Engaging with the concept of autoethnographic temporality, potentially, offers one way through which researchers can strengthen their critiques and analyses of paradoxes, shifts and dislocations of their Self and the Other within specific temporal spaces/localities and their associated patterns of powers, supremacies and social injustices.

Researcher's omnipresence

In previous chapters I discussed some incongruencies between auto ethnographic approach and positivist orientations, in which the subject of investigation is observed from outside by a detached and impartial truth-seeking narrator. In contrast, autoethnography emphasizes the importance of the connection between the researcher and the subject under study by placing researchers at the very centre of their intersections with times, places and relations. The insertion of the researcher into the core of autoethnographic inquiry replaces narrator's invisibility with ubiquity of their presence throughout the text, widening researchers' functions beyond the rituals of collecting and interpreting data. Indeed, when we write our autoethnographic narratives, we do not separate our thoughts, memories or emotions into specific study-related segments, slicing them up in a surgical way into chunks of data. Rather, we appreciate our life experiences as a seamless flow through which we recall and re-live a previously experienced event or feeling in order to evoke authentic emotional responses through our autoethnographic writings. This leads me to suggest that within the methodological context of Symbiotic Autoethnography, the researchers' concern should be that of acknowledging their presence as ubiquitously detectable across all their related experiences. In this sense, autoethnographers' omnipresence can be understood as the researcher's all-enveloping simultaneous presence in every aspect of their autoethnographic inquiry, including those that seem to fall outside the immediate temporal and contextual relevance.

Before delving into a more detailed discussion about the concept of researcher's omnipresence, it is worth mentioning that, historically, the notion of omnipresence has been associated with theological interpretation of God's divine power of being present everywhere at the same time. A number of studies (McGuire and Slowik, 2012; Benedek and Veszelszki, 2016; Cowling and Cray, 2017; Inman, 2017), however, take the notion of omnipresence out of its religious context, suggesting its potential for metaphysical explorations of such concepts as time, truth, space, location and reality. For example, Piacenti, Rivas and Garrett (2014) utilize the concept in their ethnographic study to demonstrate how the physical position of our bodies 'can be transcended by the spatial reach of computer-generated words, creating an existential omnipresence indicative of the world's cosmopolitan elite' (p. 230). Dervin and Machart (2015) write about the omnipresence of culture in their explorations of intercultural encounters that move the concept of culture beyond its common understanding.

In my search for both comprehensive and harmonious ways of theorizing about omnipresence in the context of a narrative inquiry, I choose to follow the steps of Barad (2007, 2018), who uses her interpretations of quantum physics 'to trouble the scalar distinction between the world of subatomic particles' (Barad, 2018, p. 56) and that of sociocultural and political fields. To avoid the risk of digressing into ultracrepidarian ponderings about the fundamentals of quantum theory, I lean here on Ball (2017) in my attempt to provide a cognitive bridge between the concept of researcher's omnipresence and the behaviour of quantum particles. As we all know from our school programmes, in classical physics, any particle always has a definitive identifiable position. In quantum physics, however, the position of particles is defined by, what is called, a *superposition*, which is associated with their paradoxical ability to occupy, under certain conditions, two or more positions at the same time. Ball (2017) provides an accessible interpretation of this phenomena, referring to the famous 'double-slit' experiment, the results of which shaped our current understanding of quantum particles' behaviour over two hundred years ago, well before quantum theory existed. In the 'double-slit' experiment, the experimenter shines a beam

of light on a barrier with two closely spaced parallel slits in it and then studies
the pattern it produces on a screen behind the barrier. When the 'double-slit'
experiment is performed with quantum particles, such as electrons, these
particles behave like waves, which means that they can undergo diffraction (i.e.
spreading beyond the gap) when a stream of them passes through the two slits,
producing an interference pattern. To understand the relevance of this result to
the notion of superposition, Ball (2017) invites us to imagine that the quantum
particles are sent through the double slits one by one and their patterns on the
screen can also be observed one by one. The uncomfortable discovery at this
stage points to the fact that each single particle does not travel through the slit in
a straight line but still produces interference patterns (mush as waves do), even
though it has no other particles to interfere with. This seems to imply that each
particle passes simultaneously through both slits and interferes with itself. As
explained by Cresser (2009), 'this propensity for quantum system to behave as if
they can be two places at once, or more generally in different states at the same
time, is termed "the superposition of states" ' (p. 5). And although, of course,
this is only a very basic description of an extremely complex phenomenon with
its associated conditions and speculations, it is the notion of superposition
that I find particularly useful for illustrating my thinking behind the concept
of researcher's omnipresence. Similarly to the quality of quantum particles
to be in several places at the same time, autoethnographers in their writing
transcend the constraints of physical times and spaces, allowing themselves to
be present simultaneously across and within all their experiences, localities,
memories, feelings, illusions and relations. Ellis's (2013a) powerful description
of autoethnography has a close association with the concept of researcher's
omnipresence in its focus on the blurred boundaries between being, knowing,
feeling and thinking in our autoethnographic writings:

> autoethnography is not simply a way of knowing about the world; it has become
> a way of being in the world, one that requires living consciously, emotionally,
> reflexively. It asks that we not only examine our lives but also consider how and
> why we think, act and feel as we do. (p. 10)

This view of autoethnographic writing as a 'form of continual life review' (Ellis,
2013b, p. 35) resonates strongly with the concept of researcher's omnipresence,
substantiating the capacity of autoethnographic writing to transcend temporal
and spatial boundaries. Furthermore, the suggested interpretation of researcher's
omnipresence elucidates that there is no single and fixed time or location from
which autoethnographers obtain their knowledge; rather, their sources of

knowledge are everywhere, like those quantum particles that are 'spanned all over space without distinction and real spatial separation' (Masi, 2019, p. 154). This is not to say, however, that researcher's omnipresence implies researchers' disengagement from the local sites of emotional, political and economic struggles. On the opposite, it aims to augment researchers' vistas, inciting the former to move their narratives from a static single location towards multiple sites of a contextualized world of powers and privileges. As argued by Grant (2019), an autoethnographic 'self' as a sociocultural entity enables autoethnographers to interrogate and critique wider practices and power imbalances in order to make advances in social justice. In this sense, using the concept of researcher's omnipresence deliberately as an epistemological resource allows researchers to use their subjective experience to theorize about these wider practices outside the formal time–space boundaries of their study, creating a richer and more intimate picture of the world. Here we can also detect one of the junctures, where the concept of researcher's omnipresence connects symbiotically to the previously discussed notion of temporality. Indeed, a symbiotic approach brings together the two concepts by troubling past/present and here/there dichotomies and blurring lines between precise chronological and geographical localities and their subjective autoethnographic explorations. Pole and Morrison (2003) express similar thoughts in relation to different forms of ethnographic research, suggesting that 'a close temporal and spatial relationship between researcher and the generated or collected data has the capacity to facilitate a fuller, more holistic account of social action or a discrete location' (p. 49).

In addition to negating temporal and spatial boundaries, my interpretation of researcher's omnipresence as part of a symbiotic approach also interferes with dichotomous roles of autoethnographers as outsider/insider researchers. I argue, as does Van Maanen (2011), that in autoethnographic practices, researchers face challenges of smudged boundaries between the positions of an outsider and an insider researcher, as autobiographical details mount in their 'confessional tales':

> The attitude conveyed is one of tacking back and forth between an insider's passionate perspective and an outsider's dispassionate one. Perhaps, no other confessional convention is as difficult for the writer as maintaining in print this paradoxical, if not schizophrenic, attitude towards the group observed. A delightful dance of words often ensues as fieldworkers present themselves as both vessels and vehicles of knowledge. (p. 77)

Indeed, the paradoxes of being the subject and the object of investigation create a unique dynamics within autoethnographic research, pushing autoethnographers towards disrupting the insider/outsider boundaries of classical ethnographic traditions. To understand better this dichotomy in relation to researcher's omnipresence, I consider it helpful to juxtapose it to Anderson's (2006) concept of a complete member researcher (CMR) status in the context of his understanding of analytic autoethnography. In his work Anderson refers to Adler and Adler's (1987) notions of opportunistic and convert CMRs as two possibilities of researchers' positioning in relation to the subject of their study. Opportunistic option suggests that researcher already is a member of the group prior to starting their research, whilst in the case of convert CMRs, researcher starts with making a decision about conducting research and then converts to becoming a full member of the cultural group or setting under study. Though both of these types of CMR indicate researcher's *insider* position within the researched environment, which is, broadly, congruent with symbiotic autoethnographic approach, the fundamental difference between CMR status and researcher's omnipresence lies in the notion of membership.

First, membership seems to indicate a definitive time framework that allows researcher to enter and to leave specific cultural settings by 'applying for' and 'cancelling' their membership at particular points. Yet, autoethnographic researchers, more often than not, already naturally belong to that cultural environment and, thus, do not have to make choices of entering a cultural group or a setting. As pointed out by Duncan (2004), 'in an autoethnography, the researcher is not trying to become an insider in the research setting. He or she, in fact, is the insider. The context is his or her own' (p. 3). In relation to the cases when autoethnographic researchers do choose to become part of a specific cultural environment on a temporary basis, I maintain that their presence still goes beyond the membership rules of just getting into and out of the setting. Rather, autoethnographic studies involve a much complex mode of presence ('omnipresence') of researcher's multiple fragmented selves within the entire range of their life experiences that merge together in the moment of autoethnographic writing, disrupting any seemingly obvious chronological precisions and making it impossible for researcher to separate the 'moments of being' from the 'moments of researching'. Moors (2017) also questions the use of the term 'autoethnography' in relation to all reflective accounts of researcher's experiences, some of which, she argues, seem to be 'much closer to a social experiment' of an outsider researcher (p. 387) than a genuine autoethnographic lived experience:

> When one is a relative outsider to the lifeworld of one's interlocutors, participant observation involves developing relations of trust, forms of closeness and

empathy by participating in their lifeworlds (even if this always remains limited). But if one starts off as relatively close to, or part of, a particular lifeworld and already has acquired forms of experiential, embodied knowledge, one has a different point of departure. Then one moves from participating to reflecting upon one's experiences. The latter is what I would consider autoethnography. Lumping together all research that reflects on the researcher's experiences as autoethnographic fails to recognize how one's ability or inability to 'leave the field' structures one's experiences. (p. 388)

Similarly, Maydell (2010) argues that autoethnographic researchers come with an insider position by default. Thus, based on these deliberations, the concept of researcher's omnipresence as part of Symbiotic Autoethnography steps away from Anderson's (2006) view of researcher's insider position as a type of membership.

As to my second point Anderson's (2006) complete researcher membership status implies that autoethnographers, as social scientists, have another cultural identity and goals that lead to them having a social orientation that is different from that of the other group members: 'unlike their peers in the research setting(s), autoethnographers must orient (at least for significant periods of time) to documenting and analyzing action as well as to purposively engaging in it' (p. 380). In Symbiotic Autoethnography, however, the concept of researcher's omnipresence implies that autoethnographers write about the periods of their lives when they did not perceive themselves as researchers and thus, their diaries, letters, photographs or other artefacts were not produced for the purpose of documenting and analysing them later. The aspects of working 'symbiotically' with autoethnographic data are discussed in more detail in Chapter 5; however, it is worth just briefly clarifying here that it is only at the moment of writing that all these artefacts become 'data', helping autoethnographers to tame the disorderly fusion of writing and analysis. Thus, in Symbiotic Autoethnography researcher's omnipresence goes beyond becoming a member of a specific setting or a cultural group or acquiring a different social identity. Even though our autoethnographic enquiries all have a start and an end point, what lies in-between is about our continuous presence in the spaces, events, memories, conversations, thoughts, dreams and illusions, which foregrounds 'the impossibility of separating or collapsing life from/into texts' (Holman Jones, 2007, p. 230). The idea of being in-between locations and events creates a few parallels with the concept of a 'third space', which is, mainly, associated with Bhabha (1994). In his work *Location of Culture*, Bhabha develops an idea of the third space as a place of hybridity, where hegemonic powers of dominant cultures are disrupted, giving rise to 'something different, something new and unrecognizable, a new area of negotiation of meaning and representation' (p. 211). This discourse, similarly to researcher's omnipresence, highlights the uniqueness of each individual's experiences that can be seen as a hybrid of their perceptions across different locations and sites of cultural exclusions and exchanges. Yet another interpretation of third space that comes even closer to the concept of researcher's omnipresence is developed by Soja (1996), who uses the term 'thirdspace' to denote alternative ways of exploring the spatial 'in-betweenness'. Soja (1996) describes this new 'an-Other' form of spatial awareness – thirdspace – as a search space and to initiate its evolving definition by describing it as

> a product of 'thirding' of the spatial imagination, the creation of another mode of thinking about space that draws upon the material and mental spaces of the traditional dualism but extends well beyond them in scope, substance and meaning. Simultaneously real and imagined and more (both and also ...), the exploration of Thirdspace can be described and inscribed in journeys to 'real-and-imagined' (or perhaps 'realandimagined'?) places. (p. 11)

Soja (1996) also acknowledges the uncertainty and fluidity of his concept of Thirdspace, which, similarly to researcher's omnipresence, is a flexible term that 'attempts to capture what is actually a constantly shifting and changing milieu of ideas, events, appearances and meanings' (p. 2). More recently, Dwyer and Buckle (2009) referred to 'the space between' in their discussion of the dual role of a researcher as 'insider-outsider'. Drawing on Aoki's ([1996] 2005) work, the authors suggest that the binary roles of insider and outsider as two separate pre-existing entities can be bridged by using a hyphen between them, which can be viewed not as a path but as 'a dwelling place for people, acting as a third space, a space between, a space of paradox, ambiguity and ambivalence, as well as conjunction and disjunction' (p. 60).

These deliberations in few strokes bring to the fore the central idea behind the concept of researcher's omnipresence that is about troubling unhelpful dichotomies and blurring lines between space and time, between 'past' and 'present' and between 'here' and 'there'. Driven by methodological consonance, Symbiotic Autoethnography embraces researchers' movements across spaces and locations. Taking a traditional autoethnographic study beyond chronological times and physical locations the focus is on a particular place or a 'thread'; ethnography examines processes of cultural continuity and change across multiple settings. In doing so, ethnography involves a 'peripatetic, translative mapping of brave new worlds' (Marcus, 1995, p. 114).

In contemporary society, these new worlds include social spaces, amongst them the internet, social media and cyberspace. By making autoethnographers aware of their omnipresence, a symbiotic approach aims to help researchers to discard these unhelpful dichotomies as foundation of a deterministic view of the world. By way of insisting on the acknowledgement of researcher's omnipresence as part of autoethnographic inquiry, symbiotic autoethnographers assert the inevitably paradoxical nature of autoethnographic research practices and guide autoethnographers towards 'making connections of how entangled relationalities that do not appear to be proximate in space and time constitute a force' (Barad, 2007, p. 74). The next part of the discussion is devoted to evocative storytelling as one of the ways autoethnographers can make these connections with relationalities in the context of a symbiotic approach.

Evocative storytelling

As mentioned in previous chapters, autoethnography as a theoretical approach to qualitative research has developed as a result of researchers' resistance to positivist claims about the existence of single objective 'truth' that is out there waiting to be discovered. Consequently, ethnographers and, later on, autoethnographers devoted their efforts to advancing multiplicity of 'ways of knowing' and acknowledging the presence of the researcher's views, perceptions, experiences and emotions in their research studies. In this sense, autoethnography has emerged as a space, where 'an individual's passion can bridge individual and collective experience to enable richness of representation, complexity of understanding and inspiration for activism' (Ellingson and Ellis, 2008, p. 450). This makes researchers' emotional responses to events and occurrences one of the central concerns of autoethnography and of a symbiotic approach, in particular.

Commonly, the term 'emotion' is applied to denote a broad mix of temporal behaviours that include psychological, neurological and physical responses to different stimuli. Throughout history, people used various techniques to record their emotional responses to important events and occurrences. Our prehistoric ancestors, for example, left paintings on cave walls to chronicle their significant experiences; ancient Egyptians used pyramids, obelisks and papyrus to memorialize their spiritual admonitions and significant texts; early African tribes used various forms of jewellery made from seashells, seeds, engraved stones, ivory, ostrich eggshell and animal teeth to express their emotional appreciation of wisdom, luck, hope and well-being. As noted by Dixon (2012), the word *emotion* (a translation of the French *émotion*) came into use in the English language only in the seventeenth century, even though many of the associated notions, such as 'passions', 'affections' and 'sentiments', had been the object of theoretical analysis since ancient Greece. Since then, our understanding of emotions has undergone many developments in terms of the nature and significance of human emotional responses and behaviours. Yet, as Fox (2018) observes, for generations, early interpretations of emotions in philosophy were informed by dominant appreciation of 'reason' as the ultimate human virtue and thus, emotions were considered to be antithetical to the pursuit of a rational way of life. One of the first scientific investigations focused on the meaning of emotions was carried out by Darwin ([1872] 1965), who attempted cross-cultural observations in his research and offered an argument that 'the language of emotions' (p. 366) serves an important communicative function in human evolution. Still, despite researchers' long-standing interest in emotions, it is only over the last two decades of the twentieth century that narrative research began to take interest in this concept. One of the first studies that paved a path in this direction belongs to Dewey ([1934] 2005), who wrote about the importance of emotions in creating the dynamics of narratives, where emotion 'attends the development of a plot' (p. 43). Here Dewey creates a connection between the emotionally charged narratives and their transformative powers that also affect the readers' emotional states, as they realize themselves 'they are transfigured' (p. 80). Hospers ([1956] 1997) gives powerful examples of the immense emotive effect that certain words can have on hearer and readers:

> These words don't so much *describe* the object in question as to register the speakers' *reaction* to it (original emphasis). There are emotively neutral ways of referring to certain racial groups, for example, 'African-American', but there are also emotively loaded ways of referring to them, such as the 'n-word' frequently used in the O.J. Simpson trial. The first word the raises no one's blood pressure, whereas the second word can be used as an occasion for riot and murder. (p. 25)

Later on, Oatley and Jenkins (1992) confirmed the significance of emotive narratives in helping the readers to form new schemas and new interpretations that enhance human social interactions. Similarly, Kleres (2011) makes a direct link between human experiences and their representation in specific 'narrative knowledge' (p. 183), in which narratives are inextricably emotionally structured, so that they create a consistent emotional connection with the readers. This connection is also achieved through the acknowledgement of therapeutic benefits of storytelling, which have been universally accepted centuries ago as a way of assisting people with emotional healing and treating mental health problems (Bettelheim, [1975] 1991). A notable example of using evocative autoethnographic writing as a healing tool can be found in Spry (2001), who rejects scholarly preferences for impersonal, non-emotional narratives, confessing that her own profound healing from sexual trauma happened only through the autoethnographic performance of her 'embodied critical passions' (p. 726), which allowed her to position herself as an active agent with narrative authority. Whitinui (2014) writes about a culturally informed research practice in relation to 'Maori ways of knowing' (p. 456), which has the potential to 'heal' through writing about self as 'learning' in emotionally powerful and creative ways. A number of other authors (Tomaselli, Dyll and Francis, 2008; McMillan and Ramirez, 2016; Burke, 2019; Grant, 2020) also reiterated the therapeutic effect of evocative storytelling that can serve as another channel for securing better connection between autoethnographers and their audiences.

In addition to highlighting the importance of making connections between the narratives and their readers, relatively recent studies (Hochschild, 1979; Denzin, 1984; Williams and Bendelow, 1996; Barbalet, 1999) on the sociology of emotion drew attention to the ways in which emotions could be perceived not just as innately personal but as socially and culturally constructed patterns of human behaviour:

> The development of a sociology of emotions is crucial to our understanding of social life. Emotions are 'social things', they are controlled and managed in our everyday lives and transcend the divides between mind and body, nature and culture, structure and action. In this way, they hold the key to our understanding of social process and can push forward the boundaries of sociological investigation. (Williams and Bendelow, 1998, p. xv)

This new interpretation of emotions as sociocultural constructs has reshaped theoretical field related to emotional expressions, placing emotions at the centre of our understanding of social phenomena. As confirmed by Bericat (2016), our emotions emerge in specific social situations and thus, understanding emotions can lead to understanding the situation and social relation that produces it. Simonova (2019) also reminds us that emotions reflect our subjective reactions to social situations and structures and, thus, the study of emotional dimensions 'provides a kind of access to live and genuine human experience' (p. 157), which find their way into a multitude of disciplinary studies. Indeed, our emotions pervade all aspects of human condition, including our social and cultural experiences across personal and professional lives. Acknowledging that emotions are, essentially, of a social nature enabled researchers to widen the horizons of their research approaches through including emotional dimension as a fundamental element in their explorations of social and cultural phenomena. As suggested by Pelias (2019), creative researchers can add significance to their narratives through evoking the intellectual complexity of their subjects by 'writing into and creating emotional space' (p. 23).

It is at the intersection of making emotional connection with the readers and, simultaneously, exploring subjective emotional responses to various social and cultural occurrences that I recognize the links with Symbiotic Autoethnography. Indeed, it is almost impossible to find an autoethnographic study that would disregard the importance of emotive aspects of both their narratives and the anticipated emotional reactions of these narratives on their audiences. Autoethnographers often focus on the explorations of emotionally laden objects of study that involve such phenomena as illness, death, pain, injustice, grief or abuse, to name just a few examples. In their engagement with these objects of study, autoethnographers attempt to enter their inner world of emotions to provide a deeper and more intimate exploration of events and phenomena under investigation. As described by Poulos (2020), the value of autoethnography is in the degree of its evocative potency, as 'there is nothing quite like reading an autoethnography about a broken relationship, or a traumatic experience, or a tragic loss and finishing with tears streaming down your cheeks' (p. 209).

Considering the significance of this aspect of autoethnographic research, it is not surprising that my decision to include 'evocative storytelling' as another aspect of a symbiotic approach is substantiated by a wide range of literature on the subject (Ellis, 1997; Richardson, 2000a; Ellis and Bochner, 2016; Gale, 2020; Wyatt, 2020). Undeniably, autoethnographic studies have to include evocative stories where 'emotion is privileged' (Denzin, 2014, p. 40), since when the researchers emphasize the personal, a new kind of theorizing occurs through juxtaposing of emotion, voices, temporality and points of view, enabling us to read, 'reacting and reflecting with all our senses' (Ellis and Bochner, 2016, p. 9). At this point we can also detect a locus of symbiosis between the previously discussed aspects of temporality and researcher's omnipresence with evocative storytelling. In Symbiotic Autoethnography, our autoethnographic narratives are inseparable from our omnipresence in times and locations and our associated emotional responses to events and encounters. These emotional responses to various life experiences create in our brains certain patterning systems, which facilitate our ability to store and interpret these experiences. Kensinger and Murray (2012) suggest that these patterning systems are commonly known as 'emotional memory', which is used to denote human ability to remember experiences in association with the emotional reactions they evoked. Truly, our recollections of events always seem to be more vivid when they are related to strong emotional feelings aroused by them. However, Graci and Fivush (2017) emphasize that remembering personal experiences does not involve a simple recollection of facts and observations but rather requires persons to turn these temporal emotional episodes into meaningful narratives that serve as 'an indicator and a facilitator for organizing and understanding events and ourselves' (p. 489). Similarly, in Symbiotic Autoethnography, the narratives go beyond simple dispassionate description of events, providing more comprehensive cognitive connections between our emotional memories of temporal spaces, location and relations. Thus, using evocative storytelling can be seen as the channel through which autoethnographers symbiotically embed linguistic representations of their emotions into their narratives to facilitate the process of meaning-making for both their readers and themselves.

In addition, a symbiotic approach entails researchers' acknowledgement of the potency of their evocative writing to display 'multiple layers of consciousness, connecting the personal to the cultural' (Ellis and Bochner, 2000, p. 739). An amalgamation of evocative writing with social and cultural stimuli that triggered these emotional responses creates a symbiotic connection between the researcher's experience and the cultural phenomena under study. Examining these phenomena through emotional lens opens new possibilities for autoethnographers to challenge more traditional research practices, asking questions similar to those posed by Ellis and Bochner (2000):

> Why should caring and empathy be secondary to controlling and knowing? Why must academics be conditioned to believe that a text is important only to the extent it moves beyond the merely personal? We need to question our assumptions, the meta rules that govern the institutional workings of social science – arguments over feelings, theories over stories, abstractions over concrete events, sophisticated jargon over accessible prose. (p. 756)

Such production of 'emotional knowledge' can be seen as a deliberate attempt to go against the grain of widely accepted ways of knowing, where alternative ways of generating knowledge tend to be disregarded. In the context of Symbiotic Autoethnography researchers are expected to use their emotions not only as a connecting channel with their readers but also as a catalyst to social action, where emotions locate researchers in specific social circumstances rather than abstract space. Yet there are certain risks associated with producing evocative narratives.

For Poulos (2020) one of the major perils of writing in evocative style is that 'in the name of a powerful, striking, evocative, compelling, startling, disruptive story, we might sacrifice the chance, or abdicate our responsibility, to trace and develop the broader implications of our work, thus leaving our audiences wondering what (if anything) to do (other than feel) as a result of reading our work' (p. 209). Similarly, Harris and Holman Jones (2019) warn us of the danger of replacing sustainable social action with emotional musings, suggesting that emotions should serve as a circuit, not an endpoint of autoethnographic research. In response to these concerns, it is important to confirm at this point that, in Symbiotic Autoethnography, evocative storytelling and analytic scrutiny are not seen as mutually exclusive, even though they are often presented in contrast (particularly, in reference to Ellis and Bochner's (2000) and Anderson's (2006) work). Vryan (2006), helpfully, corroborates that viewing analytic autoethnography as an alternative to evocative might create an impression that if a work is too evocative, then it is incapable or less capable of engaging in analytical exercise. Such segregation between evocative and analytic autoethnographies creates another unhelpful dichotomy, leading to a false assumption that critical analysis is discordant with emotive texts and that emotionally charged narratives are, somehow, incompatible with analysis. One of the researchers, who argues strongly for appreciation of emotion in research, is Behar (1996), who claims that research, which does not 'break your heart', is not worth doing. In support of this claim, Nash (2004) argues that such sentiment 'is a scandal to those hardline social scientists in her this sibling who believe that empirical investigators must wear bionic masks in order to totally immunise themselves to the distorting effects of human emotion' (p. 49). Importantly, using evocative approach in the context of Symbiotic Autoethnography creates additional opportunities for giving voice to marginalized populations through 'politically imaginative' (Durham et al., 2020, p. 289) ways of conveying cultural knowledge. Hughes (2020), for example, uses evocative poetic verse as part of the autoethnographic exploration of his experiences of social justice as a Black male education professor at one of the US universities. His research grew out of the need to respond to increasing attacks on scholar-activists, who engage in critical race theory and, specifically, to one of the 'rules' of White supremacy that require academics to 'avoid emotions', because emotions can undermine the information they intend to share. As form of a protest against such 'rule', Hughes starts his autoethnography

> with a free verse poem that draws from anapestic and iambic pentameter interspersing 'da-da-dum' and 'da-dum' meters to conjure feelings sometimes

of seasickness and sometimes of soothing rhythms and rhymes similar to the pentameter associated with Dr. Suess. (p. 153)

Similarly, Davina Woods (McKenna and Woods, 2012), an Indigenous Australian lecturer, writes about the capacity of evocative approach to autoethnography to assist in restoration of Indigenous emotional well-being that was mutilated by the onslaughts of colonization and the deliberate acts of pillage and larceny. She suggests that artful autoethnographies awaken researchers to alternative ways of knowing through exploring Indigenous cosmologies and belief systems illustrated in paintings, carvings, dance and other forms of art.

Hence, in a symbiotic approach, emotion is seen as a way of knowing about a cultural phenomenon that is expressed in diverse styles of evocative writing and performance. The role of emotion in this symbiosis serves almost as a methodological glue that holds together our emotions and their related social and cultural context. In this sense, a symbiotic approach impels researchers to give space to their emotive, moving, impassioned and, at times, provocative accounts, as, in agreement with Bochner and Ellis (1996), I argue that autoethnographers do not anticipate their readers just to sit back as spectators but want them 'to feel and care and desire' (p. 24) through emotionally and analytically charged narrative that combines personal, social and cultural in symbiotic autoethnographic writing. To take one step further Klevan and Grant's (2020) idea of 'friendship as method', I suggest that using 'emotion as method' would enable researchers to acknowledge and justify their move to a symbiotic approach away from the constraints of objectivity and towards a wide range of evocative ways of storytelling, including dance and drama performances, arts, graphics, digital multimedia, videos and photographs, to name but a few. In this way, Symbiotic Autoethnography offers a unique capacity to capture the attention of different audiences, which otherwise would remain unreachable through conventional practices of knowledge exchange. Multimodality of evocative storytelling can be used in a symbiotic approach to 'publicise and politicise the sentimental' (Pham, 2011, p. 23), whilst exploring ourselves and others within a specific cultural milieu.

Interpretative analysis

As mentioned in the previous section, a symbiotic approach discards the detachment of evocative writing from analytic work, thus, I include interpretative analysis as another essential feature of Symbiotic Autoethnography. Whilst in the context of quantitative methodologies researchers consider the process of interpretation as objective, replicable and generalizable, qualitative narrative studies are characterized by their inherent interpretive nature. Autoethnographies, in particular, are shaped and informed by the researchers' subjective interpretations of the cultural phenomena under study. Grant (2019) stresses the importance of analytical interpretation as one of the key ways of exercising a balanced approach to autoethnographic studies, where all three components – 'auto', 'ethno' and 'graphy' – of the overarching term need to be in evidence. The author warns novice researchers against producing stories which have little or no analysis, theory or sociocultural interrogation, arguing that

> when the seductive promise of cultural interrogation stated at the beginning of a paper remains unfulfilled by its end, the cultural status quo is left untroubled. Writers of such work might best be described as autoethnographic sheep in wolves' clothing. Many of them also often seem to work in theory-free zones, happily displaying the naive realist assumption that their particular world is the world in a universal sense. (p. 89)

Indeed, the aim of autoethnographic studies is to produce a representation of the social through a deep interpretative analysis of the researcher's own experiences that reflect wider social, political and cultural contexts. In relation to a symbiotic approach, interpretative analysis is seen as the way of amalgamating researchers' autoethnographic data with its simultaneous interpretation in temporal culturally sensitive contexts, where researcher's presence is ubiquitous. In the following few paragraphs, I will try to elaborate on both the key aspects of symbiotic interpretation and the significance of exercising culturally sensitive approach to our interpretative analysis.

The concept of interpretation as a type of human activity extends well beyond the boundaries of autoethnographic research, having multiple applications in culture, law, mathematics, neuroscience and a few more fields of inquiry. Etymologically, the origin of the word 'interpret' goes back to Sanskrit 'prathe' ('to spread abroad') and ancient Greek 'phrazein' ('to point out, show, explain, declare, speak'). Originating from the theory of hermeneutics as the methodology used for interpretation of obscure biblical and philosophical texts, the most common definition of interpretation in its philosophical sense is associated with the activity of making sense of various objects, symbols and concepts under consideration. Later on, the concept of interpretation was extended to refer to the process of making sense of something we try to understand or, as explained by Maitlis and Christianson (2014), a process that involves creating intersubjective meaning and, thereby, 'enacting a more ordered environment from which further cues can be drawn' (p. 67).

In terms of the analytical part of interpretation, the process of analysis, in general terms, refers to researchers' attempts to generate meaningful insights from the collected data, using various techniques, tools and strategies. In methodological sense, analysis is a relatively recent concept, even though the techniques of breaking complex notions into smaller parts with the purpose of gaining a better understanding of them goes back to ancient Greek geometry and philosophy. Expectedly, word 'analysis' originates from the ancient Greek 'analyein' ('break up, release, set free'). Despite the fact that today this concept is widely applied to many disciplines and subjects of inquiry, its application to qualitative research is not straightforward. Some of the controversies associated with analysing qualitative data include complexities of separating methods of data collection from data analysis, intricacies of representation as well as the obscurities related to the nature of knowledge produced, to name just a few. These issues intensify even further when it comes to autoethnographic inquiry, as it is the type of research where methodological tools of data generation, analysis, interpretation and representation merge together in the ways in which theory and practice become holistically interwoven (Leavy, 2015).

The issues of working 'symbiotically' with autoethnographic data are discussed in detail in Chapter 5, so here I intend to outline some of the more general aspects of interpretative analysis as an essential component of a symbiotic approach. The concept of interpretative analysis in the context of Symbiotic Autoethnography is built, mainly, around Denzin's (2014) understanding of interpretation as a process that 'works forward to the conclusion of a set of acts taken up by the subject while working back in time, interrogating the historical, cultural and biographical conditions that moved the person to experience the events being studied' (p. x). With this in mind, I suggest that interpretative analysis in a symbiotic approach aims at merging autoethnographic narratives within a sound theoretical basis that is critically interpreted with consideration of the researcher's omnipresence across their spatio-temporal experiences. As noted by Spry (2001, p. 713), 'good autoethnography is not simply a confessional tale of self-renewal; it is a provocative weave of story and theory'. Allen-Collinson (2012) also reminds us that, whilst autoethnographic research incorporates very personal, evocative and poetic accounts, it also requires the researcher to engage in highly analytic and theoretical work. In addition, Adams, Holman Jones and Ellis (2015) specifically note that for autoethnographers, 'theory and story have a reciprocal, symbiotic relationship' (p. 89), where theory explains the nuances of the cultural experiences, whilst story illustrates and embodies these experiences. One of the crucial aspects of creating such symbiotic relationship depends on the researchers' ability to create meaningful links between their stories and critical interpretation of how such stories help us to transform the world and ourselves within it:

> The 'critical' in critical autoethnography reminds us that theory is not a static or autonomous set of ideas, objects, or practices. Instead, theorizing is an ongoing process that links the concrete and abstract, thinking and acting, aesthetics and criticism. (Holman Jones, 2016, p. 228)

Furthermore, this approach to interpretative analysis also suits a type of sensitivity in which 'no one right form of knowledge exists, and multiple viewpoints are acknowledged and valued' (Duncan, 2004, p. 3). This line of reasoning channels my discussion of interpretative analysis towards the understanding of what 'truth' is in relation to autoethnographic narratives, where we acknowledge the absence of epistemological certainty about 'what can be known'. Here Rorty's (1989) views come particularly useful, as he asserts that 'truth' cannot be out there and exist independently of the human mind: 'the world is out there but descriptions of the world are not' (p. 5). In the context of a symbiotic approach, one of the ways of reconciling autoethnographic research ambitions with the denial of absolute and subjective truth is to consider autoethnographic stories as momentary interpretation of the events with the purpose of discovering not the *truth* but the *meaning* behind the former. As explained by Weedon (1987, p. 173), 'modes of subjectivity, like theories of society or versions of history, are temporary fixings in the on-going process in which any absolute meaning or truth is constantly deferred'. Similarly, Garratt (2014) also argues that the researcher's 'interpretive omnipotence is imbued in the fragmentary moments of fictive and corporeal reality, where meanings associated with and attached to others' actions arise in an ethical context that initially promises, but ultimately defers "truth"' (p. 343). Hence, I suggest that autoethnographers in their interpretative analysis aim to 'defer truth' and, instead, focus on discovering the meaning behind their experiences of specific cultural phenomena. This way they will be able to create new knowledge 'symbiotically' by merging their temporal versions of reality with multiplicity of perspectives, events, relations and voices. However, problematizing the notion of 'truth' also brings with it an array of questions that would require autoethnographers' reflective engagement to help them consolidate their position. One of these questions is related to an uncomfortable obscurity associated with the notion of 'fact' as applied to autoethnographic research. Morse (2018), for example, brings to our attention an interesting point about the degree of resemblance between 'factual' events and their interpretations, arguing that this quota serves as a demarcation line between interpretative research analysis and journalism:

> Judging how closely the interpretive description resembles the actual events depends on the intended use of the description. Both the journalist and the qualitative researcher have agendas at the beginning of their enquiries. This agenda comes, in journalism, from the issue being investigated; in qualitative research, it depends on the question being asked and the theoretical frames that the researcher is using. More important, underlying these agendas is the disciplinary stance: Do we wish the description to represent the facts? Or do we wish the description to represent the meaning of the event or situation to the participant? (p. 805)

These questions not only outline the differences between the two fields of inquiry but also bring to the surface more fundamental issues in relation to the notion of 'fact' as applied to autoethnographic research. Due to the temporal and ubiquitous nature of autoethnographers' journeys, researchers often feel a need to anchor their story to certain chronological 'facts'. Analogously to the concept of 'truth', the notion of 'fact' is also far from being pure and simple, yet it is one of the ways we attempt to grasp certain aspects of reality from the position of accepted rules of thinking (Schutz, 1953). So, whilst still operating in accord with the position that bare facts do not exist, I suggest that in a symbiotic approach, autoethnographers chose to use specific chronological anchor points as an opportunity to offer their interpretation of the events as momentary readings of their 'facticity' rather than 'fact'. Facticity is defined in the English Oxford Dictionary as 'the quality or condition of being fact'. Denzin (2014) provides a helpful cognitive bridge between the notions of 'fact' and 'facticity', describing the latter as how facts 'were lived and experienced by interacting individuals' (p. 13). This means that the purpose of autoethnographers' interpretative analysis is not to confirm historical events as 'facts' – that is, 'the dissolution of the Soviet Union occurred on 26 December 1991' – but rather to present their 'conditions of being fact' by offering their interpretation of what it meant to be in the Soviet Union on that day. As argued by Varga and Guignon (2014), though the facticity of each individual situation creates some constraints on our possible self-interpretations, we have the ability to choose how we interpret things and, in these interpretations, we decide how things are to count or matter.

This way of reconciliation of 'facts' with 'interpretation' is voguishly discussed by Gabriel (2015), who poses, with a certain level of sarcasm, that accepting the world around us as a hidden cultural construction turns historical matter of facts into some kind of hallucination. Indeed, such radical readings of 'truth' and 'facts' are neither flawless nor straightforward. They are as messy as the reality that we try to describe and that is precisely why they are a good match. Thus, the intention of symbiotic autoethnographic studies is not to suggest the existence of or discover one single truth or reality but instead use the 'facticities' and interpretations of researchers' fractured experiences of different sociocultural systems to craft a type of a 'working truth' or a 'truthful fiction' (Denzin, 2014, p. 13) based on their version of reality within a specific 'frame of reference' commensurate with their research question. This standpoint resonates directly with the earlier opinion from Warren (1935), who argued that

> we can but describe the universe from certain relative standpoints, each of which constitutes a frame of reference from which to try to view the whole. Some frames of reference, indeed, surpass others and man may find or approximate that vantage-point of outlook which is most adequate for him. But final knowledge, true from any angle of perspective, is a blissful dream. (p. 182)

Indeed, in Symbiotic Autoethnography researchers' interpretations are not presented as 'truth' but rather as 'the social reality of the narrator' (Etherington, 2004, p. 81), the aim of which is to make sense of the relationship between the researcher and a cultural phenomenon under study. These interpretations present a blend of researchers' reflections on their experiences, their theoretical deliberations, their memories, feelings, dreams and illusions as viewed through their subjective view of the world.

In addition to the questions related to the concepts of 'truth' and 'fact', an important feature of interpretative analysis in the context of a symbiotic approach is associated with exercising culturally sensitive attitude in our interpretative analytical assumptions. This particularly applies to stepping away from Western-centric intellectual roots towards divergent cultural perceptions of power, justice and racial relations. As explained by Yavas (2015), the concept of 'Western-centrism' (including Euro-centrism or American/European-centrism) is originally derived from a Greek term 'ethnocentric/ethno-centrism' and is used to denote perceptions for Western superiority as applied to specific times and spaces. In this context, 'West' is perceived in contrast to 'other', which is mostly associated with Middle Eastern (Orient) countries that are perceived to have unconventional and dissimilar 'history, tradition of thought, imagery and vocabulary' (Said, [1978] 1995, p. 5). Capan (2018) convincingly articulates how Euro-centrism as a system of knowledge is re-articulated through the temporal and spatial dualities that situate 'Europe' as a space separate from the 'non-West', where hierarchies are assigned to the West (rational, modern, developed) and the non-West (spiritual, traditional, underdeveloped). Yet, our perception of Western-centric discourses as dominant and veritable has shifted dramatically in the last few decades. Researchers (Bhabha, 1983, 1994; Sibley, 1995; Tuhiwai Smith, 1999; Chakrabarti, 2012; Silova, Rappleye and You, 2020) have started to seek out, reveal and reflect on marginalized perspectives, endeavouring to reimagine and transcend dominant Western-centric assumptions in their interpretative analysis of cultural phenomena. Expectedly, these processes have affected the nature of autoethnographic research, which also redirected itself towards context-sensitive cross-cultural narratives, reflecting the plurality of cultural discourses. With this in mind, in a symbiotic approach, a layer of additional responsibility is placed on autoethnographers to ground their interpretative analysis in the values of de-Westernized and de-colonialized thinking that interrogates and challenges established cultural clichés and contributes to creating anti-oppressive forms of knowledge. Yet, as Pillow (2019) warns us, this kind of theorizing can only come from an in-depth engagement with the themes of feminism, Women of Colour and decolonization, as often researchers' interpretative analysis is confined to a mechanical insertion of few citations with limited relevancy, which 'perpetuates arrogant reading, blinding, blurring and blocking capacity to acknowledge different world views and forms of critique' (p. 120). Indeed, it is the autoethnographers' responsibility to interpret various cultural phenomena in a way that avoids, what Fricker (2007) refers to as, 'hermeneutical injustice', that is, 'the injustice of having some significant area of one's social experience obscured from collective understanding owing to a structural identity prejudice in the collective hermeneutical resource' (p. 155). At stake, in the issues discussed above, is the persistent focus on the ways through which we can interpret the multiple cultural encounters, using sensitivity and high levels of reflective and reflexive awareness on the part of the researcher. With this in mind, one of the foci of a symbiotic approach is on autoethnographers' lenticular perception of cultural phenomena under study, which enables sophisticated interpretative analysis of complex blends of emotions, temporalities, localities, boarders and margins as both bodily experiences and as sites of social and political struggles. In this sense, Symbiotic Autoethnography locates researchers in wider philosophical debates, proposing a symbiosis of researchers' theoretical considerations with their autoethnographic experiences and evocative narratives. As observed by Grant (2019), achieving this balance between theoretical rigour and evocative expression is a demanding task, which requires careful preparation and commitment to produce novel intellectual work.

To summarize, I suggest that interpretative analysis in a symbiotic approach involves autoethnographers' deep engagement with multifaceted theoretical notions that are critically interpreted with consideration of the researcher's cultural sensitivity to the phenomenon under study. This approach would move autoethnographic research beyond the primacy of Western-centric epistemologies that obfuscate and distort local knowledge. In addition, this aspect of Symbiotic Autoethnography is inseparable from researcher's evocative storytelling and their omnipresence across their temporal experiences, as interpretative analysis is impossible outside the multidimensionality of its context. The next chapter continues this line of discussion, shifting the focus towards political and transformative capacities of a symbiotic approach as grounded in autoethnographers' specific personal and political vistas.

Political (transformative) focus

Current trends in autoethnographic research indicate a significant move from conventional ethnographic foci on local cultures towards multilocational, multidimensional and multidisciplinary areas of investigation that blur the boundaries within self/other and local/global dichotomies, cutting across the spaces in-between. These facilities of autoethnographic research provide ripe grounds for social construction of knowledge that places emphasis on transformative or emancipatory processes for both the researcher and the wider sociocultural domains of which the researcher is a part (Starr, 2010). In what follows, I outline the key dimensions of political and transformative aspects of a symbiotic approach as related to, first, autoethnographic capacity to detect and challenge oppressive sociocultural and political practices and, second, transformative effect of autoethnographic writing on the researchers themselves.

Autoethnography has evolved as a 'method of justice' (Salvo, 2019) from critical ethnography, in which the researcher was expected to advocate for the emancipation of marginalized groups in society. In line with this development, the political focus of a symbiotic approach intertwines closely with the feature of interpretative analysis, indicating the need for autoethnographic researchers to problematize and politicize their narratives, moving them 'beyond a world of harmonious social order into a political radical world where dissensus and power conflicts prevail' (Doloriert and Sambrook, 2012, p. 84). Autoethnographers' engagement in reflexive writing about the issues of social justice result in politically charged discourses that disrupt the neutrality of research landscape and critique the damaging influences of power control, oppression, inequality and discrimination. In this sense, any autoethnography has to be political, because everything around us is political. This idea is not new, as it is a commonly accepted assumption that our every action – or inaction, for that matter – represents a certain political stance and thus, any claims of being 'apolitical' or 'neutral' cannot be substantiated. As stressed by Lather (1986a), 'once we recognize that just as there is no neutral education there is no neutral research, we no longer need apologize for unabashedly ideological research and its open commitment to using research to criticize and change the status quo' (p. 67). Indeed, the purpose of our autoethnographic narratives cannot be limited to just outlining personal experiences of a cultural phenomenon but need to be written against the canvas of dominant expressions of particular sociopolitical power relations. Autoethnographic stories disrupt representational sociocultural landscapes by locating autoethnographers' experiences in dissonance with dominant systems of power, allowing disruptions of silences to take place. They have a potential to challenge those narratives, attitudes and perceptions which collectively proliferate systems of oppression and privilege, producing marginalized experiences. In this sense, autoethnographic research contributes to a body of work in which radical forms of academic writing destabilize and discard dominant discursive dichotomies and explore new ways of interrogating established hierarchies and relations of power within them. Through autoethnography 'radical politics of possibility is made visible' (Denzin, 2014, p. 31). In addition, Reed-Danahay (2001) highlights the way in which critical or radical autoethnographies could also problematize representation and identity in research through the researchers' self-disclosure of their experiences of inequality and social injustice. The political nature of autoethnography has been emphasized by a number of authors (Ellis and Bochner, 2000; Chang, 2008; Spry, 2011b; Pillow, 2019; Grant, 2020), all of whom see it as a pertinent avenue for making a positive change in the world through presenting their narratives as 'the string theories of pain and privilege forever woven into fabrics of power/lessness' (Spry, 2011b, p. 497).

However, as rightly pointed out by Benzecry and Baiocchi (2017), separating what constitutes 'political' from what we consider 'social' is not an easy task. In their attempt to make a distinguishment between these concepts, the authors suggest that ethnographers interpret the notion of 'political' in three distinct ways, which they refer to as *polis, demos* and *elector*. Each of these ways is associated with a specific domain of activity as well as preferred social locations and research strategies:

> The first, … polis, revolves around the question of who is counted or included in the political community. The second, demos, is concerned with the rhetorical make up of a political community, as in the contours of its imagined communities. The third, elector, in which the political is understood as the production of subjectivities, is most often associated with questions of governmentality. (p. 234)

These suggestions provide a helpful template for identifying political aspects of Symbiotic Autoethnography. Following analogous way of thinking, I suggest that one of the key political aspects of a symbiotic approach needs to be focused on researchers' political awareness. The word 'political' originates from the ancient Greek 'politikos', which means 'belonging or pertaining to the polis'. Historically, poleis were distinguished from other types of administrative communities by specific activities that were ruled by their bodies of citizens. Today 'political' is, generally, understood as the practices and meanings associated with basic issues of social power, such as organization, governance and legitimation. In the context of Symbiotic Autoethnography, 'political' relates, specifically, to the practices and meanings that occur across the intersection between the personal and the social realms. In this sense, autoethnographers' political awareness involves their explicit focus on the interplay between their personal experiences and the dominant powers, operating within their cultural environments, as well as the voices of those affected by these powers. Ellis (2020) reiterates that the issues of social justice become even more critical to consider in autoethnographic work in the current turbulent sociopolitical climate:

> It is challenging autoethnographic writers to critically consider what we want our stories to do. It is forcing us to reflexively interrogate our contributions to social justice. For autoethnographers with privilege, particularly white autoethnographers, it continues to be essential to engage self-reflexivity and work toward decentring privilege. It is more important than ever for autoethnographers to ask: Who are we writing for? Who are we writing to? What do we want our work to do? (p. 203)

From this perspective, Symbiotic Autoethnography is, principally, concerned with the problematic question of the role of autoethnographic research in stimulating meaningful social change. Thus, the contention of Symbiotic Autoethnography is that no autoethnographic narrative can lay claim to being purely theoretical in the sense of its content being divorced from contemporary political conditions and discourse. Even though some narratives will not have a direct call for political action, they will still contribute, whether intentionally or unintentionally, to the pertinent research debates within associated sociopolitical and cultural domain. A symbiotic approach to autoethnography aims to challenge canonical ways of doing research, insisting on presenting our autoethnographic narratives as conscious political acts focused on the issues of social justice. A number of researchers (Madison, 2010; Faulkner, 2017; Gale and Wyatt, 2019; Harris and Holman Jones, 2019; Hughes, 2020; Tillmann, Norsworthy and Schoen, 2022) refer to the concept of *activism* in relation to this aspect of autoethnographic research. Their studies present autoethnography as a space in which researchers' narratives and performative practices are always shifting and moving in rhythm with the issues of inequity and injustice as 'assembling and dissembling bodies that are active in always territorializing space and in world making' (Gale and Wyatt, 2019, p. 528). This makes any autoethnographic study a type of a leftist political project, where autoethnographers become activists through their engagement with social justice agendas.

Against this background a symbiotic approach can be seen as inherently oriented towards social justice, as it helps to escape hierarchical processes of knowledge production, replacing abstract theorization with embodied lived experiences of otherness, dislocation, marginalization, exclusion and violence. Thus, political focus as an integral feature of Symbiotic Autoethnography implies researchers' critical engagement with discourses of power and associated tensions and contradictions within the cultural context under study. Denzin (2018) stipulates that all inquiry is political and therefore, autoethnographic researchers do not need to be apologetic about the overly political nature of their narratives, as this direction helps us to seek forms of praxis and inquiry that are emancipatory, collaborative and empowering. Multiple examples of autoethnographic studies confirm researchers' commitment to political focus of their interpretative analytical efforts. Chew, Greendeer and Keliiaa (2015), for example, use their autoethnographic narratives to problematize Westernized language policies through the exploration of the roles of Indigenous graduate students in preserving Indigenous language heritage. Durham et al. (2020) use their autoethnographic study 'The future of autoethnography is Black' to argue that autoethnographic writing can serve as a vehicle for politically imaginative, life-sustaining and creative ways of conveying cultural knowledge of Black African diaspora across space, body and time. Bishop (2021) writes about her experiences of being an aboriginal woman within the Australian education system as a site of ongoing colonialism. In her research she utilizes Indigenous autoethnography as a space from which she attempts to expose dominant research methodologies and push forward the type of autoethnographic research where Indigenous knowledge is not 'ridiculed and delegitimised'. These studies, amongst many others, confirm a pivotal trajectory for autoethnography as a politically focused approach to knowledge-making. Such facility of autoethnographic approach is particularly important in situating autoethnography within the fabric of decolonial experiences, giving voices to 'people who have suffered in silence for too long' (Ellis and Bochner, 1996, p. 24). I deliberately avoid using the word 'postcolonial' here and throughout the book, concurring with Tuhiwai Smith's (1999) reference to the iconic statement by Bobbi Sykes, an Australian-born lifelong campaigner for Indigenous land rights, who asked at an academic conference on post-colonialism: 'What? Post-colonialism? Have they left?' (p. 24). Our sensitivity to the nuances of specific cultural structures and our orientation towards the issues of social injustice are central to Symbiotic Autoethnography. It is, therefore, not by chance that this autoethnographic approach aims at encouraging researchers to merge their personal voices with political contexts in, what Ellingson and Ellis (2008) call, a constructionist project, where the dichotomy of what should be private and what should be public is no longer appropriate. Hence, including political focus as another facet of a symbiotic approach is in line with the researchers' commitment to make connections between autoethnographic praxis and issues of social justice, acknowledging its potential on both micro and macro levels. This takes our discussion towards the transformative capacity of Symbiotic Autoethnography as operating on a micro (individual) level.

The political aspect of Symbiotic Autoethnography is inseparable from the transformative capacity of autoethnographic writing, where a researcher's interrogation of personal perceptions and actions leads to the transformation of the researcher's Self. Such prominent autoethnographic researchers as Ellis (2004), Chang (2008), Spry (2016), Harris and Holman Jones (2019), Bochner (2020), Poulos (2021), all link transformative capacity of autoethnography to its political nature, seeing it as 'an avenue for doing something meaningful for yourself and the world' (Ellis and Bochner, 2000, p. 761). Holman Jones (2016) explicitly confirms that autoethnography is a politically resistive and transformative activity, whilst Starr (2010) argues that autoethnography allows the introspective exploration for enhanced cultural understanding of self and others and has the potential to transform self and others in building cross-cultural alliances. Bochner (2020) refers to these transformative faculties as 'autoethnographic temperament'. This is how he describes a step-by-step process of rigorous autoethnographic self-scrutiny that leads to personal transformations:

> You listen closely to yourself talking; you talk back to yourself, commenting directly on what you hear yourself saying; you don't stop there but rather insist on keeping the conversation going, interpreting and reinterpreting, discovering something strange about the self you started with in an effort to transform yourself into a new being. The conversation moves in the direction of edification as you show a willingness to be your own worst critic – picking at scabs, exposing warts, vacillating between angst and anger, striving for an acute self-consciousness and a shameless subjectivity. (Bochner, 2020, p. 85)

Indeed, it is almost axiomatic that our life experiences broaden our perspectives and, consequently, our engagement with writing about these experiences has implicit transformative effect. However, in the context of Symbiotic Autoethnography, researchers' experiences also include movements between times and spaces, both physical and imaginary, as well as their blurred and fragmented memories, thoughts and illusions. Thus, one of the aims of Symbiotic Autoethnography is to draw these dimensions together to provide a more holistic approach to the transformative potential of autoethnographic narratives. The idea of transformative effect of our experiences resonates strongly with Mezirow's (1991) transformative learning theory that seeks to elucidate the ways in which our learning shifts how we view the world around us through changing our frames of reference. According to Mezirow (1991), learning starts with a 'disorienting dilemma' (p. 153) that is an accretion of transformed meanings that calls for a change of current perspectives, practices or actions. As the author explains, these transformations can be painful, as 'they often call into question deeply held personal values and threaten our very sense of self' (Mezirow, 1991, p. 168). Truly, any change or a transformation requires a disruption of certain structures and established sociopolitical and cultural boundaries, where personal merges with political. In this sense, Symbiotic Autoethnography can be seen as a transformative approach with a political utility, since commitment to social justice and positive change is repeatedly ascertained by researchers as the key impetus for choosing autoethnography. Ellis and Calafell (2020) challenge autoethnographers to engage with the political aspects of the contexts in which they are writing and working, so that they can align their personal transformations with their politics and reflexively interrogate their contributions to social justice. A symbiotic approach enables this engagement to take place, as it allows autoethnographers to capture their lived experience from across spatio-temporal dimensions, giving them access to the depth of political intricacies that other approaches cannot reach. Autoethnographers' symbiotic immersion in the political and transformative focus of their subject matter and the culture under study helps to generate the view of the politics 'from within' and thus, has the capacity to expose subjective meanings behind particular political concepts, powers and practices. These intimate disclosures of local practices and social relations, in their turn, can generate more varied discourses that deepen, or even transform, our understanding of cultural phenomena and related issues of political concern. As noted by Doloriert and Sambrook (2011), one of the signs of a good quality autoethnography is 'a feeling of moving from old selves to new selves' (p. 596). By accommodating and acknowledging the transformative impact that autoethnographic research has on the researchers themselves, we also acknowledge that these personal transformations enable us to become explicitly aware of the impact of political powers in charge of the lives of individuals. Thus, in Symbiotic Autoethnography the unity of political and transformative aspects forms a conceptual synergy that enables representation of researchers' experiences as 'personal, political and palpable' (Spry, 2011, p. 15). Numerous authors and contributors to the recent volumes on autoethnography (Stanley and Vass, 2018; Boylorn and Orbe, 2020; Iosefo, Holman Jones and Harris, 2021; Ferdinand, 2022) challenge autoethnographers to reflexively interrogate their interpersonal and intercultural experiences of race, gender, ethnicity and sexuality within larger systems of power, oppression and privilege. Encouraged by these pleas, I suggest that, in the context of a symbiotic approach, autoethnographers are eloquent in their consideration of the inescapable issues of politics that beset the fabric of our cultural experiences and practices. As I mention elsewhere (Beattie, 2018b), a human society can be seen either as a chaos of incomprehensible absurdity with its unpredictable and unconstrained happenings or as a vibrant, intricate and enigmatic edifice of political, cultural and economic liaisons that require continuous decoding and interpretation. One of the key roles of Symbiotic Autoethnography is to radically rethink how we decode and interpret these tensions and contradictions of contemporary political discourse in our attempt to find ways of making advances in social justice. As powerfully portrayed by Grant (2018), autoethnographers, the most impactful of whom are wolves rather than sheep in their ability to critically call out oppressive sociocultural practices, are 'cultural tricksters or gadflies whose role is to trouble the complacency of normative cultures and challenge their assumptions' (p. 114). This, once again, confirms a close connection between political and transformative capacities of autoethnography, where autoethnographers' personal experiences get permeated with ideological and political values. In Symbiotic Autoethnography, autoethnographers' sensitivity to the pervasiveness of political powers within specific cultural contexts is seen as paramount, as it not only produces new 'local knowledge' but also creates a fertile ground for autoethnographers' reflections on how this new knowledge came about. This brings us to the main theme of the next chapter on reflexivity as another essential feature of Symbiotic Autoethnography.

Reflexivity

The impossibility of eliminating researchers' presence from their studies has been widely accepted in research circles, as researchers' expectations and interpretations of the data have been acknowledged to be deeply influenced by their subjective thought patterns, cultural backgrounds and methodological choices. Prior to this paradigmatic 'reflexive shift', researchers' focus was on a neutral and objective presentation of their studies and obscuring the details of their research processes rather than explicating their personal assumptions, feelings, beliefs and agendas. The word 'reflexive' comes from the medieval Latin *reflexivus*, meaning 'turned back' or 'bend back'. As Babcock (1987) explains, the word 'reflexive' as a concept first appeared in English in 1588 to denote the capacity of mental operations to be turned back upon the mind itself. However, the author also notes that this concept had been frequently confused and used interchangeably with its near synonym – 'reflective':

> To be reflexive is to be reflective; but one is not necessarily reflexive when one is reflective, for to reflect is simply to think about something, but to be reflexive is to think about the process of thinking itself. In its present usage, reflection does not possess the self-referential and second-level characteristics of reflexivity. (p. 235)

Terminological variations related to reflexivity could be also found in later references to the concept in the work of such prominent theorists and researchers as Malinowski (1967), Merton (1948), Popper (1957), Geertz (1983), Clifford (1988), Giddens (1990) and Bourdieu and Wacquant (1992). And yet, despite some conceptual disparities, researchers, generally, agreed that any investigative inquiry needs to go further than examining theoretical and methodological constructs, bringing into the studies researchers' personal imprints that, consciously or subconsciously, govern all key aspects of their research. More recently, reflexivity as a concept grew beyond the common perception of it as a relationship between the researcher and the research procedures, permeating all aspects of social research and presenting itself in various forms of researchers' reflexive efforts. It is no longer a luxury, as writers can no longer presume to be able to produce an objective non-contested account of their experiences (Denzin, 1997). Responses to this shift involved attempts to widen the possibilities for acknowledging manifold influences of the researcher on the research. Pillow (2003), for example, identifies four different aspects of reflexivity that work together to provide the researcher with a form of self-reflexivity as confession: reflexivity as recognition of self, reflexivity as recognition of other, reflexivity as truth and reflexivity as transcendence. In her discussion, Pillow (2003) leads researchers towards the idea of 'reflexivity of discomfort' (p. 192), which challenges researchers to use reflexivity not just as a methodological tool of gathering data but as a tool for interrogating complicit relationships with ethnocentric powers and knowledge in qualitative research:

> Thus, a reflexivity that pushes toward an unfamiliar, towards the uncomfortable, cannot be a simple story of subjects, subjectivity and transcendence or self-indulgent tellings. A tracing of the problematics of reflexivity calls for a positioning of reflexivity not as clarity, honesty, or humility, but as practices of confounding disruptions. (Pillow, 2003)

Gergen (2000) suggests that such forms of self-exposure have led to the flourishing of autoethnography as a research approach, where investigators explore in depth the ways in which their personal history saturates the phenomena under study and where the juxtaposition of self and subject matter is used to enrich the investigation. Similarly, Patton (2015) defines reflexivity as a way of emphasizing the importance of self-awareness, political and cultural consciousness as well as ownership of the researcher's perspective. Anderson (2006) also confirms pertinence of reflexivity within autoethnographic praxes, seeing it as a tool for engaging in 'self-conscious introspection guided by a desire to better understand both self and others through examining one's actions and perceptions in reference to and dialogue with those of others' (p. 382).

In terms of practical engagement in reflexive praxis, Pillow (2006) puts forward an argument that the way researchers utilize reflexivity depends on their approach to the subject of investigation. In most cases, autoethnographies are informed by researchers' interpretations of cultural phenomena as multifaceted, impenetrable, obscure and fluid. Thus, their reflexive practice would entail various forms that allow certain level of plasticity to accommodate manifold aspects of the subject under study. This is particularly relevant to Symbiotic Autoethnography with its multiple facets that create a mosaic reflection of the autoethnographer's self, blurring the boundaries between social, cultural, political and personal. In Symbiotic Autoethnography reflexivity is seen as a powerful impetus that compels researchers to think more carefully about their deep-rooted dependence on specific cultural contexts and sociopolitical environments in which the researchers operate. Specifically, symbiotic reflexivity entails researchers' consistent and conscious engagement in different forms of reflexive activities as applied to theoretical, methodological and ethical aspects of their study. These three components form the basis of symbiotic reflexivity that is defined in this context as the researcher's simultaneous consideration and scrutiny of their own epistemological, methodological and ethical assumptions in terms of examining both the possible underlying sociocultural sources of these assumptions and the ways in which they inform the construction of the phenomenon under study. Using these three planes of symbiotic reflexivity provides distinct opportunities for autoethnographers to create their 'writing stories' (Richardson and St. Pierre, 2005, p. 959) through their symbiotic engagement in 'writing about the process of writing and the context in which that writing occurred' (Wall, 2008, p. 40). In the next few paragraphs, I will look at each aspect of symbiotic reflexivity in more detail.

One of the main concerns of symbiotic reflexivity is the impact of researchers' views on the nature and sources of knowledge and the conditions required for a belief to constitute knowledge, all of which constitute main questions of epistemology. A number of authors suggest different variations in their interpretations of this facet of reflexivity as applied to qualitative research. Johnson and Duberley (2003), for example, refer to researchers' theoretical positioning in relation to, what they call, 'epistemic reflexivity' (p. 1288), which they describe as researchers' thinking about how their own social location influenced the shape and outcomes of research. The authors conclude that 'a key role of epistemic reflexivity is to negate the world as an objectively accessible social reality and denaturalize hegemonic accounts by exposing their modes of social organization and reproduction' (p. 1289). Similarly, Dowling (2006) writes about this form of reflexivity as 'epistemological reflexivity',

where the researcher is required to ask such questions as: 'How has the research question defined and limited what can be "found" and how could the research question have been investigated differently?' Therefore, epistemological reflexivity encourages the researcher to reflect upon the assumptions (about the world, about knowledge) that are made in the course of the research and it helps the researcher think about the implications of such assumptions for the research and its findings. (p. 11)

Boylorn and Orbe (2021) see critical reflexivity as inherent in autoethnographic work, as the former can be utilized by autoethnographers to document their moments of revelation, their emotional responses to various cultural phenomena and the experiences of self-empowerment.

With consideration of these deliberations, Symbiotic Autoethnography aims to move epistemological reflexivity beyond simple accounts of activities noted in researchers' reflexive journals towards continuous reflexive efforts focused on their representations of the world, which, potentially, contribute to either maintaining or changing of existing societal structures and relations of power within them. In this way, in a symbiotic approach, researchers' epistemological stances can also be seen as sensory systems of power and, thus, their positions need to be acknowledged with consideration of their effects on how specific cultural phenomena are interpreted. As suggested by Neufeld (1993), reflexive turn in post-positivist research prompted researchers to re-examine the foundations of their theoretical (i.e. epistemological) assumptions at a deeper level of discourse, leading their inquiries towards problematizing and deconstructing the choices made at the epistemological levels. Indeed, if our epistemological positions are, primarily, representations of specific sociocultural and political influences, then 'theorizing about our theorizing' allows our autoethnographic narratives to be seen in relation to our reflexive interpretations of our positioning. Alvesson and Skoldberg (2017) agree that any research is most likely to have a positive impact on both practice and theoretical knowledge if researchers continually question 'the taken-for-granted assumptions and blind spots in their own social culture, research community and language' (p. 11). Borrowing from these authors, I maintain that in Symbiotic Autoethnography both 'recipe-book research' and 'theorizing in a vacuum' should be replaced by researchers' deep reflexive re-examination of underlying sociopolitical and cultural influences on their paradigmatic and epistemological perspectives. These reflexive efforts are focused not only on researchers' reflections on theoretical literature but, most importantly, on their interactions with and relations to particular cultural and political terrains. Such perception of symbiotic reflexivity resonates with Spry's (2001) perspective on autoethnographic texts as a product of researchers' bodily standpoints, as the researchers are continually recognizing and interpreting the residue traces of culture inscribed upon them from interacting with others in contexts, making the researcher 'the epistemological and ontological nexus upon which the research process turns' (p. 711). Indeed, since autoethnography obliterates the subjective/objective dichotomy, autoethnographers relinquish idiosyncratic position of a 'truth narrator' and present their views as simultaneously socially, culturally, politically and personally situated. In the case of Symbiotic Autoethnography, the distinction between the researcher and their theorizations is also fully abandoned, as researchers' personal investments in their theoretical interpretations are not only explicitly acknowledged but become one of the main aspects of their inquiry. These theoretical deliberations on cultural and political phenomena through the lens of personal experiences provide a powerful tool for unveiling examples and practices of social injustice and exclusion, at the same time offering reflexive analysis of the impact of these practices on the researcher's theoretical positions.

As discussed in previous chapters, social, political and cultural factors create a complex societal fabric, and researcher's cultural reflexivity can help us with having a better understanding of the internal contradictions and nuances of external structures of power that shape local sociopolitical conditions. Ultimately, the act of epistemological reflexivity in Symbiotic Autoethnography requires researchers to make a conscientious effort of presenting to the readers a genuine authentic account of the ways in which their theoretical situatedness has been influenced by specific cultural and political circumstances. However, as mentioned at the beginning of this chapter, unlike other forms of qualitative research, Symbiotic Autoethnography invites researchers to use epistemological reflexivity as part and parcel of their broader reflexive practice, which also extends to their methodological and ethical assumptions, all of which intersect, merge and drift in a continuous flow of researchers' reflexive thinking. Thus, the next part of this chapter will focus on methodological reflexivity as an integral part of a symbiotic approach.

The 'reflexive shift' in social sciences that occurred around the 1980s affected the ways in which researchers presented the accounts of their investigations as well as associated methodological processes and tools. As Etherington (2007a) points out, researchers had to acknowledge that their work needed to demonstrate not only what they discovered but also how they discovered it. O'Reilly (2009) also confirms that in writing about ethnographic research, researchers began to look more critically at the ways in which their fieldwork had been produced and started to use methodological devices that presented ethnographies as fiction rather than fact. This position coincides with a symbiotic approach, which aims to accept and celebrate the diverse multifaceted and messy nature of researchers' experiences, rejecting clinically neat and tidy methodological frameworks. The main premise of methodological reflexivity in a symbiotic approach is based on the argument that methodological approaches are defined and selected by the researcher, who makes conscious choices about the ways of approaching and exploring the phenomenon under study. Throughout this process, reflexive autoethnographers have to give careful consideration to all aspects of their research design, paying particular attention to recognizing broader structures of power that influence their choices. The core of these arguments can be effectively supported by drawing on the conceptual interpretation of methodological reflexivity proposed by Pillow (2003), who urges researchers to extend their reflexivity beyond the grid of traditional methodological categories of data, method and member checks towards a reflexivity that calls for

> the necessity of an ongoing critique of all of our research attempts, a recognition that none of our attempts can claim the innocence of success (even in failure) – with the realization that many of us do engage in research where there is real work to be done even in the face of the impossibility of such a task. This is a move to use reflexivity in a way that would continue to challenge the representations we come to while at the same time acknowledging the political need to represent and find meaning. (Pillow, 2003, p. 192)

This form of reflexivity resonates with a symbiotic approach, where autoethnographers' positionality, as influenced by sociopolitical context of their studies, permeates their engagement with the research participants and the whole process of working with the data. As Pels (2000) explains, methodological reflexivity systematically takes stock of and inserts the positions and perspectives of the researchers into their reports about the world. Thus, researchers' methodological choices cannot be considered 'neutral' or incidental, as they define the 'politics of research' that is framed by researchers' theoretical preconceptions about how certain cultural phenomena should be represented. The concept of symbiotic reflexivity gains a firm traction in the context of these deliberations, as the features of theoretical and methodological aspects of reflexivity intertwine in a symbiotic relationship, where autoethnographers' beliefs, values and choices shape the ways in which their autoethnographic stories are presented. This takes us to the next facet of symbiotic reflexivity that is related to autoethnographers' ethical principles and decisions. Ethical considerations within a symbiotic approach are discussed in more detail in Chapter 7, so here I aim to focus mainly on their reflexive nature.

Researchers and theorists, generally, agree on the importance of epistemological and methodological reflexivity, however, their discussions about research ethics are often confined to commonly accepted ethical frameworks and principles rather than researchers' reflexive efforts in relation to their ethical consideration. Guillemin and Gillam (2004) agree that the connection between ethics and reflexivity is rarely made clear, since reflexivity is, largely, seen as an aspect of research rigour rather than preparing researchers for their encounters with ethical issues. The authors argue that merging reflexivity with ethical practice helps researchers to realize that ethical issues do not stop after the requirements of procedural ethics have been satisfied and that the researchers must continuously consider all ethical concerns. As Clayton (2013) rightly points out, in some cases ethical reflexivity is limited to procedural or technical approaches to ethics, involving a 'tick-a-box' of formulas and rules related to informed consent, anonymity agreements and member checking processes and less attention to particularities of the research context. Parr (2011) also argues that such approaches can obscure rather than illuminate ethical decisions, which should be placed at the heart of the research process, compelling researchers to continually revisit, reassess and interrogate their world views and beliefs and their impact on how their inquiries are conceptualized, initiated and lived. In line with these arguments, in a symbiotic approach, autoethnographers' ethical reflexivity is seen as central to their reflexive processes and interwoven with epistemological and methodological reflexivity. Indeed, autoethnographers' ethical stances cannot be separated from their 'view of the world' as reflected in every aspect of their research process. Altheide and Johnson (1994) provide us with an example of how 'an ethnographic ethic' combines different points of researchers' reflexivity in relation to such aspects of ethics as

(1) The relationship between what is observed (behaviours, rituals, meanings) and the larger cultural, historical and organizational contexts within which the observations are made (the substance);

(2) The relationship between the observer, the observed and the setting (the observer);

(3) The issue of perspective (or point of view), whether that of the observer or the member(s), used to render an interpretation of the ethnographic data (the interpretation);

(4) The role of the reader in the final product (the audience); and

(5) The issue of representational, rhetorical, or authorial style used by the
     author(s) to render the description or interpretation (the style). (p. 489)

In the same lines of reasoning, symbiotic ethics involves autoethnographers'
continuous and simultaneous reflections on different foci of their studies
throughout their autoethnographic writing. This, of course, brings a great deal
of complexity into the symbiotic reflexivity, where researchers' reflexive praxes
go beyond the established 'tick lists' of ethical procedures and considerations,
inviting researchers to look deeper into the existing and potential ethical
situations and pre-empt their responses to such situations in an ethically sound
manner. One of the ways of going beyond the 'tick list' approach to ethics could
be associated with thinking reflexively about the symbiosis between the adopted
ethical stance and autoethnographers' position in relation to such aspects of
their study as imbalance of power between the researcher and the researched,
Eurocentric and/or ethnocentric asymmetries in data interpretations,
consideration of intersectionality in relation to participants' gender, sex, race,
class, sexuality, religion, disability, physical appearance and so on.

It is worth clarifying at this point that, even though Symbiotic
Autoethnography serves as a space for researchers' personal stories, these
stories do not exist in isolation from researchers' interactions and interrelations
with the multiplicity of the above-mentioned issues. Throughout our
autoethnographic journeys, our fractured segments of Self are disturbed,
managed and shaped by the encounters with the multifaceted Other: the Other
as the characters of our stories, the Other as our participants and the Other
as our reflexive Selves. In a symbiotic approach, these multiple Other(s) form
a polyvocal autoethnographic narrative, where each of the voices has equal
significance in representing the mesh of sociocultural connections with the
purpose of not 'looking harder or more closely, but of seeing what frames our
seeing' (Lather, 1993, p. 675). This takes me to the next feature of Symbiotic
Autoethnography – polyvocality.

Polyvocality

The concept of polyvocality as a methodological and ethical feature of qualitative
research is not new. Bakhtin (1981), Quantz and O'Connor (1988), Tobin (1989),
Anderson (1989) and Conquergood (1991) all wrote about the issues related
to representing multiple voices in researchers' studies. Bakhtin (1981), for

example, argued for the construction of a dialogical narrative that involves using multiple voices, which emerge throughout the process of writing. He referred to such polyvocality as 'dialogic imagination', suggesting that the speeches of the authors and narrators and the speeches of characters are those fundamental compositional unities that permit 'a multiplicity of social voices and a wide variety of their links and interrelationships (always more or less dialogized)' (p. 263). Anderson (1989) builds on Bakhtin's ideas, linking 'multivoicedness' (p. 261) within ethnographic studies to socially organized ideologies that have the power to either legitimize or silent individual voices:

> Multiple voices within the individual and within the community are in a constant struggle for legitimacy. Thus, neither a unified individual nor a consensual society is possible because both inward and outward speech are dialogical and social. (p. 261)

Similarly, Hermans (2001) confirms that polyphonic construction of a particular theme allows the feeling of continuous meaning to flow through using dialogical relations of various voices, adding multifacetedness and richness to research studies. Yet, polyvocality in research is not without controversies, as noted by a number of researchers in both their earlier and more recent debates about qualitative research practices. Mclaren (1992), for example, urges ethnographers to re-examine the categories they use in light of new multiple voices that are being sounded from the margins and which had been previously silenced by the social practices of power structures. The author expresses particular concern about using these voices as a means of marketing 'otherness' to culturally annex 'them' for the benefit of 'us'. Instead, Mclaren suggests that researchers interrogate the repressed 'otherness' within their own presumptions and take the multiplicity of voices beyond the display case towards 'the meaning of identity as a form of cultural struggle, as a site of remapping and remaking historical agency within a praxis of liberation' (p. 90). In the same line of reasoning, Gergen (2000) suggests that polyvocality opens the door to new forms of research methodology,

> in which multiple voices are given entry into the interpretive arena – voices of the research participants, the scientific literature, the private views of the investigators, the media and so on. However, the challenge of polyvocality is more radical in that we are sensitized to the possibility that all parties to the research may 'contain multitudes'. The question is whether researchers enable participating parties (and themselves) to give expression to their multiplicity – to the full complexity and range of contradictions that are typical of life in postindustrial society. (p. 1041)

These arguments illustrate that the concept of polyvocality brings with it an array of interwoven issues with a particular focus on the complexities and controversies associated with representing the Other. Thus, I consider it useful to provide some background theoretical underpinning on the notions of 'the Other' and 'otherness' in qualitative research.

The debates about possible connections between the Self and the Other permeate the domain of qualitative research, where researchers search for more creative and ethically sound forms of representation. The concepts of 'the Other', 'otherness' or 'othering' are, generally, associated with differentiating discourses that juxtapose human beings as dissimilar to or the opposite to Self. In other words, 'otherness' is seen as what sets one apart. Hermans (2001) recognizes the complexity of the notion and points us towards the early works of James (1890), who, in the author's view, paved the way for later theoretical developments of multivoiced self by suggesting that Self and the Other are not mutually exclusive, since the Other is simply an extension of Self and so, to understand the Other, we need to, first, understand Self. These early assumptions informed researchers' more recent attempts to illuminate the nature of Self/Other dichotomy. As Gergen (2000) notes, with the influx of postmodern and constructionist approaches, researchers have become increasingly aware of the limitations of research authorship, which favours hierarchy of the researcher as 'the knower', reinforcing the self/other difference. These new approaches to qualitative research brought with them a sense of doubt about the possibility for researchers to represent themselves without referring to external world, where 'the 'Other' resides. To complicate things further, the acknowledgement of the Other in qualitative research has taken different trajectories in different fields of study. Dervin (2015) argues that, in psychology, 'othering' is seen as an ordinary process associated with the formation of identity, where in order to exist, one needs to make sense of other people, thus, one 'others' them as much as they 'other' the rest of us. In sociology, however, 'othering' is often perceived as a socially constructed boundary that separates majority from minority and insiders from outsiders. Thus, sociologists tend to put a critical spotlight on the ways in which the concept of 'othering' is constructed. Indeed, in the context of sociological research, the concepts of 'the Other' and 'otherness' are often interpreted in relation to specific cultural indicators, such as gender, disability, language, beliefs and traditions. Miller (2008) confirms that 'otherness', described as 'the condition of being different or "other", particularly if the differences in question are strange, bizarre, or exotic' (p. 587), often results in placing certain individuals at the margins of accepted societal 'norms' which may lead to moral and political judgement of superiority and inferiority in relation to 'us' and 'them'. Therefore, it is not surprising that in recent decades many authors (Said, [1978] 1995; Lavie and Swedenburg, 1996; Gergen, 2000; Goodall, 2006; Spry, 2018; Alexander, 2020) have stressed the importance of critical approaches to the concept of 'the Other' that would take into account the impact of power relations on constructing the benchmarks for the 'sameness' and 'otherness' in relation to different identity markers and their representations in research studies. These critical approaches have resulted in the researchers' increased attention to how the voices of 'the Other' are represented in the contexts of social stratification, privilege, colonization and power. St. Pierre (2008) also warns qualitative researchers against the 'obsession with the voices of participants as the primary, most authentic data' (p. 332), arguing that it might result in the eclipse and disappearance of other data and, thus, a weaker analysis. She suggests that conventional qualitative inquiry needs to move away from the 'hegemony of presence, of voice' to a 'methodology-to-come in which we begin to do it radically differently wherever we are in our projects' (St. Pierre, 2008, p. 332).

Against this theoretical background, autoethnography, as an innovative approach to a qualitative inquiry, offers a fertile ground for incorporating polyvocality into its epistemological and methodological stances. A number of prominent advocates of autoethnography (Ellis, Adams and Bochner, 2010; Short, 2010; Denzin, 2014; Pelias, 2019; Poulos, 2021) all emphasize that the construction of autoethnographic narratives through multiplicity of voices allows researchers to interpret cultural phenomena under study from a multiplicity of perspectives, whilst also capturing complex interplay of associated social and political powers. Adams (2006, p. 720) affirms that 'writing about the self always involves writing about others', whereas Denzin (2014) identifies the representation of multiple voices as one of the key conditions of 'authentically adequate' (p. 73) autoethnography. In response to these claims, Johnson and Strong (2008), for example, use polyvocality in their autoethnographic reflections on supervisory experiences with a master's student. The authors use the notion of 'polyphony', when writing about negotiating multiple voices (the voices of experts, research participants, personal affiliations) in their supervisory relationship. Similarly, Mizzi (2010) refers to the concept of 'multivocality' in his attempt to provide a representational space in the autoethnography for the plural and sometimes contradictory narrative voices located within the researcher's Self 'to provoke a deeper understanding of the often silent tensions that lie underneath observable behaviours in the story' (p. 2). Most importantly, researchers in the field (Ellis and Bochner, 2006; Grant, Short and Turner, 2013; Whitinui, 2014; Schmid, 2019;

Boylorn and Orbe, 2020) confirm the capacity of autoethnographic polyvocality to gather multiple silenced or marginalized voices into one chorus without expecting such contributions to conform to one another or to a dominant tone. As explained by Schmid (2019), autoethnography facilitates making links, where these have not before occurred, creating multivocal spaces for enhancing and ultimately transforming 'the music by incorporating the variety of ignored and overlooked sounds, noises and songs and so to grow community' (p. 268).

Leaning on these arguments, I suggest an enhanced interpretation of polyvocality in the context of Symbiotic Autoethnography as a space for capturing simultaneously complex entanglements of autoethnographers' narratives with the Other, where the Other includes the characters from the researchers' stories, their participants and the researchers' multiple Selves. Throughout our autoethnographic journeys our fractured segments of Self become disturbed, managed and shaped by the encounters with the multifaceted Other. These multiple Other(s) form a symbiotic polyvocal narrative, where each of the voices has equal significance in representing the mesh of sociocultural connections with the purpose of not 'looking harder or more closely, but of seeing what frames our seeing' (Lather, 1993, p. 675). In the next few paragraphs, I will look at each of these components of symbiotic polyvocality in more detail.

The Other as the characters of autoethnographic narratives

Autoethnographers, like any individual, do not live in a vacuum and therefore, their memories, experiences and feelings cannot be separated from the intricate fabric of their relations and encounters with others. These 'others' also include characters of our narratives, who might be our first schoolteachers, our childhood friends, our parents, our partners and colleagues. They might be alive, deceased or just lost somewhere in the depths of our temporal 'past' without us knowing anything about their life trajectories. Pineau (2012) refers to these others as collaborative 'ghostwriters', who she describes as 'internalized others, generally others long dead and reincarnated in any narrative moment through my articulation of them, in absentia and without their consent' (p. 459). As with any form of representation, their appearances in our stories create complex ethical issues since their consent to participation could not be obtained. Ethical considerations associated with representing the characters of autoethnographic narratives in the context of Symbiotic Autoethnography are discussed further in the book, so in this part of the discussion I will focus on my general theoretical deliberations related to the Other as the characters of our stories.

One of the most relevant theoretical perspective related to the voices of others takes us back to Bakhtin's (1981) concept of 'the dialogic imagination' based on the premise that all our actions and experiences are dialogic in nature. This also applies to our autoethnographic writing, where we conduct dialogues with the characters of our stories through 'writing in' our direct conversations with them or through reflecting on our relations to or with them and related feelings and emotions. Bakhtin's (1984) ideas can help us gain insight into what these voices mean in a wider sense during the process of constructing our narratives:

> Everywhere there is an intersection, consonance, or interruption of rejoinders in the open dialogue by rejoinders in the heroes' internal dialogues. Everywhere a specific sum total of ideas, thoughts and words is passed through several unmerged voices, sounding differently in each. The object of authorial intentions is certainly not this sum total of ideas in itself, as something neutral and identical to itself. No, the object of intentions is precisely the *passing of a theme through many and various voices*, its rigorous and, so to speak, irrevocable *multi-voicedness* and *vari-voicedness*. (p. 279)

Concomitantly, Madison (2012) makes a useful comparison of the researchers' methodological choices in relation to their positionality toward the Other, suggesting that the traditions of the autoethnographic approach involve the researcher painting a Self-portrait with consideration of the Others' view of the world/culture, whilst ethnographers paint a portrait of the Other with consideration of the painter's own view of the world/culture. In relation to autoethnography, a few authors (Richardson, 2000a; Goodall, 2005; Poulos, 2009; Spry, 2016) wrote about different experimental ways of representing researchers' experiences of and reflections on the Other to create polyvocal textual forms. Goodall (2006), for example, suggests that when we write about the self, we often reflect on our past experiences and talk with others about the past 'to create specific representations of the culture/cultural experience and to give audiences a sense of how being there in the experience feels' (Adams, Ellis and Holman Jones, 2017, p. 3). Indeed, researchers' voices can never exist in isolation from these temporal interactions that help us create meaning through writing with and about the characters of our stories, therefore, fusing their voices with our own in a symbiotic way, where it is, sometimes, impossible to distinguish where the researcher's 'I' becomes 'a wilful embodiment of "we"' (Spry, 2016, p. 48). These deliberations readily accommodate the theoretical stance adopted by a symbiotic approach, which encourages autoethnographers to both acknowledge and problematize the tensions invoked by inserting other characters into our research. In Symbiotic Autoethnography, the voice of the narrator gets populated by other voices that are situated in, what I would call, an autoethnographic polyphonic space. Within that space, symbiotic autoethnographers disturb a static view of the Other as characters of their stories by inducing new meanings and interpretations into 'the partial presence of a temporal conversations constituted by others' voices, bodies, histories and yearnings' (Madison, 2012, p. 11). These new meanings and perspectives emerging from the narrator and other characters do not necessarily complement each other but interact dynamically to produce new ways of perceiving the phenomenon under study. In this way, when writing about the characters of our stories, autoethnographic 'I' becomes symbiotically fused with a specific cultural context to which these characters belong. Yet, as pointed out by Chadwick (2021), embedding the voices of others into our research remains an ambiguous, slippery and paradoxical process that involves oscillating between belief and doubt, speech and silence, presence and absence, since 'speaking for "others" is wholly suspect' (Richardson, 2000b, p. 254). Similar but, perhaps, slightly different issues are associated with embedding the voices of participants as the Other in our autoethnographic narratives, which is discussed in the next section.

The Other as the research participants

Though involving participants in an autoethnographic study seems to contest the value of 'auto-' within its methodological principles, a number of authors (Connelly and Clandinin, 1990; Anderson, 2006; Adams, Ellis and Holman Jones, 2017; Chang and Bilgen, 2020) argue that participants' voices strengthen autoethnographic rigour by adding more depth, empathy and richness to the researcher's perspective. Adams, Holman Jones and Ellis (2015) emphasize that 'the insights we acquire from talking with and listening to others can deepen and complicate our own stories' (p. 55). This thought resonates strongly with Anderson's (2006) earlier theorization about analytic autoethnography, where a 'dialogue with informants beyond the self' (p. 385) is presented as one of the key criteria of critical autoethnography. The author argues that

> solipsism and author saturation in autoethnographic texts are symptoms rather than the underlying problem. They stem from failure to adequately engage with others in the field. No ethnographic work – not even autoethnography – is a warrant to generalize from an 'N of one'. (p. 386)

As with other aspects of autoethnographic writing, the question of involving participants as the Other in our research is not without problems and controversies. Moen (2006), for example, brings to our attention the dilemma associated with different interpretations of specific events by the researcher and the participants, which can reveal tensions related to the interpretive authority of the researcher and vulnerability of the participants. Spry (2016) expresses similar concerns related to arrogating the voices of the Other in autoethnographic research. She calls for 'self-less autoethnography' (p. 38), where a dialogical performative space is not created by researchers' pure ambition to re-discover their own Self through appropriating the stories of the Other but using autoethnography as a decolonizing tool to bring forth the issues of power and privilege 're-written and rescored with others' (p. 18). Morse (2002), Sparkes (2013), Winkler (2018b) all remind us that our stories do not only belong to us but also to the participants who shared with us their view of the world. As Gannon (2013) observes, writing about one's experiences inevitably involves writing about others, which brings researchers into new relationships with their own experiences, creating 'a mobile textual and material assemblage' (p. 230) within which the researcher and others are always in circulation. Murphy and Kraidy (2003) also draw our attention to the point that, despite the capacity of polyvocal texts to recognize the multiple dimensions of cultural phenomena through historically and ideologically located disparate voices, multivocal texts run the risk of positioning the Other in the narrative as more comfortable and proactive than they, actually, have been during the research process. The authors explain that

> rhetorical devices such as 'co-researchers' and 'cultural interlocutors' have been applied to soften disparities between voice, text, ethnographer and power, but these labels may not necessarily function to make ethnographic descriptions any 'thicker'. Rather they may serve only to help fashion descriptions that appear more communal, open and empowering than, say, 'informant' or 'subject'. Moreover, they can be abused as the incorporation of the Other as an active speaker in an ethnographic text often erases rather than challenges relations of power, making one wonder if the elaboration of polyvocal texts actually democratizes ethnographies or if multivocality merely camouflages the authoritative voice of the writer. (Murphy and Kraidy, 2003, p. 316)

Leaning on these deliberations, I suggest that in Symbiotic Autoethnography the voices of participants intertwine with the researcher's personal experiences to paint a richer picture of the cultural phenomenon under study, allowing the reader to 'feel the feelings of the other' (Denzin, 1997, p. 228). As suggested by Trahar (2006), each meeting with participants can be considered a snapshot of a moment in time, where the researcher and the participants are being uniquely embedded in their current lives and 'as we converse we are changed by our interactions, each person's story affecting the other's and new selves are forming through this constant reconstruction' (p. 83). Hence, using researcher's Self as the only source of information needs to be reconsidered, contemplating instead a polyvocal interchange with the Other as participants, which, according to Taft-Kaufman (2000), allows multiple untold stories to be accessed and validated as conceptually and critically framed by experiences that exist beyond the writer's own. In this way, autoethnographers working with their participants symbiotically allow their own stories, narrated from the perspectives of both a subject and object of their study, to be supported, negated, disrupted and upturned by the participants' voices that conjointly construct a complex fabric of social reality through their lived experiences. These lived experiences extend beyond the researcher's single version, creating, instead, a polyvocal inquiry into the cultural phenomenon, where the researcher's voice succumbs to, merges with or transcends the voices of the Other in ever-shifting symbiotic balance of auto- and ethno-. Most importantly, even though autoethnographers accept their foremost contribution to their studies as the researcher in charge of methodological, theoretical and analytical tools, in a symbiotic approach, their position becomes one of the participants, as the voices of Self and Others fluctuate continuously throughout their narrative, creating overall a dynamic polyvocal textual space, where the voices of all participants, including their own, become equally significant. Hammersley and Atkinson (2007) agree that 'once we abandon the idea that the social character of research can be standardized out or avoided by becoming a "fly on the wall" or a "full participant", the role of the researcher as active participant in the research process becomes clear' (p. 17). This recognition of the researcher's own voice as one of the participants allows autoethnographers to engage in polyvocal storytelling in an empathetic and respectful way, which 'demonstrates to others, who are involved in or implicated by our projects, that they matter too' (Adams, Ellis and Holman Jones, 2017, p. 8). Thus, symbiotic polyvocality of research that involves participants requires autoethnographers' explicit reflexive and reflective engagement with the issues of the researcher power and privilege to ensure that their narratives are told *together* with the participants rather than *about* the participants. Yet, it is worth mentioning here that the recent debates about polyvocality of research problematize the assumption that adding more voices can result in better research quality (Winkler, 2018b). In a similar vein, symbiotic polyvocality is not about the numerical quantities but about the ways we can take the participants' voices beyond the words spoken towards broader shared understanding of the cultural phenomenon under study. More specific discussions related to a symbiotic approach to ethical issues and data analysis associated with involving participants in autoethnographic studies are considered further in the book, whilst the next few paragraphs are devoted to discussing the Other as researcher's multiple Selves.

The 'Other' as researchers' multiple Selves

Another challenge for any qualitative researcher is related to the issue of representing their own Self, which takes us back to Denzin and Lincoln (2005), who refer to this kind of questions as the 'crisis of representation', arguing that qualitative researchers no longer can directly capture lived experience, as these experiences are created by the researchers themselves. Allen-Collinson (2012) takes this idea a step further, suggesting that autoethnography as a genre ascended from that 'crisis of representation' within qualitative research, challenging some of the very foundations and key tenets of more 'traditional' forms of research in its requirement for the researcher explicitly to situate and 'write in' her/himself as a key player. One way of theorizing about the researcher's Self can be linked to Lyotard (1984), who used the concept of a 'postmodern Self' to explain that it existed not as an isolated island but as a part of an intricate fabric of relations that became more complex and mobile than ever before: 'Young or old, man or woman, rich or poor, a person is always located at "nodal points" of specific communication circuits, however tiny these may be' (p. 15). This means that researchers' complete immersion in this intricate fabric of relations makes it impossible for the former to merely explore the interplay between culture and their own Self. Researchers have to write about themselves as an embedded part of this fabric, zooming backwards and forwards, inwards and outwards, thus, making 'distinctions between the personal and the cultural to become blurred, sometimes beyond distinct recognition' (Ellis and Bochner, 2000, p. 739). Engaging in this form of writing, in its turn, creates multiple points of departure for the researcher, which, according to St. Pierre (2000), results in dislocation, internal disorientation, fragmentation, scattering, contradiction and instability of the researcher's Self. Hermans (2001) confirms that there is no one essential core Self, but rather, it is composed of manifold positions, as a result of the global interconnections between communities and cultures. Thus, rather than thinking in terms of an essential core self, the author proposes 'a view that decentralizes both self and culture to a considerable degree without losing track with the notion of unity' (Hermans, 2001, p. 275). And though a simultaneous presence of several Selves is a condition that is traditionally seen by the Western medicine as a pathology associated with schizophrenia or multiple personality disorder, in relation to qualitative research, the existence of one core Self, according to Collins (1988), is a myth imposed on us by the requirements of social contacts. As Collins (1988) explains, in reality our multiple Selves are constructed as a result of various fluctuating roles that we play in different life situations: 'We are compelled to have an individual self, not because we actually have one but because social interaction requires us to act as if we do' (p. 256).

To avoid diving too deeply into the domain of psychology or psychiatry, I redirect my discussion here back to the field of autoethnographic research with a specific focus on the issues of representing researcher's multiple Selves. Specifically, in the context of a symbiotic approach, the researcher's Self is seen as a constellation of multiple, often conflicting, partial identities, contrasting the 'fiction of a single true, authentic self' with a 'reflexive self' (Denzin and Lincoln, 2000, p. 1060) in the continuous presence of the Other. Yet, researchers' multiple Selves do not and cannot exist in separation from the Other. To escape an impending dichotomy of Self/Other, I suggest that, in a symbiotic approach, Self is not represented within the narrative in opposition to the Other, first, to avoid engagement with another unhelpful binary of Self/Other and, second, to re-establish that there is no one stable and static Self as there is no one constant and fixed Other. As explained by Subreenduth and Rhee (2010), the 'Self-Other' dichotomy restricts the possibilities of qualitative researchers, as the use of a hyphen between Self and Other continues to signify 'a linear occurrence – exactly what we intend to disrupt as we speak of/about for example the field-home, personal-professional and identity politics' (p. 341). Similarly, Gergen (1991) uses a postmodern view to explain the breakdown and erasure of one single Self, which is cast adrift in a world, where 'we become pastiches, imitative assemblages of each other; each of us becomes the other ... we appear to each other as single identities, unified, of whole cloth' (Gergen, 1991, p. 71). Thus, researchers' encounters with the Other are seen here in symbiosis in a way described by Chang (2008) as a 'give-and-take' process, where Self learns values, norms and customs from others, whilst also contributing to the continuity of the others as a cultural community. Consequently, 'self becomes mirrored in others and others become extension of self' (Chang, 2008, p. 27). Researchers' representation of the Other in this sense will be achieved through close alignment and juxtapositions of their Selves with the Others' selves to indicate their 'acceptance of our multiple selves in our many fractured ways of being, to acknowledge and be aware of how this acceptance and acknowledgment influences wider relationships at both a particular level and a cultural level' (Short, 2010, p. 36). Such symbiotic fusion of the researcher's multiple Selves with the multiplicities of the Other confirms the intent of autoethnography to provide a deep contextual critique of a cultural phenomenon through drawing on a complex interplay between the researcher's personal experiences of and influences on that cultural phenomenon. As explained by Grant (2010), autoethnographic writing

> blurs the categorical distinctions between self and culture, as culture is expressed through self and vice versa. We move through culture and culture moves through us. In this sense, we are both the inventors of culture and simultaneously invented by it. This does not mean that the self of the ethnographer is taken as a social agent to be described definitively, once and for all. Rather, she or he should be viewed in relational terms within a continuously changing and fluid configuration of relationships. (p. 113)

Thus, in symbiotic polyvocality the notion of the Other as researchers' multiple Selves broadly captures the simultaneity and multiplicity of the voices that emerge from the researchers' engagement with their fragmented Self: Self as a researcher, a participant and as a representative of a particular culture, time and locality. Each of these multiple Selves produces different voices, where each of these voices is shaped by specific sociocultural vistas, epistemological positionings, political powers and professional practices. As noted by Etherington (2007b), knowledge produced this way is 'situated, transient, partial and provisional; characterized by multiple voices, perspectives, truths and meanings' (p. 30).

In summary, the concept of polyvocality as one of the constituent parts of a symbiotic approach aims to highlight the importance of acknowledging and reflecting on the complexity of researchers' simultaneous engagement with multiple forms of the Other: the characters from their stories, their participants and their multiple Selves, as they interact with each other in a wider sociocultural and political context. Thus, in symbiotic polyvocality, 'voice' ceases to be an individual or personal occurrence, gaining potential to expose deeper societal concerns and imbalances of power, as the former give rise to new illuminations or instigate new inquiries.

Part 3

'Doing' Symbiotic Autoethnography

5

Working Symbiotically with Autoethnographic Data

Introduction

Our life experiences are dispersed across spatial and temporal dimensions, making it problematic to capture them through linear methodological structures and conventions. This is particularly relevant to Symbiotic Autoethnography, where autoethnographers face the challenges of positioning themselves as both the object and the subject of their investigation entwined in a complex simultaneous interplay of multiple Selves with the Other and with the cultural phenomenon under study. As noted by Denzin (1997), in autoethnography, the subjective Self of the researcher is reflected on with the purpose of understanding of the social world from the perspective of the interacting individual. Conquergood (1991) refers to this aspect of autoethnography as 'embodied practice', where researchers try to combine 'the Being There of performed experience with the Being Here of written texts' (p. 193). Pillow (2019) brings out attention to the fact that the main methods of research, such as seeing, hearing and recording, have been recently intensely debated, resulting in calls for 'an end to data' and questions of whether data even matters or exists, raising fundamental questions about how research is thought and conducted. Indeed, being placed within a research study, where one's life becomes 'data', creates an unaccustomed experience of knowledge production 'that literally moves our musculature and rhythms of our breath and hearts, as corporeal knowledge conjoins cognition through enfleshment knowledge' (Madison, 2010, p. 7). This type of 'embodied' knowledge production often requires autoethnographers to engage in the ways of working with data that goes against the grain of traditional research conventions based on inflexible prescriptions and technical requirements at the expense of creativity, imagination and innovation. Going against conformity and compliance requires researchers' courage and determination to produce autoethnographic texts, which emerge 'from the researcher's bodily standpoint as she is continually recognizing and interpreting the residue traces of culture inscribed upon her hide from interacting with others in contexts' (Spry, 2001, p. 711). As noted by Wyatt (2020), it is not always possible to make these connections between events and our Selves and yet, we keep trying, because

> continuity, however fabricated – as in made, not as in untrue – connects us to our/selves; and it connects us to a sense (however fabricated) that we are 'selves'. We make these links in hindsight, in tentative, provisional stories – ours but not ours – that we piece together. It's like re-assembling fragments of a broken vase someone we love has dropped. If we are bold, we allow the fragments' sharp edges to draw blood. (p. 60)

In this part of the book I outline some of the strategies of 'doing' autoethnography symbiotically, at the same time refusing any implicit assumptions that this way is the standard against which other autoethnographic approaches should be gauged. In addition to theoretical deliberations, my discussion here also contains examples from my doctoral thesis, which illustrate my attempts to grapple with the complexities of autoethnographic data in the process of creating new meaning.

What is data in Symbiotic Autoethnography?

Naturally, the very first question that arises, when talking about working with autoethnographic data, is – what is considered as data in a symbiotic approach? The answer to this question is, paradoxically, both simple and complex, as in Symbiotic Autoethnography, everything is regarded as data. This is not too different from the general perception of what autoethnographic data encompasses. Ellis and Bochner (2000) argue that in autoethnography, where the researcher is the subject, the researcher's interpretation of the experience becomes the data. Bullough and Pinnegar (2001) also confirm that, when it comes to autoethnographic research, what counts as data expands greatly, creating for the researchers 'the difficulty of representing, presenting, legitimating, analysing and reporting one's own experience as data' (p. 15). Alerby and Bergmark (2012) warn us against relying on predefined methodological procedures, arguing that, 'given the notion that reality cannot be reduced to two separate qualities – mind and body – researchers have to develop inclusive methods to grasp the complexity of reality' (p. 96).

In a symbiotic approach, however, a particular complexity of working with autoethnographic data involves researchers combining, juxtaposing and manipulating various fragments of data, whilst being omnipresent across all their experiences throughout times and spaces. This approach aligns well with autoethnographers' commitment to creating unique personal interpretation of cultural phenomena as far from being a unitary and static occurrence 'untainted by experience, but in reality, completely fluid' (Powell, 1996, p. 1483). In this sense, a symbiotic approach challenges common appreciation of established methodological procedures, whilst giving autoethnographers freedom to engage in the interpretation of data as a fluid multifaceted concept that has the capacity to make use of ruptured realities, fragmented thoughts, tangled emotions and disorientated bodily experiences. As argued by St. Pierre (1997), if we wish to engage in the risky practice of re-describing the world, we need to reject the existing categories and think differently about the word 'data' and to find a different strategy of sense-making that can embrace 'emotional data, dream data and sensual data' (p. 177). Lather (2006) maintains the same line of reasoning, suggesting that such interruption of long familiar habits in the production of knowing contributes to the proliferation of countervailing practices that are 'about saying yes to the messiness, to that which interrupts and exceeds versus tidy categories' (p. 48). Figure 3 illustrates the complexity of working with autoethnographic data in a symbiotic way, where the boundaries between traditional and 'out-of-category' (St. Pierre, 1997, p. 175) forms of data become blurred to the point at which the sources of data cannot be positively determined or predefined. In contrast, the data pool here is presented as a multidimensional 'cloud' of researcher's emotions, feelings and bodily senses captured in the act of writing, where fragments of data intertwine, collide and merge with each other in an intricate and, at times, unexpected and uncomfortable way. This fluidity of data is, of course, impossible to capture in a two-dimensional image, so I will have to rely here on the readers' imagination to visualize the spatial and shifting nature of data in symbiotic autoethnographic approach.

The complexity of a symbiotic approach to autoethnographic data resonates, somehow, with Brinkmann's (2014) notion of 'stumble data', which troubles what counts as traditional data, suggesting that researchers should think of data as any material brought about by 'astonishment, mystery and breakdowns in one's understanding of life events, big or small' (Alvesson and Karreman cited in Brinkmann, 2014, p. 722). Indeed, such approach erases the lines between life, autoethnographic writing and traditional ways of collecting data, as, according to the author, research is part of the life process. In this sense, in Symbiotic

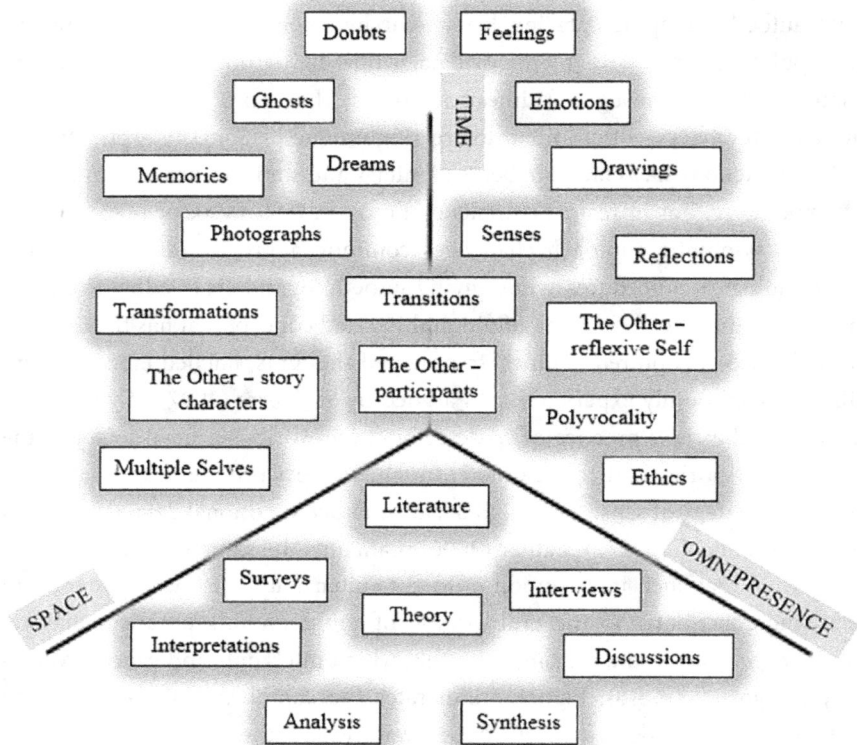

Figure 3 Working with autoethnographic data symbiotically.

Autoethnography, data is placed in and between bodies in the 'rupture and rapture' (Spry, 2011b, p. 497) of writing that exceeds the constraints of traditional data collection and analysis, allowing researchers to perform the impossible, moving in and out of the data 'with words and blood and bones' (Spry, 2011b, p. 498). This brings a symbiotic approach into a close connection with the concept of embodiment, since the 'pathology' of an inescapable fragmentation of the researcher's Self into multiple Selves thrusts them towards a raised level of self-awareness and, consequently, the issues of the researcher's living body/ subjective self. This is a salient part of working with autoethnographic data symbiotically. Prominent theorists and researchers in the field of qualitative studies (Reed-Danahay, 1997; Ellis, 2004; Chang, 2008; Denzin, 2014; Ellingson, 2017; Leigh and Brown, 2021) endorse the significance of that connectedness of researchers' bodily experiences to the cultural and social in a study of specific phenomena. In relation to autoethnography, Van Wolputte (2004) suggests that autoethnographic narratives can be seen as an important means of evoking, assimilating and reconceptualizing the ways in which our Selves are perceived in terms of the distinctions between mind and body, subject and object, psychological and biological, gender and sex, culture and nature. This view places the idea of 'extended' autoethnographic Selves in a stark contrast with the Cartesian mind–body dualism that is based on privileging the rational mind over the emotional body. Such dualism is grounded in the assumption that there is one centralized 'I' responsible for the process of reasoning or thinking that is essentially different from the body and other material extended in space (Hermans, 2001; Butler and Dunne, 2012). As explained by Turner (2009), from a dualist point of view, the 'body' exists outside the 'social world' or, even, is opposed to it and 'hence the body from this standpoint cannot be of interest to sociologists' (p. 513). Postmodern thinkers, such as Derrida (1976), Kristeva (1982), Butler (1997) and Langellier (1998), critiqued the false dichotomy of body and mind, demonstrating in Braidotti's (2006) words that 'the truth of self lies in its interrelations to others in a rhizomatic manner that defies dualistic modes of opposition' (p. 161). Similarly, Csordas (1994) claims that embodiment is intrinsically part of our being in-the-world and as such 'it collapses the difference between subjective and objective, cognition and emotion, or mind and body' (p. 276). In the context of autoethnographic research, this view is also supported by Langellier (1998), who suggests that embodied autoethnographic writing could destabilize social and political relations, because it enabled a story of the body to be told through the body, making cultural conflict concrete and accessible. De Freitas and Paton (2009) also add that autoethnographic writing 'is the embodiment of an otherness that undermines the presence of the self' (p. 494).

Perceptibly, the location of embodied praxis in Symbiotic Autoethnography draws on the existing consensus in research circles, which sees the researcher's body as the primary sociocultural product. On the one hand, such perception problematizes a whole series of binary oppositions and dichotomous categories, governing the ways we understand bodies, their relations to other objects and to the world; and on the other hand, it displaces the privileges assigned to mind or to the psyche over the body: 'it involves understanding the interaction of the social and the individual in terms of the production and inscription of bodily surfaces' (Grosz, 2001, p. 31). Hence, in Symbiotic Autoethnography, working with the data is anticipated to be grounded in researchers' embodied experiences, as a practice that privileges the body as 'an intensely sensuous way of knowing'

(Conquergood, 1991, p. 180). Researchers are encouraged to use their 'stored embodiments' (Hokkanen, 2017, p. 26) to reflect on their bodily reactions to specific times, spaces and cultures as well as to the process of autoethnographic writing itself. As explained by Alexander (2014), the meaning of embodiment is in the tripartite construction of, first, the physical disposition of the body; second, its presumed positionality against socially constructed norms; and finally, its recognition of a state of being as one's social orientation of the body in time and place:

> Such a construction seeks to address not only how a body is socially marked (e.g., claimed, categorized, or marginalized) but how we embody – own, disown, resist, mourn, celebrate, torture, or politicize the skin we live in, establishing the structural disposition of that body. How we do our body as a performative act of being, as well as how we use our body (and bodily experience) as a site of critical theorizing in scholarly discourse and in the everyday – as we tell our stories. (p. 1169)

In this sense, embodiment within Symbiotic Autoethnography represents an intention to completely abolish the mind/body dichotomy, enabling researchers to tell their stories as a joint experience of the body and the mind, where the latter is no longer perceived as something superior and independent from the body. Rather, when working with the data symbiotically, researchers see and represent their body as a canvas that bears the markings of the cultural phenomenon under study; the markings that are often fragmented, contradictory, perplexing and incoherent but, nevertheless, based on real lived experiences. Reflections on these embodied feelings represent another opportunity for researchers to appreciate a symbiotic mind–body autoethnographic praxis of working with the data that calls upon the body as a site of knowledge production. It is important to note that the embodied nature of autoethnographic writing and qualitative research in general contributes to the political thrust of our research studies, where researchers' actual material bodies become central for a praxis-oriented social justice autoethnography (Johnson, 2018; Ellis and Calafell, 2020; Leigh and Brown, 2021). Indeed, if we accept that Symbiotic Autoethnography draws attention to embodied ways of exploring the world, then lived experiences of the bodies can be used to connect researchers, as the agents of knowledge production, to their experiences of social power, oppression, injustice, inequality and domination. This way individual experiences of the body become fragments of the data that is embedded in the political focus of Symbiotic Autoethnography (as discussed in Chapter 4), enabling researchers to bring to the surface concealed underlying issues of oppressive discriminatory social structures and to call for action towards positive societal change. As Johnson (2018) clarifies, an embodied approach as a way of recognizing the degree to which our bodies are implicated in the reproduction of social power works on both structural and individual levels, where the 'structural shifts correspond with authentic transformations in attitude and where legal rights and freedoms are experienced at the core of our beings and manifested in our everyday interactions with others' (p. 2). In the next part of our discussion, I will focus on some of these specific fragments of data that form the intricate fabric of autoethnographic symbiotic approach.

'Discerning' the data vs data collection

Unquestionably, at the heart of any type of research lies the process of collecting data. Since we have agreed in the previous chapter that, in Symbiotic Autoethnography, everything is data, the next question that arises here is whether we can apply conventional methods of 'data collection' to Symbiotic Autoethnography. Traditional methods of data collection in qualitative research predominantly involve interactive interviewing and/or asynchronous surveying of participants followed by a subsequent analysis of the spoken or written responses. In Symbiotic Autoethnography, however, data is extracted from the researcher's own spatio-temporal embodied experiences of a cultural phenomenon under study. This means that conventional methods of data collection need to be reconsidered in the context of Symbiotic Autoethnography with a focus on 'discerning' rather than collecting data, where 'discerning' is understood as a process of imaginative and creative techniques of recognizing relevant and potentially valuable fragments of experiences within the complex fabric of the researcher's life journey that could contribute to a better understanding of the cultural phenomenon under study. The process of discerning data requires a great deal of rigour to ensure that the data is meaningful, manageable and bears well-defined internal coherence with the aims and objectives of the autoethnographic inquiry. Researchers' efforts here need to focus on creating a, what Saldana (2021, p. 199) calls, 'through-line' (Saldana, 2021, p. 199) in the multidimensional data – a strand that provides a symbiotic connection between the fragments of data aiding the process of constructing the autoethnographic narrative. This process offers limitless possibilities in the choice of data sources, making it possible to discern data not obtainable through more traditional ways of data collection. Yet, it also brings about the challenges of circumscribing a specific selection of data from the multiplicity of field notes that might include, but are not limited to, memories, feelings, experiences, dreams, photographs, various memorabilia, records of interviews with participants, entries from reflexive journals and diaries as well as researcher's reflections on relevant literature and theoretical perspectives. Duncan (2004) also suggests that, although autoethnographic reports are presented in the form of personal narratives, they do not consist solely of the researcher's opinions but are also supported by other data that can confirm or triangulate those opinions, using such sources of data as participant observation, interviewing and gathering documents and artefacts. Yet, in the context of a symbiotic approach, researchers need to be mindful of relying too heavily on traditional ways of collecting and selecting data, given the idea that these methods rarely reflect the complexity of the cultural phenomena under study. Hammersley and Atkinson (2007) point out these challenges in relation to any type of qualitative research, arguing,

> Field notes are always selective: it is not possible to capture everything. And there is a trade-off between breadth of focus and detail. What is recorded will depend on one's general sense of what is relevant to the foreshadowed research problems, as well as on background expectations. Moreover, as we shall see, the character of field notes may well change, in terms of focus and detail, over the course of the research. The completion of field notes is not an entirely straightforward matter, then. Like most aspects of intellectual craft, some care and attention to detail are prerequisites: satisfactory note-taking needs to be worked at. It is a skill demanding repeated assessment of purposes and priorities and of the costs and benefits of different strategies. (p. 141)

These ideas are fully relevant to a symbiotic approach, where the ways of discerning the data are not distinctly prescribed but, instead, emerge gradually from the body of the researcher's interaction with the cultural phenomenon under study. In this way, the process of discerning the data in Symbiotic Autoethnography comes closer to the perception of the world as far from being a unitary and static phenomenon 'untainted by experience, but in reality, completely fluid' (Powell, 1996, p. 1483). This position challenges commonly accepted appreciation of established methods of data collection, whilst giving researchers the freedom to engage in the interpretation of 'data' as a fluid multifaceted concept that has the capacity to make use of ruptured realities, fragmented thoughts, tangled emotions and disorientated bodily experiences.

> The chaotic data fragments defy boundaries, resist unity and disturb the consistency of my story, a story that is necessary to make sense. To maintain that tenuous story line, the data is projected onto paper in the anticipation that some warrant of 'accuracy' is born out of its tangible graphic presence ... However, like walking towards the horizon, the promise of certainty keeps fading away, as I approach it. And the sense of doubt refuses to leave. (An extract from my Reflexive Diary)

As argued by St. Pierre (1997), if we wish to engage in the risky research practice of re-describing the world, we need to reject the existing categories and think differently about the word 'data' and to find a different strategy of sense-making that can embrace 'emotional data, dream data and sensual data' (p. 177). Lather (2006) maintains the same line of reasoning, suggesting that such interruption of long familiar habits in the production of knowing contributes to the proliferation of countervailing practices that are 'about saying yes to the messiness, to that which interrupts and exceeds versus tidy categories' (p. 48).

To make the process of discerning the data more manageable, it might be useful to distinguish two symbiotically connected layers of what might be considered as, first, possible sources of data (white boxes) and, second, more tangible forms of data (grey boxes) discerned from these sources, even though the boundaries between these two will always remain blurred and the categories within them fluid and overlapping (see Figure 4).

Yet, despite this attempt to, somehow, streamline the process of discerning the data, the fragments of data often 'leak' into each other, mixing real with imaginary, rational with emotional, temporal with spatial and personal with political, creating a symbiosis of fluid and intertwining data fragments. In such complex symbiosis of data, words, both written and spoken, lose their dominance, giving way to memories, emotions, dreams, feelings, sounds and silences. Acknowledging this complexity along with recognizing the inaptness of language instruments for communicating evocative nuances of the data present one of the key tasks for autoethnographers in the context of a symbiotic approach. Discerning words alone is not sufficient for Symbiotic Autoethnography, as pauses, laughs and silences are equally significant in representing researchers' experiences, since the former exemplify different ways of perceiving the world available to human beings, which go beyond the limitations of language instruments.

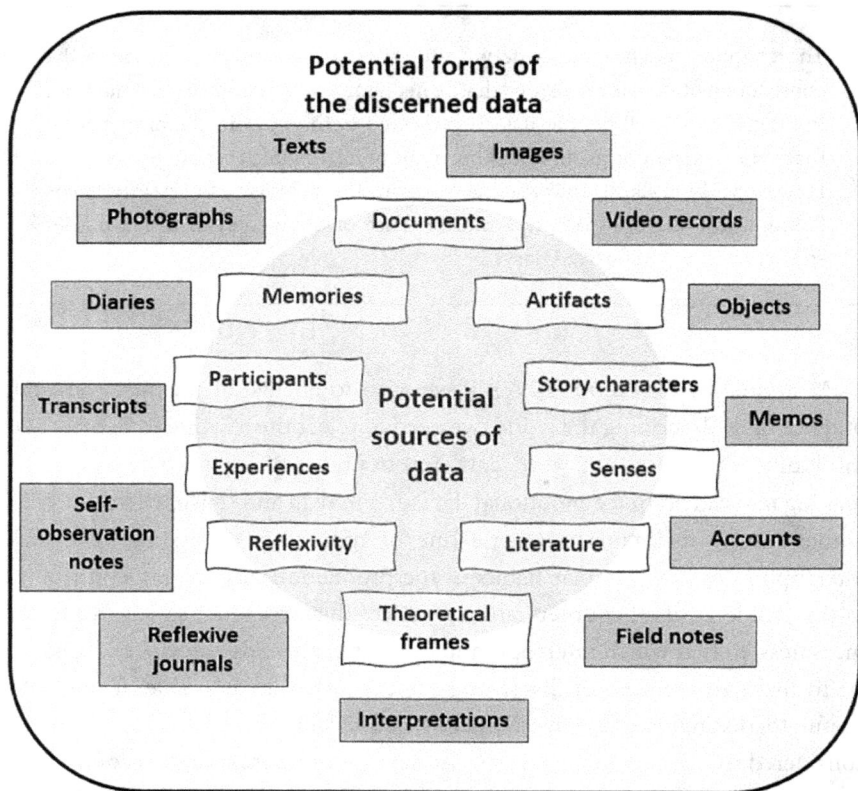

Figure 4 Discerning data in Symbiotic Autoethnography.

This way of thinking has led me to the concept of 'tacit knowledge', developed by Polanyi (1966), who suggested that 'we can know more than we can tell' (p. 4). His argument is, originally, exemplified by an example of driving in a nail by the strokes of a hammer:

When we use a hammer to drive in a nail, we attend to both nail and hammer, but in a different way. We watch the effect of our strokes on the nail and try to wield the hammer so as to hit the nail most effectively. When we bring down the hammer we do not feel that its handle has struck our palm but that its head has struck the nail. Yet in a sense we are certainly alert to the feelings in our palm and the fingers that hold the hammer. They guide us in handling it effectively and the degree of attention that we give to the nail is given to the same extent but in a different way to these feelings. The difference may be stated by saying that the latter are not, like the nail, objects of our attention, but instruments of it. They are not watched in themselves; we watch something else while keeping intensely aware of them. I have a subsidiary awareness of the feeling in the palm of my hand which is merged into my focal awareness of my driving in the nail. (Polanyi, [1958] 2005, p. 57)

In his later work, Polanyi (1966) refers to this kind of knowing as 'tacit dimension', suggesting that individuals continuously process wide range of visual, conceptual and sensory data in their attempts to make sense of something and yet, this process of discovery is often difficult to articulate adequately by means of language. To explain his concept of 'tacit knowledge', Polanyi (1966) offers us another example, based on our ability to recognize a human face amongst millions of other faces without being able to explain our thinking behind the process of recognition. Despite multiple incongruities and controversies associated with Polanyi's arguments, some aspects of his ideas resonate with the autoethnographic writing and, especially, with the process of discerning data in Symbiotic Autoethnography. First, it is the acknowledgement that language as our interpretive frame has its limitations in terms of its capacity to communicate the whole range of our experiences with all their complexities and intricacies. And second, it is the process of connecting these 'unspecifiable particulars' (Polanyi, 1966, p. 24) into a comprehensive entity in a way we, sometimes, cannot define. This is where the concept of symbiosis comes handy, encouraging researchers' attempts to discern the data that is not, necessarily, immediately obvious or explicable, discarding the illusory division between 'real' and sensory, verbal and unspoken, embodied and impalpable, social and personal, rational and emotional. In the next few sections I attempt to show examples of working symbiotically with some of the autoethnographic data, which might be particularly challenging to 'discern'.

Dreams

In this context, even dreams can be considered significant in the process of discerning data, if they somehow influence the researcher's interpretation of events, experiences and lines of thinking. St. Pierre (1997), for example, suggests that dream data is another form of transgressive data. She goes as far as questioning whether dreaming can be named as a method of data collection, arguing that, since her study was based on examining her own subjectivity, which has always been, at least partially, produced by dreams, it seemed appropriate and even necessary to adopt the view that dreaming is a process of inquiry. To support her point, St. Pierre turns to Foucault's (1986) work 'Of Other Spaces', where he makes a direct connection between 'the space of our dreams' and 'the space of our primary perception' (p. 23). St. Pierre then concludes that dreams cannot be discounted as a form of data, as the latter add another layer of depth to researchers' analytical efforts, keeping interpretation in play in some dislocated space of their texts, producing dissonance, alterity and confusion, whilst enabling and legitimizing 'a complexity of meaning that science prohibits' (p. 183). Similarly, Goode (2019) maintains that the nature of narrative research allows dreams to be used as data, supporting her view by references to the work of Steedman, an academic historian, who combines chronological framework of history with psychoanalytic mode of storytelling that 'allows the dream, the wish, the fantasy, to be presented as evidence' (Steedman cited in Goode, 2019, p. 49) in her exploration of the idea that writing history is an interpersonal process of interaction with the 'spirits' or 'ghostly presences' of historical subjects from the past (Goode, 2019). Long and Manley (2019) take the idea one step further in their interpretation of a concept of 'social dreaming'. In their edited volume, the authors and the contributors argue that dreams are relevant to the wider social sphere and have a collective resonance that goes beyond the personal narrative. Indeed, in Symbiotic Autoethnography, dreams represent a justifiable source of data as they influence, whether consciously or subconsciously, our perceptions of the world with all its sociocultural and political controversies, disparities and problems. Our 'dream data' does more than simply mirror our daytime experiences: it represents an activity that affects researchers' lives, decisions and thinking. Thus, in a symbiotic approach, the process of discerning data shifts from 'hard data' to a symbiosis of dreams, events, memories, times and spaces with a focus on the researcher's attempts to understand better a specific cultural phenomenon.

Memories

Another non-traditional category that is vital in the process of discerning data in Symbiotic Autoethnography is related to our memories and memory work. Wall (2008) brings to the researchers' attention the fact that in a more traditional research culture there still persists favouritism towards 'hard' data rather that a pure reliance on memories in the process of qualitative analysis. Yet, Wall (2008) justifiably questions whether these memories would have been viewed as more legitimate if they were brought to life during an interview by another researcher, despite the fact that both the interview transcript and her autoethnographic text would be based on the same set of memories. Keightley (2010) highlights the value of memory work, noting that it involves a process of sense-making as a lived process of time and the experience of it, which has a potential value for qualitative research both as an object and technique, since the researcher's turn to memory

> enables the role of the past in the present to be explored. Ruptures and continuities, past events and forgotten episodes can be investigated, not as objective historical occurrences but as constructed and reconstructed accounts of the past acting in and on the present. If the frameworks of meaning in memory and remembering are to be understood, memories themselves must be treated as texts to be analyzed. (p. 67)

Using memories in research studies has been appreciated over the years by a number of theorists and researchers (Bruner, 1987; Polkinghorne, 1988; Plummer, 2001a; Chang, 2008; Bochner and Adams, 2020; Silverman, 2021). In Symbiotic Autoethnography, memories elicited from our past in the moment of writing ('present past') allow alternative histories and marginal accounts to be uncovered and reconstructed in specific social and cultural contexts. Chang (2008) confirms that personal memories tap into the wealth of information about self and 'what is extracted through the memory can be written down as textual data' (p. 72). Hokkanen (2017), however, warns us that not all memories may be analytically useful: some are irrelevant to our research, even though their analysis may be useful for personal development or other aspects of our lives. Hokkanen (2017) also notes that our memories of highly emotional experiences and events are not necessarily accurate, even though we sometimes feel that every detail and even the visual appearance of the situation are forever ingrained in our memory. Thus, taking notes about feelings and emotions is an important part of practice for researchers, as it will support their memory accounts in later stages of research. Yet, Goode (2019) argues that in relation to re/membered testimonies, the factual 'truth' of what the individual claims is less important than its 'emotional truth' and that the content of what is narrated is less important than the ways in which it is expressed. This view aligns with Plummer's (2001b) earlier claim that majority of life story researchers no longer believe that 'simple, linear or essential, real truth about a life can be gleaned through a life story; or indeed that a researcher can have any clear, superior access to knowledge about a life' (p. 400). Plummer offers five analytical levels of memory work, including psychological or individual memory, narrative memory, collective memory, generational memory and popular memory. In relation to psychological or individual memory, the focus is on what a person can recall and how well they can recall it, whereas narrative memory is focused on highly selective stories that people tell about their past, which seem to develop into autonomous motives. In collective and generational memory work, researchers call on, what Plummer (2001b) defines as, 'the social frameworks of memory' (p. 402), where life stories emerge from collectively organized societal narratives about a specific phenomenon. This type of analytical approach to memory work is closely linked to generational memory, where a sense of belonging to a generation may become the key to unlocking such frameworks, highlighting the memories associated with events that happened generations earlier. Finally, Plummer (2001b) identifies 'popular memory', where the focus is bringing to the surface and returning back to their communities 'the memories of class, traditional communities, oppressed minorities, Indigenous peoples, the colonized, the marginalized, the depressed and oppressed' (p. 402), which have either never been told or have been lost. Following a similar approach, Roessner and Teresa (2020) write about the differentiation between 'public memory' as a sanctioned official type of memory ('history') and cultural memory, suggesting that our 'diverse, fragmented and mutable' (p. 160) fragments of memories are most clearly understood as a comparison of various 'official' and alternative versions of it.

Though these analytical categorizations of memories might help some researches in discerning their 'memory data', in Symbiotic Autoethnography, the focus is on researchers' simultaneous engagement with temporally connected present memories of the past that are symbiotically fused to help the researchers step into the shoes of their various former Selves, as Bochner (2020) puts it, in order to arrive at interpretations of the epiphanies they had lived through and to make whatever unifying sense they could of them. Bochner (2020), writing about the process of working with the memory data, acknowledges that his intention was to probe and examine his memories, self-investigating by turning the memories of significant incidents inside out and upside down, resulting in the text, which 'worked the hyphens of scholarly and literary form: memoir and essay, evocative and analytic autoethnography, story and theory' (p. 81). These ideas gain firm traction in the context of a symbiotic approach to working with autoethnographic data, including memory data, given that any categorization within this process creates a risk of disrupting the symbiosis of the seven features of symbiotic autoethnographic narrative as discussed in Chapter 4. Thus, discerning memory data in the context of a symbiotic approach is not about the attempts to classify this data or to verify its 'accuracy'. Rather, it is about recognizing pertinent memory fragments within the researcher's life

At this point of my story I am retracing my own steps to the beginning of my journey, pushing my memory to bring up my first recollections of events that can be made visible on paper in a form of words with their countless meanings, where, once again, misinterpretations, disorientations and perplexities aim to suggest different ways of seeing. Moving back and forth between the images of the past bonded with my present Self feels like pressing a pen against a piece of paper, moving it back and forth along the same line until the paper is pierced by the abrasion, in the same way my past memories and my present feelings press against each other, as I am waiting for the words to escape from the worn-out seams. (An abstract from my Reflexive Diary)

journey as remembered and captured in the moment of writing, in symbiosis with the researcher's reflexivity, omnipresence, polyvocal evocative storytelling and interpretative analysis with consideration of the political (transformative) nature of their narratives.

Truly, as supported by Goodson (2014), the production of autobiographical memories can be seen as an ongoing process of knowledge production, where the capacity of our memory work to dis-embed our understanding of the world becomes central to this knowledge, as 'in doing so we move beyond the birth right scripts we inherit ancestrally into the production of new scripts and visions' (p. 127). In my own research based on a symbiotic approach, my personal memories have enabled me to bring back to life a few powerful events that have been imprinted on my mind for over twenty years, allowing 'alternative histories and marginal accounts of the past to be uncovered and reconstructed in social and cultural history' (Keightley, 2010, p. 61), whilst challenging, along with St. Pierre (2009), Denzin (2014) and a few others, an exclusive reliance on voice, presence and experience as the only unproblematic window to the past. In addition, reflecting on my memories provided me with new understandings of the cultural phenomena under study, merging symbiotically with further understandings, as I engaged with my participants' stories entering, adjusting, rapturing or balancing my own recollections. Writing about these merged present memories of the past is never an easy task, as words try to escape the impermanence and mutability of our thoughts. As noted by Bochner (2020), when we attempt to fit language to our experiences, we encounter the process of transforming our original experiences into something else – something remembered:

the chasm between experience and words; between the chaos and fragmentation of living a life and the smoothing orderliness we often bring to it when we write; between what we can say about the past now and what we imagine took place then; between how we mourn or celebrate the past and what shape our grieving or rejoicing gives to our future. Remembering, then articulating what we remember, is always an activity under the influence of the present, fusing what one desires, what one imagines and what may actually have occurred. (p. 82)

These ideas provide a natural cognitive bridge towards the next part of our discussion related to discerning our feelings, emotions and silences as sources of data in Symbiotic Autoethnography.

Feelings, emotions, sounds and silences

Hammersley and Atkinson (2007) express their perception of researchers' personal feelings of anxiety, surprise, shock or revulsion not just as the motive for narcissistic self-absorption but as data of analytic significance. The authors argue that not only researchers' feelings enter into and colour the social relationships they engage in during fieldwork, but such personal and subjective responses unavoidably influence one's choice of 'what is noteworthy, what is regarded as strange and problematic and what appears to be mundane and obvious. One often relies implicitly on such feelings; therefore, their existence and possible influence must be acknowledged and, if possible, explicated in written form' (p. 151). Altheide and Johnson (2011) express similar views in relation to any type of ethnographic research, suggesting that good ethnographies 'reflect tacit knowledge, the largely unarticulated, contextual understanding that is often reflected in nods, silences, humor and naughty nuances' (p. 590). Hokkanen (2017) echoes these views on non-traditional data, arguing that the analysis of subjective feelings may reveal important cultural assumptions and tacit understandings that affect interpreting practices in different social settings.

Indeed, our feelings and emotions are a large part of who we are, as we continuously engage with the world around us through our subjective reactions to various experiences. Not only our emotional responses to these experiences govern our actions, but they also provide the emotional 'screen' upon which our understanding of the phenomenon is inscribed. Once again, the task of autoethnographers in the context of a symbiotic approach is to discern the fragments of 'emotional' data that are relevant and analytically useful for their autoethnographic inquiry. As argued by St. Pierre (1997), researchers' 'emotional labor' (p. 177) is an important part of fieldwork and another way of making themselves uncomfortable. Yet, as I argued previously, the feeling of discomfort associated with autoethnographic writing is central to the process of interpretative analysis. This particularly applies to discerning 'silences as data', as in the context of a symbiotic approach, paradoxically, silences are also considered to be voices distinguishable within a complex fabric of autoethnographic discourse. The significance of silences in research data has been highlighted by a few researchers and theorists (Heidegger, 1962; Scott, 1993; Lather, 1996; Boler, 2004; Mazzei 1997, 2004, 2007; Silverman, 2020; Aiston and Fo, 2021). Heidegger ([1962] 1978) saw keeping silent as an essential aspect of discourse, explaining that 'anyone who keeps silent, when he wants to give us to understand something, must "have something to say"' (p. 342). Spivak (1976) wrote about silences as secondary material that were not just a simple adjunct to a primary text but valuable data, which 'inserts itself within the interstices of the former, filling holes that are already there' (p. xxiv). Foucault (1978) added an aspect of power to these debates, claiming that discourses were not subservient to power or raised up against it, any more than silences are; thus, we must make allowance for the complex and unstable process whereby discourses both transmit and produce power and, 'in like manner, silence and secrecy are a shelter for power, anchoring its prohibitions; but they also loosen its holds and provide for relatively obscure areas of tolerance' (p. 101). More recently, Mazzei (1997) theorized about being haunted by the silences in the conversations and her engagement with these 'inhabited' silences as the data, where a silent absence became as important for her as a voiced presence. In her later work, Mazzei (2007) challenges the ways in which traditional approaches to working with data censor and discipline researchers towards eliminating all silences as data

> because it does not make easy sense and transgresses the disciplined data easily hearable, knowable and nameable. These transgressive silent texts that we cannot 'hear', but that speak to us nonetheless, require a different attentiveness and listening in our research settings. These silent texts are audible only within a problematic of silence that is errant, wayward and that rebels against those practices of censoring and over-writing as it irrupts our received notions of what is granted a hearing as we analyze the conversations and verbalizations by participants in our research settings. (p. 632)

As researchers begin to 'listen to the silences' behind their own autoethnographic stories or the words of their participants, the data discerned from these silences provides a fruitful ground for theorizing about the nature of these silences. As argued by Denzin (1997), it is those gaps and silences which 'provide the flesh and bone – the backdrop against which meaning is established' (p. 38). Listening 'symbiotically' to silences involves recognizing the complexity of interplay between spoken and unspoken, looking into the depth of researchers' own and the participants' motives behind the act of being silent. Although an auditory representation of silences is the same in every case, the meanings behind these silences always vary depending on a symbiosis of specific circumstances, motivations and cultural preferences. Engaging in the process of discerning silences as data enables new meanings to emerge from the empirical material, which is 'not always observable or immediately "present" but rather was discovered in the hidden, the covert, the inarticulate: the gaps within/outside the observable' (Mazzei, 2003, p. 358).

Such a symbiotic approach to silences, which occur within researchers' own reflections, inner dialogues with multiple selves or during interviews with participants works against the binary interpretations of autoethnographic data as blanks/speech, silence/utterance, absence/presence. Researchers' omnipresence becomes almost palpable in the process of discerning such data, as the sounds of silence enter their already complicated polyvocal 'present past' memories, tangled with their reflexive and interpretative contemplations. Nevertheless, discerning and interpreting silences also adds to a constant concern about 'losing meaning', whilst trying to make sense of the data, as warned by Walker (1991). The process of capturing silences in symbiosis with other fragments of data feels very much like taking a snapshot with a camera without knowing what the actual photo is going to look like. In the spaces between the click of the camera and the final

---

Working with the silences as data in my Symbiotic Autoethnography was about making gestures towards unfamiliar and strange, towards previously concealed and suppressed, towards disruptive and problematic; it was about uncovering these hidden silences in-between the interactions of my multiple Selves with the multiple Others as a way of discovering a deeper socio-cultural understanding of the subject under study. These silences were significant and yet, almost impossible to capture, as they expanded beyond the boundaries of my narrative account. Nonetheless, I was acutely aware that the silences were there for a reason. (An extract from my Reflexive Diary)

image there is always a sense of doubt, ambiguity and hesitation about whether any meaning can be ascribed to the occurrences, words, gestures and anything in between.

'In the moment of writing' experiences

Autoethnographers' current or, as I prefer to call them, 'in the moment of writing' experiences represent another source for discerning data in the context of a symbiotic approach. These experiences are embedded in self-observational reflexive narratives that chronicle researchers' representation of experiences, feelings and thoughts as they happen in the process of autoethnographic writing. Close to this understanding of 'in the moment' experiences as data comes Chang's (2008) suggestion that self-observational data encompasses researchers' actual behaviours, thoughts and emotions as they occur in their natural contexts. Yet, in Symbiotic Autoethnography, distinguishing self-observational data from a flow of 'in the moment' experiences that are embedded into the fabric of autoethnographic writing presents a practically impossible task. Wall (2008) reflects on a similar issue associated with ethnographic research, asking a well-founded question: if our 'lived experience can be equated to traditional ethnographic participant observation (being actively involved in the field), it is interesting to ask "how much participation is participation enough?"' (p. 42). The answer to the posed question might lie in the symbiotic approach, which endorses the view that self-observations are symbiotically intertwined with researchers' reflexivity and thus, the 'amount of participation' in self-observation becomes infinite, as the autoethnographers' involvement in their own studies is a fundamental aspect of symbiotic or, for that matter, any other type of autoethnography. Hence, self-observation and reflexivity in relation to 'in the moment of writing' experiences are two sides of the same coin, as researchers cannot write about their experiences without using their reflexive autoethnographic lens. Reflexivity as one of the key features of Symbiotic Autoethnography has been discussed in more general terms in Chapter 4, so, to avoid repeating myself, in the next few paragraphs I will focus specifically on 'in the moment of writing' experiences as data in Symbiotic Autoethnography.

In Symbiotic Autoethnography, the process of self-observational reflexive writing involves researchers' attention to and scrutiny of their experiences and thoughts that transpire in the moment of writing their autoethnography, whilst simultaneously considering these experiences alongside their epistemological, methodological and ethical assumptions related to the phenomenon under study. Researchers use these 'in the moment' experiences in symbiosis to both turn their 'autoethnographic gaze' at themselves as well as looking across and beyond their research journey in their attempt to interpret the confluences, diversions, intersections and blind alleys of their inquiry. Discerning data from such indivisible fusion of self-observations with reflexivity is a challenging, if not an impossible, part of working with autoethnographic data, as researchers engage in a reflexive praxis of 'turning back of the experience of the individual upon her- or himself' (Mead, 1934, p. 134); examining place, biography, self and other to understand how they shape the analytic exercise (Macbeth, 2001); avoiding the pitfalls of treating the self as individualized and self-contained (Herman, 2001); and considering inherent ethical questions where the Other may come to be harmed as much as the Self (Roth, 2009). These snippets from literature substantiate general complexity and ambiguity of working with reflexive self-observational data, whilst also providing a rich theoretical ground for outlining the process of discerning such data. In a symbiotic approach, the key emphasis within this process is placed on researchers' capacity to reveal and critically reflect on how their 'in the moment of writing' fluid and fleeing experiences inform the process and the outcomes of their inquiry. Rather than trying to extract

---

I am in a state of a constant transformation. ... I am being transformed by the 'chronological past' that previously seemed familiar, but now – looks strange; and by the temporal 'present past', which initially felt unknown, but now feels strangely recognisable. This creates a strong feeling of being stuck in liminality of my fluid multiple Selves. That eerie blurred feeling of being 'betwixt-and-between' the old and the new Self, whilst constantly changing into somebody else, who is both familiar and unknown. The encounters and collisions with the Other as well as intermediary impermanent artefacts of experiences continue to fill my mind with countless layers of memories, fractured images, obscure phrases and foreign spaces, as I keep writing about them. I am still drifting ... I am still transforming ... Yet, the process of 'writing about my writing' feels almost therapeutic, as the words try to perforate the layers of liminal entities held together by my narrative, promising – probably, falsely – a closure, a sense of relief, a remedy, or even better, the exact reasons behind my compulsion to write. (An extract from my Reflexive Diary)

fragments of these experiences and feelings, the task of the researcher here is about acknowledging and reflecting on the transformational impact of the actual process of autoethnographic writing on their own thinking.

Indeed, the transformative and fluid nature of our reflexive self-observations interspersed with our interactions with the Other defer any possibility of closure, as our autoethnographic reflexive Self keeps shifting and changing in the process of writing, disrupting the very exercise of static textual representation. As Starr (2010) highlights, this process requires researchers to remain continuously visible in the text by interrogating interrelations between the self and the others, the self and the context and the self and the social, all of which may transform the researcher's own beliefs and actions, the meanings associated with them and the contexts in which they occur. Yet, as pointed out by Pelias (2005), reflexive writing is 'much more selective than rambling rhetoric' (p. 416). McIlveen (2008) similarly highlights that reflexivity in research and practice 'is a process which in itself proffers new understandings and actions – transformation. Therefore, as a vehicle for reflexivity, autoethnography is one way to improve the rigor of the process of generating critical consciousness within researchers' (p. 18). These ideas resonate with a symbiotic approach, where engaging with self-observational reflexive data is not about trying to produce a Xerox-copy of the researcher's experiences but about exposing their doubts, emotions and disorientations as they give rise to new illuminations or instigate new inquiries. Specifically, in the context of Symbiotic Autoethnography, self-observational 'in the moment of writing' data blends with reflexivity in the way which makes it impossible for the former to be distilled from multidimensional reflexive narratives: self-observations in Symbiotic Autoethnography mean reflexivity and reflexivity means self-observation. Hence, discerning self-observational data involves almost 'double reflexivity', when researchers are expected to reflect on their reflexivity in a, potentially, 'endless spiral of introspective reflexive iterations, which surface the multiple discourses immanent in any social space, thereby, avoiding discursive closure' (Johnson and Duberley, 2003, p. 1288). In simple terms, this means 'writing reflexively about the process of autoethnographic writing'. Such tactic of 'double reflexivity' will allow researchers to consider symbiotically the ways in which the 'in the moment of writing' data has been both generated and, simultaneously, embedded in their studies.

More traditional sources for discerning data in a symbiotic approach include participants' voices, documentary artefacts and relevant literature, as discussed below.

Voices of the participants

Involving participants in Symbiotic Autoethnography embraces the value of polyvocality of autoethnographic narrative, whilst also dissolving the power imbalance between 'researcher-as-subject' and their participants. Ethical issues associated with including the voices of participants in Symbiotic Autoethnography are discussed further in the book, so in this part of the discussion I will just briefly outline some of the key issues related to working with the associated data symbiotically.

Naturally, every autoethnographer will have different aspirations and purposes related to involving participants into their own autoethnographic story. St. Pierre (1997), for example, included into her pool of participants her dissertation committee members, members of writing groups at two different universities, her mentor, her mother, her aunt and cousin, her friends, members of seminar and conference audiences, the women of her dreams, the authors she read, journal editors, journal referees and so on. As she further explains,

> All these others move me out of the self-evidence of my work and into its absences and give me the gift of different language and practice with which to trouble my commonsense understanding of the world. They help me move toward the unthought. I hope that the naming of this practice, the collection of response data, will be an incitement to discourse and that other researchers will address this disruptive, unplanned, uncontrollable, yet fruitful fold in their work so that we can begin to collect data about response data and study the transgressions they enable. (p. 185)

These deliberations resonate strongly with a symbiotic approach, which suggests that including participants' voices into the process of discerning autoethnographic data contributes to the polyvocality and reflexivity of the study, as discussed in previous chapters. Generating this data can take multiple forms, including traditional or multi-modal interviewing, focus groups, cognitive mapping, online forums, surveys, to name just a few. Yet, despite the abundance of available tools for working with research participants, it is important to keep in mind that the aim of involving participants in Symbiotic Autoethnography is to gain deep insights into their subjective experiences, perceptions and feelings, thus, researchers' choices need to be in congruence with the practices of narration and storytelling. For example, unstructured or semi-structured in-depth interviews might be more suitable to this approach rather than a traditional questionnaire. As noted by Chang (2008), this approach 'broadens the database by including others of similarity' (p. 65) as co-participants in autoethnographic study, whilst still keeping the main focus on the study anchored in the researchers' personal experiences. As noted by Roulston (2018), 'research interviews as a method rely on researchers selecting participants based on a particular collectivity with an associated corpus of knowledge about which they are called on to speak' (p. 323). Specifically, in Symbiotic Autoethnography, a 'free flow' approach is suggested in working with participants, regardless of the selected ways of data collection, as such tactic provides wider scope for individual perspectives and experiences to emerge, allowing the participants' stories to lead the direction of the narrative. These points are also reflected in the size of the sample in the context of Symbiotic Autoethnography, which prioritizes the depth of the data over the sample size. Sandelowski (1995) confirms that there are no specific formulas in qualitative research that allow the researchers to determine a priori the size of a sample, suggesting that the researcher's main goal is 'to ensure that the sample size is small enough to manage the material and large enough to provide a new and richly textured understanding of experience' (p. 183).

In addition, in a symbiotic approach, the processes of collecting and discerning the participants' data are based on the idea that any selected techniques are not neutral tools of data gathering but 'active interactions between people leading to negotiated, contextually-based results' (Fontana and Frey, 1998, p. 62). These interactions need to be considered not just a source of data gathering and data discerning but as a valuable experience of initiating and developing meaningful relationships with the participants as those who have unique knowledge on the subject under investigation. As argued by Karnieli-Miller, Strier and Pessach (2009), defining what counts as knowledge in a researcher–participant exchange is not the sole privilege of the researcher, since participants bring their own perspectives on the research agenda. More information and some practical examples of working with the participants' data in a symbiotic way are included in Chapter 7, so I am going to move this discussion to the subject of artefacts as data in a symbiotic approach.

Artefacts

Other sources of data in Symbiotic Autoethnography may include various textual and non-textual artefacts, such as letters, drawings, diaries (written, audio or video), documents, photographs, memos, to name just a few.

Plummer (2001a) describes these sources of data as 'documents of life', explaining that

> the world is crammed full of human personal documents. People keep diaries, send letters, make quilts, take photos, dash off memos, compose auto/biographies, construct websites, scrawl graffiti, publish their memoirs, write letters, compose CVs, leave suicide notes, film video diaries, inscribe memorials on tombstones, shoot films, paint pictures, make tapes and try to record their personal dreams. All of these expressions of personal life are hurled out into the world by the millions and can be of interest to anyone who cares to seek them out. (p. 17)

And with consideration of our modern technologies, we can also add to this list such sources of data as posts on social media websites, text messages, blog and vlog entries, emails, which is unlikely to be a complete catalogue, considering the speed and the range of new technological advances. The significance of a symbiotic approach in this context lies in opening up opportunities for autoethnographic researchers to look symbiotically at their experiences of various artefacts beyond paradigmatic boundaries of language and text, situating their narratives in synergy with multimodal sensory (i.e. visual, olfactive, aural, tactile) experiences of these artefacts.

Senses are central to human experiences, emotions, culture and relations, providing significant information about the world around us. A 'sensuous methodology', where multiple senses are explored in the research process, has been utilized in a number of recent studies (Low, 2015; Allen-Collinson et al., 2018; Powis, 2019; Hunter, 2020; Allen, 2021). For example, Allen-Collinson (2018) with colleagues drew on sociological and anthropological theorizations of the senses and 'sensory work' to investigate the sense of thermoception, as the lived sense of temperature. Based on four long-term autoethnographic research projects, the authors examined whether thermoception could be conceptualized as a distinct sense or is more appropriately categorized as a specific modality of touch. The key findings from the study revealed the importance of thermoceptive senses as alternative physical-culturally specific bodily ways of knowing and sense-making. Allen's (2021) study had a focus on another form of sensuous methodology known as smellwalks, which required a reorientation of the senses to temporarily emphasize the information received from an active form of smelling to examine the researcher's environment that diverged from normal smell perception. According to Allen (2021), in attuning to the invisible, intangible, mundane and small details of life via smell, smellwalks opened opportunities for new embodied and material knowledge about her lockdown experience in a suburban town in Aotearoa-New Zealand.

Indeed, knowing how to infer meaning from our sensory experiences is considered the very basis of human existence. Opening an old letter, touching a scarf knitted many years ago by a loved one, listening to a familiar song or seeing a photo on a Facebook page can create a surge of emotions that might be essential for better understanding the multiplicity of societal impacts on our experiences.

Privileging the material nature of artefacts over the sensory formations activated by their physical presence limits the authentic significance of the former, whilst also reducing the scope of researchers' interpretative potential. Symbiotic Autoethnography enables the emergence of narratives that support our understanding of the cultural phenomenon under study through the exploration of these sensory reactions to artefacts, making them important sources of data. This approach involves moving away from the conventional fixation on extracting meaning from a text to make way for sensing and 'sensory interpretation' of the artefacts, placing emphasis on feeling rather than

At the bottom of one of the drawers of my old desk, I have spotted a piece of bright red cloth. It was my pioneer tie! All of a sudden, touching its silky fabric brought back a swarm of memories from my childhood, taking me back to the times when I was a pupil in a Soviet school. My mind walked me again through its corridors, where every space was occupied by sculptures of Marx and Lenin, red flags with the images of sickle and hammer, photographs of enthusiastic muscly factory and agricultural workers, Pioneer and Komsomol oaths on the walls and multiple banners with fervent communist slogans. Throughout my school years rigorous adherence to specific rituals and obligatory respect for the symbols of Communist Party were considered a priority. I was taught that a Red Pioneer kerchief symbolised a particle of the blood of people who died in their fight for our bright communist future and so, being admitted into the Pioneer organisation was seen as a great honour. My old pioneer tie. … How many times I washed and ironed it. … I could still smell the odour of that cheap Soviet soap, coming from it. And I suddenly remembered the day, when I first got it. On turning ten years old, like every self-respecting 'Oktiabrenok' (the pre-stage for becoming a Pioneer), I removed a red star with the face of a young, curly-haired Lenin from my chest and, taking a solemn oath, tied a red pioneer tie around my neck. (An extract from my Reflexive Diary)

detached construal of an argument. Thus, discerning data from the researcher's symbiotic engagement with various artefacts will, once again, involve reflexive autoethnographic writing, which problematizes the conflation of the materiality of objects with their multisensory modalities in a melange of object-sense-time-space. In this way, a symbiotic approach makes it possible to arrive at an embodied multisensory personal understanding of the cultural phenomenon in symbiosis with its contextual interpretation of the associated sociocultural milieu.

Literature

Following the principles of a symbiotic approach, literature is considered an integral part of Symbiotic Autoethnography and as one of the forms of data. Onwuegbuzie and Frels (2016) argue that the word *data* refers to a body of information that can be extracted from many sources, which allows us to presume that 'the literature review process can be viewed as a data collection tool – that is, as a means of collecting a body of information pertinent to a topic of interest' (p. 49). Chang (2008) also suggests that literature serves as an important form of data that enables researchers to contextualize their personal stories within the public history. Moreover, as highlighted by Ravitch and Riggan (2017), the ability to gain information from literature represents one of the hallmarks of scholarship, as only by situating our work within the existing scholarly milieu are we able to accomplish one of the main goals of any research study – contribution to collective knowledge on the subject. Indeed, working with literature as a source of data allows autoethnographers to demonstrate the intellectual depth and rigour behind their theoretical deliberations as well as providing a broader context for the cultural phenomenon under study. Specifically, in relation to a symbiotic approach, working with literature involves a complete integration of researchers' efforts of critical engagement with literature into a persuasive autoethnographic narrative that connects their subjective experiences with wider scholarly perspectives on the subject.

As mentioned previously, Symbiotic Autoethnography, in general, defies any linear or clinically sterile approaches to a qualitative inquiry. With this in mind, having a traditional stand-alone 'literature review' chapter would go against its main aim of producing an autoethnographic story that symbiotically fuses researchers' subjective experiences with their continuous critical contextual interpretations of a particular cultural phenomenon. As mentioned in relation to one of the key features of Symbiotic Autoethnography – Interpretative

Analysis – researchers are expected to amalgamate their autoethnographic data with its simultaneous interpretation in temporal culturally sensitive contexts, where researcher's presence is ubiquitous. This process of interpreting the researchers' autoethnographic data takes place within the underlying landscape of existing scholarly research, guided by well-established principles of engaging with literature, such as detailed analysis, reflexivity and a conjectural synthesis of perspectives. This approach is different from stand-alone literature reviews, which, quite often, resemble annotated bibliographies. As explained by Axelrod and Cooper (2018), the difference between a literature review and an annotated bibliography is analogous to the difference between still pictures and a movie: a literature review is similar to the process of connecting still pictures into a meaningful storyline, whilst an annotated bibliography just represents a collection of still pictures. The metaphor of creating a movie, using still pictures, has some relevance to working with literature symbiotically. Yet, it lacks the concept of a dialogical connection between the literature and the researcher, which Wall (2008) describes as 'conversing' with the literature rather than just interjecting researcher's perspectives into identified gaps in the literature:

> By approaching my autoethnography as a two-way conversation with the literature, I not only challenged the received wisdom of the field but also learned to think about my experience as an adoptive parent in a way that challenged and changed me. (p. 48)

Similarly, Gergen (2000) suggests that a major challenge for the future of qualitative research is generation of relationship and integral connectivity through the development of dialogic inquiry, in which 'the outcome is determined not by a single individual, or by a plenary of separate voices, but within the dialogic process' (p. 1041). It is that polyvocal colloquy, where the voice of the researcher intertwines with the ideas, concepts and theoretical frames found in literature, which is the defining feature of working symbiotically with literature as data. To understand better the process of discerning this data, it might be helpful to think about it as a process of creating a painting, where the painter's choices of colour nuances are made with careful consideration of how they contribute to the overall portrayal of the subject of their artistic imagination. Drawing on this analogy, relevance of selected literature to the overall aim of autoethnographic study becomes the pivotal point in the process of discerning the relevant data. Maxwell (2006) makes a similar observation, arguing that relevance of selected literature has important implications for the design, conduct and interpretation of the subject under investigation. Thus, researchers' efforts need to be aimed at reviewing not the works that deal with the topic in the defined field but at selecting the relevant literature artfully to support and explain the choices made specifically for *their study*, rather than educating the reader about the debates in the chosen area. In the context of a symbiotic approach, the relevance of selected literature is determined by its discernible connections with both the 'auto-' and the 'ethno-' aspects of the phenomenon under study as well as its capacity to create and maintain a polyvocal argument concomitant with the aims and objectives of the study. As discussed in previous chapters in this book, various genres of autoethnographic writing interweave 'auto-' and 'ethno-' in different ways and each invites a foregrounding of and a focus on different fields of literature and theoretical frames. In a symbiotic approach, any genre of autoethnographic writing is considered to be a vehicle for exploring wider sociocultural contexts through engaging in and contributing to scholarly debates. How autoethnographers discern, interpret and write about these debates shapes new trajectories for the advancement of knowledge about cultural phenomena, as autoethnographers become movers and shakers of the existing insights and traditional perceptions.

To summarize, working with literature as data in Symbiotic Autoethnography involves, first, amalgamation of researchers' interpretative analytical deliberations with their autoethnographic narrative; and second, discerning relevant literature based on its relevance to the subject of autoethnographic inquiry and its potential to create meaningful connections between the researcher, the literature and the cultural phenomenon under study. In this sense, a symbiotic approach does not offer one specific answer regarding the best ways of synthesizing and interweaving literature into the structure of autoethnographic narratives. Instead, it emphasizes a wide scope of creative latitude in working with literature as shaped by the experiences and expertise of individual researchers as well as the nature of their autoethnographic inquiry.

Symbiosis of data and analysis

The similarity between painting a picture and working with literature symbiotically, as outlined in the previous chapter, serves as a helpful cognitive bridge to the next point of my discussion – a symbiosis of data and analysis. When looking at or creating a painting, we do not perceive each individual brushstroke separately but appreciate the overall impression of the painting through the totality of its artistic features. In the same way, in Symbiotic Autoethnography, the brushstrokes of data cannot be separated from the entire flow of researchers' interpretive analytical deliberations. As discussed in previous chapters, the underlying tenets of Symbiotic Autoethnography are shaped by a general rejection of highly structured approaches that advocate for clear demarcation between methods of data collection and data analysis. Similarly to Greenough (2017), in a symbiotic approach I attempt to engage in an 'undoing methodology' (p. 9), which releases the researcher from methodological constraints, allowing 'an intuitive, reflective and creative analysis of the information gained' (Greenough 2017). Consequently, in a symbiotic approach, the stages of generating and discerning data fuse with other aspects of research, prompting working with data in a simultaneous reflexive engagement with its interpretative analysis, evocative qualities and political focus across spatio-temporal dimensions of the researcher's experiences. Indeed, writing Symbiotic Autoethnography is similar to painting a picture, where colours, textures and media coalesce, dissolve and imbricate to represent the painter's impression of a subject or a theme. This approach is similar to Denzin and Lincoln's (2008) description of montage in relation to interpretive practices, which involve aesthetics of representations that go beyond the pragmatic or the practical. The authors explain that montage is a method of editing cinematic images, where a picture is made by superimposing several different images on one another, creating something new, as in a jazz improvisation that creates

> the sense that images, sounds and understandings are blending together, overlapping and forming a composite, a new creation. The images seem to shape and define one another; an emotional gestalt effect is produced. Often, these images are combined in a swiftly run sequence. When done, this produces a dizzily revolving collection of several images around a central or focused picture or sequence; such effects signify the passage of time. (Denzin and Lincoln, 2008, p. 6)

Gannon (2017) echoes the idea of similarity between working with qualitative data and musical improvisation, suggesting that the motif of music and incorporation of jazz elements and other experimental forms 'reinforce the textual versatility of autoethnography and its underpinning by aesthetic and literary sensibilities' (p. 13).

Nevertheless, the issues associated with narrative data and its analysis remain contested in research circles and continue to be widely debated (Clough, 1999; Pillow, 2003; Guttorm, 2012; Byrne, 2017; Boylorn and Orbe, 2021; Adams, Holman Jones and Ellis, 2021). As noted by Clandinin and Connelly (2000), a narrative inquiry contains aspects of temporality, the personal/social and the place, creating a three-dimensional research space, within which researchers move during data collection, analysis and representation. Another useful contribution to the debate comes from Richardson (2000a), whose theorization about a method of inquiry leads us towards its interpretation as a way of understanding ourselves reflectively as well as freeing us from 'trying to write a single text in which we say everything at once to everyone' (p. 929). 'Writing is validated as a method of knowing' (Richardson 2000a), Richardson concludes. MacLure (2003) argues that, for some, this entails creating new textual practices that 'disturb the usual conventions of research writing and baffle the boundaries between literature and science, self and other, data and analysis, fact and fiction, mastery and surrender' (p. 172).

In the field of autoethnographic studies, in particular, the multiplicity of forms and types of autoethnographic data require researchers to search continuously for the new ways of its representation and analysis. Pillow (2003) welcomes this direction of travel, suggesting that new approaches to qualitative inquiry have the potential to challenge traditional ways of representation we come to, whilst acknowledging the political need to represent and find new meaning. According to Pillow (2003), 'the qualitative research arena would benefit from more "messy" examples, examples that may not always be successful, examples that do not seek a comfortable, transcendent end-point but leave us in the uncomfortable realities of doing engaged qualitative research' (p. 192). Similarly, Richardson and St Pierre (2005) encourage autoethnographic researchers to 'think of writing as a method of data analysis' (p. 970). In this sense, as confirmed by Adams, Holman Jones and Ellis (2015), it is not possible to separate 'doing autoethnography' with 'writing autoethnography' (p. 67). St. Pierre (2008) also argues that conventional processes of research methodology are linear and do not fit well with the processes of data collection, analysis and interpretation, which, often, happen simultaneously. She suggests that 'we should seriously rethink the organisation of the conventional qualitative research report because it artificially isolates those data (literature and voices of participants) in different sections and thus contributes to weak analysis' (St. Pierre, 2008, p. 331).

In response to these claims, over the years, autoethnographers engaged in the exploration of various forms of presenting and analysing autoethnographic data. In some ways, autoethnographers have become 'solo performers' who deploy 'the duplicity of artistry and journalism, expert testimony and witnessing' to 'create, enact and incite' (Holman Jones, 2005, p. 782) new possibilities in the field of autoethnographic research. Gergen (2000), for example, writes about using a stylized representation, which replaces traditional realist discourse with forms of writing cast in opposition to 'truth telling', including various forms of fiction, poetry or autobiographical invention. According to the author, the use of stylized representation 'signals to the reader that the account does not function as a map of the world (and indeed, that the mapping metaphor is flawed), but as an interpretive activity addressed to a community of interlocutors' (Gergen, 2000, p. 1030). Guttorm (2012) also tries to step away from traditional forms of data representation with distinct chapters on methodology and data analysis, which, according to her, are not reflective of the multifaceted (not only words but also noises, smells, movements) complexity of data. To avoid the limitation of conventional modes of working with autoethnographic data, the author chooses poetic writing, which enables her to

> cross boundaries and dichotomous concepts and to refrain from sureness and producing freezing metaphors. For example, to be surely unsure. And that it is important/significant/even reasonable to write from this partial, nomadic place, where I am and where I travel, still not meaning I have to write an autobiography, but just to take this place and stop thinking about whether this specific writing is this or that in some pre-existing category. (Guttorm, 2012, p. 600)

Similarly, LeBlanc (2017) abandons 'the artificial material and discursive boundaries between data, data collection, data analysis and representation', making it her goal 'to craft a narrative that puts things in motion rather than capturing them in some still-life' (p. 795). To facilitate such weaving of method, data and analytical interpretation, LeBlanc (2017) uses a number of interconnected interpretative strategies, such as diffractive analysis, assemblage analysis, rhizoanalysis and pastiche.

Despite the general agreement amongst the researchers that there is no one single recipe that would serve the analytical demands of all autoethnographic studies, a few authors offered a number of strategies for the autoethnographic data analysis, including bricolages (Levi-Strauss, 1962), pastiche (Jameson, 1991; LeBlanc, 2017), layered accounts (Ronai, 1995), multi-vocal vignettes (Mizzi, 2010), assemblages (Bettez, 2015; Alexander et al., 2019), evocative storytelling (Adams, Holman Jones and Ellis, 2015), epiphanies (Denzin, 2014). As the researchers persevere in their search for innovative ways of analysing multifaceted data, the list of interpretative strategies continues to grow and so, examining each one separately would take this discussion far beyond its original scope. Thus, I intend to just briefly outline here only few of the approaches in addition to those mentioned above. Seidel (1998), for instance, suggests that working with qualitative data is analogous to composing a symphony based on three notes: Noticing, Collecting and Thinking. These three notes combine to create a complex non-linear process of data analysis, which 'evolves and develops in an iterative and recursive fashion' (p. 12) and, as the analysis develops, the researcher learns to think differently about the data they have already collected. Following a similar line of reasoning, Dye et al. (2000) use a metaphor of kaleidoscope, where the loose bits of coloured glass represent data bits, whilst the two plain mirrors represented categories and 'the endless variety of patterns in a kaleidoscope represented the constant comparison of data bits in the unending journey to create category arrays' (p. 6). Their theoretical deliberations resonate with Denzin and Lincoln's (2000) appreciation of qualitative researcher's role as a bricoleur or a maker of quilts, who 'uses the aesthetic and material tools of his or her craft, deploying whatever strategies, methods, or empirical materials are at hand' (p. 4). Taking a more inventive turn, Norris (2008) refers to collage as an arts-based research approach to meaning-making through the juxtaposition of a variety of pictures, artefacts, natural objects, words, phrases, textiles, sounds and stories. Bazeley and Kemp (2012), using what seems to be a popular analogy of a researcher-as-artist, write about combining the strategies of bricolage, mosaics and jigsaws for integrating the process of data analysis in mixed-methods social research:

> Just as artists vary in their ability to create a holistic image from the elements they place together, so also researchers might vary in the degree to which they are able to integrate their component data items. But the greater the degree of integration, the more likely it is that the combined product will create an impression that is quite different from and richer than, the separate components. (p. 59)

Yet, although such abundance of approaches that push the boundaries of convention is becoming more wide-ranging in autoethnographic research, more traditional ways of working with autoethnographic data, such as thematic approach, constant comparative analysis, phenomenological approaches and discourse analysis, to name just a few, also remain popular choices in the arsenal of interpretative strategies.

So, what can a symbiotic approach contribute to such already theoretically dense area related to the ways of presenting and analysing autoethnographic data? Before trying to answer this question, it is worth emphasizing that, as I mention elsewhere (Beattie, 2018a), in terms of a 'one-size-fits-all' model for analysing autobiographical data, there cannot be a cookbook containing a single recipe that would help autoethnographers to produce a delicious dish to be equally appreciated by everybody. To rephrase a famous quote from W. Somerset Maugham about writing a novel, there are three rules to merging autoethnographic data with its analysis, but, unfortunately, no one knows what they are. Indeed, moving from fragments of autoethnographic data towards its interpretative analysis is far from being a straightforward process that can be completed flawlessly based on a set of prescribed procedures. This point of view resonates with Hammersley and Atkinson's (2007) argument related to ethnographical writing, which, according to the authors, is closely connected to analysis and where each of the multiple ways, styles, genres of ethnographic representation bring different emphases and so, 'it is important to recognize as early as possible that there is no single best way to represent any aspect of the social world' (p. 191). Nevertheless, there are a couple of strategies that are commensurate with a symbiotic approach, which I would like to discuss in the next few paragraphs: 'symbiotic writing' and 'analytical transiences'.

As discussed in previous chapters, in Symbiotic Autoethnography, researchers' analytical interpretations of data cannot be separated from autoethnographic writing. The emphasis of a symbiotic approach to working with autoethnographic data is an amalgamation of meaning-making with fragments of data in a continuous flow of the research process. As a result, the processes of discerning data and analysis intertwine to create, what I call, symbiotic writing, which involves simultaneous 'writing as data' and 'writing about data', providing the possibility of a more holistic reflexive understanding of cultural phenomena under study.

In my own research study, based on a symbiotic approach, the non-linear, fluid and overlapping methods of working with the data reflected the fragmented and multifaceted nature of my autoethnographic data, blurring the traditional distinction between the processes of data generation and data analysis. The focus of my autoethnographic research project was on contesting and challenging some of the more conventional modernist views on the leader-follower dichotomy, offering a postmodern perspective on how educational leadership might be experienced by the followers across different sociopolitical environments. Specifically, this line of reasoning shaped the overall aim of my research study, that is, to make sense of how followers with a Soviet background construct their perceptions of educational leadership at a contemporary UK university. Prompted by personal experiences of both Soviet and neoliberal environments, I attempted to bring the followers' perspectives on educational leadership to the forefront of my autoethnographic inquiry. Using a symbiotic approach to data analysis helped me to unveil a complex interplay of subversive powers as potential determinants behind the followers' constructs of educational leadership. Throughout my research project, the diversity and multiplicity of data both challenged me and offered opportunities for creating my own approach that fits best the objectives and the context of my study. Consequently, using symbiotic writing as one of the elements of a symbiotic approach, I presented the data discerned from multiple sources as a symbiosis of vignettes ('flashbacks'), autoethnographic micro-narratives, extracts from my reflexive diary and the snippets from the interview records interspersed with the fragments of my theoretical deliberations. In the examples of my symbiotic writing provided below, you will also be able to detect elements of assemblage, layered account and thematic analysis. Using 'layered account' (Ronai, 1995) gave me the desired flexibility to manipulate the fragments of data in a way which allowed it to intertwine with, disrupt and dislocate my autoethnographic narrative in a deliberate attempt to provoke new questions and re-direct the flow of discussion. As proposed by Ronai (1995), layered accounts as a postmodern ethnographic reporting technique have the capacity to embody a theory of consciousness and to become a method of reporting in one stroke:

> While the traditional narrative form force-feeds the reader a particular understanding of the world masquerading as the understanding of the world, the layered account offers an impressionistic sketch, handing readers layers of experience so they may fill in the spaces and construct an interpretation of the writer's narrative. The readers reconstruct the subject, thus projecting more of themselves into it and taking more away from it. (p. 396)

Within the layered account, vignettes or, as I called them, 'flashbacks', have been used to create a more dynamic representation of my experiences of educational leadership. Miles and Huberman (1994) define vignettes as 'vivid portrayals of the conduct of an event of the everyday life, designed to enhance the contextual richness of ethnographic research' (p. 83). I used my autoethnographic 'flashbacks' as an enriching representational strategy for autoethnographic research, bearing in mind that 'a multi-layered text allows rather than specifies a wealth of insights reaching well beyond the author's particular predicament' (Sparkes, 2002, p. 221). These 'flashbacks' can be recognized within the examples provided below as italicized paragraphs that aim to penetrate the traditional neat writing conventions with their disorderly and distracting interference – one of the signifiers of symbiotic writing.

Furthermore, my engagement with the process of reflexivity helped me to enhance my symbiotic writing with extracts from my Reflexive Diary, which I maintained throughout the entire research process. These extracts intersperse with the other data to contribute to the multi-vocality of my autoethnographic journey that is based on 'experiences of me, with others, within a context' (Short, 2010, p. 45). They can be recognized within the flow of my writing as paragraphs of text surrounded by straight line boarder.

The participants' voices have formed part of my symbiotic writing, contributing to the ambiguity and disorientation of my journey, as their voices merged and intertwined in our joint polyvocal search for the meaning of leadership across two different sociopolitical systems. In this sense my interpretation of symbiotic writing resonates with Puar's (2007) concept of assemblage, which she defines as a collection of multiplicities or 'a series of dispersed but mutually implicated messy networks' (p. 211) that allow the researchers to attune to multiple voices towards a greater understanding of the complexity of the researched subject.

In terms of deploying some elements of thematic analysis, I was guided by Ellis (2004), who described it as one of the potential layers of analysis in autoethnographic study:

> The author might or might not decide to add another layer of analysis by stepping back from the text and theorizing about the story from a sociological, communicational, or other disciplinary perspective ... 'Thematic analysis' refers to treating stories as data and using analysis to arrive at themes that illuminate the content and hold within or across stories. (p. 196)

However, I was concerned, as were St. Pierre and Jackson (2014), about analysing my data through 'brute' coding, labelling and categorizing into themes. Thus, in line with a symbiotic approach, I searched for more supple ways of data organization, which prompted me to use fluid and momentary notion of 'analytical transiences' instead of themes, where the former could be continuously constructed, deconstructed and refined by the fragments of data to accommodate transmuting views at different moments of writing. The transiences, though roughly shaped by the subject of my study, were not predefined but have emerged gradually from the body of my interaction with the data and the literature, someway resembling Michelangelo's sculpturing technique of 'gradually revealing the figure from the block rather as if it were slowly emerging from the surface of a vessel of water' (Vasari and Hemsoll, 2006, p. 27). The 'analytical transiences' created an illusion of permanence through holding together the mosaic pieces of the data to allow the emerging patterns to be captured in their momentary stillness before they got shattered again in kaleidoscopic impermanence of ever-changing patterns of thoughts, spaces, times, voices, utterances and behaviours. Through the intertwined analysis of these transiences against theoretical concepts, an interpretative analytical story has transpired that enabled new inferences of what it felt like to be a follower in a Soviet and a neoliberal educational establishment.

Yet, my symbiotic engagement with 'writing as data' and 'writing as analysis' was used to 'subjectivize' the ambiguous concept of educational leadership rather than objectify it, as, in the context of Symbiotic Autoethnography, to know reality is to participate in it (Dillet, 2017). As my mind compulsively wandered through the data, trying to construct a steady line of reasoning, my writing kept discarding any generalizable significance, as symbiotic writing 'has nothing to do with signifying. It has to do with surveying, mapping, even realms that are yet to come' (Deleuze and Guattari, 1987, p. 1). Thus, the genesis of my data within temporary 'transiences' moved the analysis through, across, between and beyond the indivisible flow of data, constantly promising but ultimately deferring any certainty of the conclusions.

Below, I provide two examples of my symbiotic writing, where data analysis merges with my autoethnographic writing in a continuous flow of my narrative. To simplify the navigation through the layers of data, the text of my 'flashbacks' is presented in italics and the participants' data is outlined by a shaded text box, whilst the extracts from my reflexive diary are surrounded by a straight line. The 'flashbacks' are intended to move randomly between my Soviet and neoliberal occurrences, contributing to and, at the same time, disrupting the dynamics of a presumed chronological neatness of a life-story.

Example one

Transience – Being 'edified'

This transience emerged from the data, predominantly, as a result of my engagement with the first sub-question of this study, which focuses on identifying possible factors that compel the followers to see educational leaders in a romanticized way. The symbiotic connection with this aspect of my inquiry has also been made through the conceptual lens of the Romance of Leadership, followed by creating a cognitive bridge between the associated modernist concepts to the postmodern ideas of 'power/knowledge' as one of the disciplinary technologies of the state, as discussed by Foucault.

Flashback One: Meeting 'the one who knows'

My heart is pumping … I am about to enter the school principal's office for the first time as a teacher of English and a new member of staff. A tight dryness in my throat … A quick consideration of my options: pretend to be sick? Faint? Just leave? No … It is too late. … The secretary is inviting me in. Zurab Zurabovich is sitting in a gargantuan-sized leather armchair at the far end of a long polished desk, engrossed in reading papers in from of him. He doesn't move. The room is airless. A massive portrait of Lenin gazes at me unsympathetically from the wall above the armchair. I take a step forward, trying to make Zurab Zurabovich aware of my presence. He doesn't move. Without turning my head, I begin to notice faded floral wallpaper peeling from the room corners and cloudy white stains left on the table varnish by the steam from hot tea cups. Seconds begin to feel like hours. Finally, Zurab Zurabovich lifts his eyes from the papers and looks at me … All of a sudden, I feel small … very small … almost invisible. I feel his power. It is almost palpable. The armchair creaks. Zurab Zurabovich slowly reaches for a pack of 'Kosmos' cigarettes in front of him, unhurriedly takes one out and lights it after breaking a couple of matches in his unsuccessful attempts to ignite a spark from a scuffed matchbox. He contentedly inhales the first puff of smoke and slowly releases it, allowing it to escape simultaneously through his mouth and his fleshy nostrils. Finally, he acknowledges my presence. 'Leaka', he breathes out my name. Being unsure whether this is a statement or a question, I just say: 'Yes'. 'Very good. Sit down.' – he slurs and continues to speak before I manage to pull out one of the bulky chairs from under the table, 'Now, the first and the only thing you need to learn here, working in my school, that you follow the rules. My rules.' He slightly raises his voice and makes a long pause, probably, giving me enough time to appreciate the importance of his statement. 'You will be fine, provided that you follow these rules. And the rule number one is – no self-initiative! If you do not know what to do or to say – you come to me and I will tell you! Do you understand? (… another long pause). I am the one who knows what to do, because I have been appointed to do this job: to tell people what to do!' He paused and leaned back in his armchair. 'Leading you lot is quite a job, you know …', he exhaled, almost exhaustingly.

I remember leaving the principal's office that day, feeling determined to do well and inspired to follow the rules of the one 'who knew what to do'. I turned out to be 'a perfect follower'. I never failed in this endeavour: I never showed initiative and never doubted the truth as communicated to me by the almighty Zurab Zurabovich. This prerogative function of the Soviet educational leaders as the Party elite and, thus, as the bearers of truth infiltrated the Soviet society across all its educational institutions, blatantly presenting itself as the only legitimate way of leading the system of education (Beattie, 2018b). From my position of a follower, Zurab Zurabovich was a regular Soviet hero – a respectable long-standing member of the Communist Party of the Soviet Union (CPSU) and a school principal for many years and so, his behaviour was perceived by me as a remarkable example of a perfect Soviet leader, whose grandiose sense of self-importance and strong preoccupation with the idea of his unlimited power of 'the knower' were fully justified in my eyes by his position. I felt small ... I felt almost invisible. ... But these emotions did not feel unnatural to me at that time, as I fully expected Zurab Zurabovich to be the one who was strong and powerful. Meindl, Ehrlich and Dukerich (1985) explain that one of the foremost elements in such romanticized view of leaders is people's deep faith in the unlimited potential of their leaders as the primary force behind all organizational activities. From this perspective, leadership is no longer defined by what leaders do but is socially constructed by the followers' experiences and their attempts to make sense of these experiences and 'it is within those sense-making processes, where leadership has assumed a romanticized, larger-than-life role' (p. 79). And for me, Zurab Zurabovich was, undeniably, just that – 'larger than life'. He performed his role with extreme confidence and aplomb, fostering amongst his staff intuitive followership abilities, where even a slight movement of his heavy eyebrows was intended to initiate our specific actions. Gray and Densten (2007) explain this phenomenon through examining the origins of the Romance of Leadership from a leader-centric perspective, gauging whether leaders held romantic notions about their leadership. The results of their study indicated that leaders distorted their self-attributions to reflect romantic or idealized images of leadership and transmitted these images through impression management to 'woo' followers into constructing romantic images of leadership. Indeed, in my attempts to understand Zurab Zurabovich's behaviour as well as his requests, I had to act as a 'naive psychologist' (Heider, 1958), ascribing the causes of all positive outcomes (and we never knew if our school had any negative ones) to his leadership skills, which were considered the beacon of perfection. I *wanted* to be like him and so did every teacher in our school. And we all strived to be efficient followers by imitating his words and actions in our day-to-day practice.

Zurab Zurabovich was not an idiot. He was just an exemplary Soviet leader, operating as a principal of a Soviet school, who had both the right type of 'knowledge' and a suitable level of 'power' to propagate and utilize it.

Under the Soviet rule or under the Soviet control, leadership is always about trying to emulate the leaders that seek perfection; ... and people believe that the nation's leader ... they believe that they can solve the most difficult puzzles, they can do heart surgery, be a philosopher, athlete, fighter pilot, almost like a personality cult, when actually, most of the times, he might be a complete idiot. (Jaydee)

However, the question that arises in my mind is – were my views on Zurab Zurabovich as 'the knower' shaped purely by my 'romanticized' perceptions of his individual skills and abilities? My story intertwines here with Jaydee's memories to create a useful entry point to a postmodern way of thinking that disrupts this narrow modernist explication of leadership influences by looking at a wider sociopolitical surrounding landscape and the powers operating within it. My fascination with Zurab Zurabovich's leadership practice and his invisible powers over me as a teacher in 'his' school links well with Foucault's concept of 'power/knowledge'. Foucault (1991) saw the formation, circulation and utilization of knowledge as a fundamental problem in our social world, where the accumulation of knowledge coupled with the mechanisms of power needed to be considered as important as the accumulation of capital. In this sense, my need to 'emulate the leader' (Jaydee) exemplifies here, what Foucault (1991) considered to be, a pragmatic conceptualization of the relations between the subjects of knowledge and the powers of knowledge production as operating concurrently. Indeed, there could not be a power relation between Zurab Zurabovich and his followers without the correlative constitution of a field of 'Soviet' knowledge, nor could there be any knowledge that did not presuppose and constitute at the same time Zurab Zurabovich's power facility. Thus, my fascination with the school principal's leadership was very much predetermined by his power as 'the knower' and the 'bearer of truth'. As Foucault argues (1972a, p. 52), 'the exercise of power perpetually creates knowledge and, conversely, knowledge constantly induces effects of power. It is not possible for power to be exercised without knowledge, it is impossible for knowledge not to engender power.'

To understand better Jane's reflections on the delivery of a Soviet 'approved' version of history, I turn here to Gillies's (2013) explication. Seeing the notion of power/knowledge as an essential circuit of a 'disciplinary' technology, Gillies (2013) makes a useful link between Foucault's concept

> And you couldn't change the way things were introduced and, especially,
> for example, in the way history was taught ... certain things that I learnt
> afterwards ... and it was so shocking ... and I only learnt it when I came here
> (the UK – my note) that the history that we studied was not actually true ...
> history that took place was different ... but even when Soviet teachers knew
> that the historical facts were not true, they were forced to deliver it that way,
> because they had to deliver what they were told. (Jane)

and educational leadership, arguing that this body of 'approved' knowledge
(in this case – distorted 'historical facts' as referred to by Jane) becomes a
pillar of power to those educational leaders who acquire it and marshal its
distribution across individuals and teams, at the same time making these
leaders subjects of that knowledge for their continued authority in the
hierarchy of powers. The data above helps to illustrate how individual Soviet
educational leaders operated within these clusters of power relations as the
subjects of knowledge that were simultaneously affected by the powers of
knowledge production of the Soviet state. Indeed, the concept of power/
knowledge as a disciplining technology was used not just by individuals, such
as Zurab Zurabovich, but by the entirety of the modern state as insidious and
pervasive powers that turn individuals into subjects of various discourses
by prescribing norms, dispositions, positions and behaviours (Allan and
Iverson, 2009) and thus, determining what 'knowledge and practices are to
be regarded as legitimate and in what knowledge forms and practices they
are prepared to invest' (Fitz, 1999, p. 313). Hence, the feelings of admiration
with our Soviet leaders, experienced by myself and my participants, were
not just single cases of romanticizing the former, but a result of a complex
'general politics of truth' (Foucault, 1977, p. 131), created by the Soviet state
techniques, which defined what counted as truth and endorsed selected Party
members as its knowers. Foucault (1977) explains that, as a result of these
procedures and techniques, new politics of truth become embedded in the
systems of power, not only changing people's consciousnesses or what's in
their heads but changing the whole political, economic, institutional regime
of the knowledge production.

The next set of data contributes further to the deconstruction of the follower's
perceptions of leaders as 'the knowers' by bringing closer together the issues of
leadership, knowledge and power.

At this point of my story I am retracing my own steps to the beginning of my journey, pushing my memory to bring up my first recollections of leadership that can be made visible on paper in a form of words with their countless meanings, where, once again, misinterpretations, disorientations and perplexities aim to suggest different ways of seeing. Moving back and forth between the images of the past bonded with my present Self feels like pressing a pen against a piece of paper, moving it back and forth along the same line until the paper is pierced by the abrasion, in the same way my past memories and my present feelings press against each other, as I am awaiting for the words to escape from the worn-out seams. This is how the journey started. (An abstract from my Reflexive Diary)

Example two

Transience Three: Being 'perfected'

This section concludes my symbiotic engagement with the data, focussing on the third sub-question of this study related to the possible factors behind the formations of the followers' preconceived prototypes of educational leaders. Following the analytical structure of the previous sections, I initially start working with the data within the modernist context of Implicit Leadership Theory, followed by the change of my analytical trajectory towards Foucauldian notions of 'technologies of the self' in my attempt to make sense of my own followership experiences and the experiences of my participants across two sociopolitical societal orders.

Flashback – a blast from the past

'Are you coming to the dean's talk this afternoon?' – I heard a colleague's question behind me. 'I wasn't sure whether it was compulsory … I have got so many things to do', I replied. 'Don't be silly. Everything that is organized and led by our dean is compulsory'. That was a conversation that took place shortly after I started working at a university as a senior lecturer. As expected, I did go to the dean's talk, since disregarding a directive was not a part of my followership template of accepted behaviours. The lecture theatre was packed with people. At 1pm sharp a cheerful woman from the front row energetically jumped on her feet, made a short opening statement and enthusiastically clapped her hands, as the dean made his way to the lectern. The dean talked convincingly about the recruitment

numbers, the market trends and the importance of generating income. His presentation slides were saturated with graphs, pie-charts and motivating quotes. 'The financial health of this Faculty', affirmed the dean, raising his voice, 'is everybody's business. Nobody is going to save you if you do not save yourselves!', he continued, 'I want you to go away now and think about how you personally can contribute to our income generation strategy'. As the image of the university's coat of arms appeared on the final slide, all the people in the lecture theatre applauded and so did I. 'Another blast from the past', I thought to myself, as my school principal's words of 'saving my drowning self' rushed through my mind. As I was leaving the lecture theatre, I stumbled upon my line manager. 'Shall we go to my office and look at your performance targets?' she asked with a synthetic smile. I was about to say that I was in the middle of writing a report, but she was already in front of me walking towards the lift. I followed.

These recurring feelings of familiarity in my encounters with leadership after my move to the UK create in my mind a perturbed disruption in meaning caused by the loss of the distinction between the past and the present and a 'massive and sudden emergence of uncanniness, which, familiar as it might have been in an opaque and forgotten life, now harries me as radically separate, loathsome' (Kristeva, 1982, p. 2).

The data above reinforces this persisting familiarity with my previous constructs of leadership, which continue to trouble me, amplifying the feeling of liminality of being betwixt and between the two realities that no longer seem to be real. In line with my previous attempts to maintain this entanglement of my multiple past and present Selves, whilst creating a more or less detectible direction

---

I often allow my memory to wander through the labyrinth of my Soviet experiences, but every time my mind enters that multidimensional world of truths and lies, good and evil, genuine and false, I find it difficult to see my way out again. Perhaps, that is because at the exit point my past and my present collide to create an obscuring layer of some kind of undetermined state of existence, within which my multiple selves are suspended in a timeless zone of being neither then or now, neither there or here ... Are my Soviet experiences really in the past or are they still here in me today, continuing to shape who I am in the ever-changing transitory space? But despite all the doubts and uncertainties, one thing remains a reality for me – for a long period of time it was my home. (An extract from my Reflexive Diary)

in my theorizing about the data, I take this discussion back to the modernist ways of constructing leadership, as suggested by the Implicit Leadership Theory. My feelings of familiarity associated with the dean's expectation of 'saving myself' suggests a strong association with ILT's central premise that perceiving someone as a leader involves a categorization of the 'stimulus person' (Lord, Foti and Philips, 1982, p. 104), or leadership in general, into already existing followers' perceptions. Sternberg (1985) adds a useful explication that these existing prototypes represent a reflection of followers' inner concept of leadership in a specific cultural context.

Aial's comment supports that, when a behaviour is shown by a leader, followers refer to their existing schema and prototype of leaders 'to assess whether that behaviour is matching before the categorisation is made, depending on the outcome of this comparison process' (Alabdulhadi, Schyns and Staudigl, 2017, p. 24). Indeed, the data indicates that both Aial and I instinctively made comparisons between our new encounters with educational leadership and our preconceived prototypes of Soviet leaders, drawing our conclusions on the results of these judgements. Furthermore, the data from my 'Flashback Seven' shows a few recognizable patterns in my Soviet and neoliberal experiences of educational leadership, where the leaders' disciplinary strategies did not involve arms, physical violence or material constraints but were exercised through a subtle and obscure agency of social cohesion and normality, serving to assure the conditions of existence and survival of the existing societal order (Foucault, 1972a). Amann (2003) provides an unanticipated substantiation for my analysis, suggesting that such perceptive congruencies between Soviet and neoliberal structures is not a unique phenomenon. He confirms that 'the growing managerial pressures on public sector in Britain, which caused dismay and incomprehension in many colleagues, are instantaneously recognisable to an old Soviet hand' (Amann, 2003, p. 468). Correspondingly, Brandist (2016) argues that a few of the neoliberal performance management regimes, such as an expectation for all academics either to excel or leave the organization, would have been recognizable to Soviet workers and management alike.

At this point I take the discussion of the followers' preconceived leader prototypes outside the Implicit Leadership Theory towards a postmodern way

In this country [UK], however, I also do feel power, but it is different [from the Soviet] … because it's not necessarily visual … it's very hidden. (Aial)

My desire to make my story coherent is accompanied by a constant concern about 'losing meaning', while trying to make sense of the data, as warned by Walker (1991). The process of capturing the data feels very much like taking a snapshot with a camera without knowing what the actual photo is going to look like. In the spaces between the click of the camera and the final image there is always a sense of doubt, ambiguity and hesitation about whether any meaning can be ascribed to the occurrence captured in a particular space and at a particular time. Can my momentary 'snapshots' of data reveal something that is enduring? (An extract from my Reflexive Diary)

of thinking in my further attempt to make a better sense of the processes that shape the formation of these prototypes.

The memory of me obediently following my line manager to her office to 'save myself' (Flashback Seven) takes me back to Foucault's concept of self-regulation as another form of objectification. Foucault's ideas are particularly helpful here as one of the ways of exploring the impact of disciplinary powers on the followers' constructs of leadership. Jaydee's comments below indicate that this form of objectification has become integrated into the structures of a neoliberal university as a technique that assures 'coercion and processes through which the self is constructed or modified by himself' (Foucault, 1993, p. 204).

These comments combined symbiotically with the data from my Flashback give a reason to suggest that university academics are subjected to the

When I started teacher training education course 10 years ago ..., my job was actually to get teachers to get the confidence to start the lesson, to develop the lesson, to do the summary and do the assessment, but now I have noticed that when you start a teacher training job, the job description says that you will be a part of the university strategy and help to raise a grade of this university to outstanding. But listen, this is not really my job ... this is a Vice Chancellor's job whose salary is 10 times higher than my salary; that's his responsibility. So in principle this idea of shared or distributed leadership – this is something that I cannot do, but then your manager will tell you: 'Oh, you are really good at that and this will also help you with the development of your leadership skills.' (Jaydee)

I noticed that there is more of a work for academics and lecturers that is called 'preparation for management', but basically you are just asked to do more for the same salary under the pretence that you will get promoted, but then again – you never get promoted. (Jaydee)

technologies of power that aim to direct their conduct into desirable channels. Specifically, this form of objectification is achieved through shaping them into self-reflective and self-developing subjects, who should aspire to become well-equipped leading agents of the government-sanctioned neoliberal discourses of performativity (Beattie, 2020). This, consequently, leads to the 'normalization' of the followers' perceptions of what educational leadership is about, imposing an additional layer of cognizance onto their pre-existing leadership prototypes. Jaydee's further comments below suggest that the formation of these 'normalized' prototypes is stimulated via engaging the followers in a variety of training programmes, development courses and leadership-focused qualifications, which, essentially, are aimed at making the followers more predictable and institutionalized, whilst 'the maverick, the eccentric, the "individual", become side-lined, marginalised and ineligible' (Gillies, 2011, p. 53).

Jaydee's frustration with this push towards the 'preparation for management' echoes Amsler and Shore's (2017) perception of such mechanism of self-improvement as an extension of the followers' responsibilities, or, what he calls, 'responsibilization'. The authors make a convincing link between a Foucauldian notion of 'self-regulation' and the neoliberal discourses of responsibilization, which they define as the condition of rational, autonomous 'self-care' as a recognized standard of 'behaviour "expected" by government, institutions, or society of citizens, employees and persons' (p. 124). Jane's observations below reveal that, similarly to the Soviet modes of objectification, these imposed responsibilities of 'self-improvement' can be amplified by the denunciating ideas of failed personal targets and lack of commitment.

It depends a lot on who is managing you personally and who is managing your professional development, because some people make ... make you feel like you are nothing and your work is not really worth anything because it is difficult to measure myself what I'm doing right or wrong. (Jane)

> I'm finding now that in England … we almost are all forced to pretend that we can be what we want to be. (Jaydee)

Significantly, Jane's comments indicate that the path to becoming a 'successful follower' at a neoliberal university is, to some extent, stipulated by the individual leaders' expectations. Yet, it is equally defined by the followers exercising power on themselves through the 'technologies of the self', where the subject 'inscribes in himself the power relation in which he simultaneously plays both roles; he becomes the principle of his own subjection' (Foucault, 1991, p. 203). Similarly to Jane, I seemed to have lost the point of reference in relation to my own performance as a university lecturer and thus, consciously accepted the directives on my self-improvement, coming from the people above me, in my attempt to modify myself according to their norms. According to Foucault (1988), one of these technologies of the self involves the subject's engagement in specific training activities, or what he calls a 'training in thought' (p. 37), through which individuals inhabit subject position and transform their existing behaviours and attitudes. Jaydee's note below resonates directly with Foucault's argument.

Indeed, as the data shows, the university academic population has been forced to internalize neoliberal agendas through the process of self-improvement, allowing the state, according to Gillies (2011), to 'improve the quality of the labour force' and shape the individuals 'in approved ways' (p. 53). This position resonates strongly with the data, confirming that the process of objectification led both my participants and myself towards the 'normalization' of our constructs of leadership, bringing our existing Soviet leadership prototypes closer to the dominant neoliberal values and standards.

This last snippet of data from Elgee substantiates the above conclusion, brining it even closer to Foucault's (1993) concept of self-regulation as another

> And somehow, we all go along with everything that we are asked to do. And we don't notice how we become the people that we criticized before. Everything becomes normal then. I can't talk about the details, but my colleagues all felt that that needs changing … we don't know how it's supposed to change but it definitely it needs changing. (Elgee)

form of objectification, where governing people by force is replaced by 'a versatile equilibrium, with complementarity and conflicts between techniques, which assure coercion and processes through which the self is constructed or modified by himself' (p. 204).

In these two examples of symbiotic writing presented in a form of analytical transiences I attempted to demonstrate one of the ways in which the complexity of autoethnographic data can be amalgamated with interpretative analysis in a polyvocal reflexive and politically charged narrative. My symbiotic autoethnographic analysis involved a fusion of different features, such as layered accounts, vignettes, assemblages and elements of thematic analysis, all of which, according to Allen-Collinson (2012), strengthen autoethnographic research and open rich possibilities through its openness to new uses and formats. My analytical transiences have been created through bridging my personal experiences and reflexive praxes with the process of my autoethnographic writing, where each fragment of data was both 'inspiring and constraining the others in a gradually consolidating loop' (Taber, 2010, p. 20), within which 'the discourse on the postmodern self will be ongoing, with no fixed resolution on the horizon' (Powell, 1996, p. 1520). Indeed, the symbiosis of data with analysis can take many different forms. As rightly pointed out by Hammersley and Atkinson (2007), one of the major problems is that 'the social world does not present itself as a series of separate analytic themes. ... We have to disentangle the multiple strands of social life in order to make analytic sense of them' (p. 193).

The examples provided here are not anticipated to be used as a static template that is applicable to any autoethnographic study in one rigid format but rather offer an insight into my efforts of going beyond the limits of traditional qualitative methodology through problematizing its emblematic categories, such as data, method, analysis and theme. In this sense, the changes in the styles of writing within my narrative are deliberate, as these variations were intended to replicate the whole range of features associated with symbiotic writing – from deeply emotional to highly analytical, creating my 'way of knowing' of the cultural phenomenon under study. In the next chapter I intend to outline the concepts of validity and reliability in the context of 'doing' Symbiotic Autoethnography before moving to the final chapter on the ethical consideration associated with a symbiotic approach.

Moving Beyond the Boundaries of Validity

Introduction

In this chapter I discuss the ways in which the traditional perceptions of validity and reliability can be disrupted by autoethnographic praxes. Here I aim to offer a number of suggestions associated with a symbiotic approach to the issues of validity and reliability as an alternative interpretation of these concepts in the context of autoethnographic studies.

Disrupting the concept of validity in Symbiotic Autoethnography

Similar to the issues of data collection and analysis, the traditional concepts of validity and reliability have also been disrupted by the unconventional quintessence of a symbiotic approach. Historically, the hallmark of rigour in scientific research has been associated with key aspects of quantitative approach, which utilizes measurement instruments, such as internal validity (i.e. the extent to which a study establishes a trustworthy cause-and-effect relationship between two variables), external validity (i.e. the extent to which the results of a study can be generalized across other situations or samples) and reliability (i.e. the degree to which research methods produce stable and consistent results). These concepts are, generally, associated with positivism (see Chapter 1 for more detailed discission of positivism), which proposes a unified methodology for all disciplines, including humanities, based on the premise that any world phenomenon can be studied objectively via scientific methods and instruments and that the discovery of general laws presents the ultimate goal of a research inquiry. As pointed out by Scheurich (1997), the concept of validity was originally associated almost exclusively with testing that became 'one of the necessary truth criteria of conventional social science research: no validity, no truth' (p. 80). Similarly, Lather (1986a) urges researchers to accept the view on validity that 'reaches beyond the obfuscating claims of objectivity used by positivism to skirt the role played by researcher values in the human sciences' (p. 66). Gergen (2000) suggests that, in view of recent substantial scepticism in research circles related to the foundations of scientific practices, the capacity of science to produce accurate portrayals of its subject matter and the possibility of scientific progression toward objective truth are all undermined.

Specifically in relation to autoethnographic studies, Bochner and Ellis (2016) explain,

> the shift to an autoethnographic paradigm unnerved those traditional social scientist, who insisted on clinging to objectivity, detachment, theory-building and generalization as terminal goals of scientific inquiry. They perceived autoethnography as a threat to the domination of their cultural practices, namely their insatiable appetite for analysis and abstractions grounded in objectivist empiricism, value neutrality and the rationalist ideal of prediction and control. (p. 45)

Doloriert and Sambrook (2011) also agree that within qualitative research there are those that dismiss anything but positivist notions of validity and reliability, as they 'equate being rational in social science with being procedural and criteriological' (p. 593). Over the years, a number of authors (Lincoln and Guba, 1985; Ellis and Bochner, 2000; Duncan, 2004; Kelley, 2014; Hays and McKibben, 2021) attempted to reconcile these 'criteriological' differences, suggesting alternative interpretations of validity and reliability in the context of qualitative studies, including autoethnography. Lincoln and Guba (1985), for example, suggest replacing the conventional criteria with such alternatives as credibility, transferability, dependability and confirmability. Ellis and Bochner (2000) suggest that validity in autoethnography means seeking verisimilitude as the means of evoking in readers 'a feeling that the experience described is lifelike, believable and possible' (p. 751), whilst describing reliability as a process of checking of the researcher's story against the interpretations of the people involved and finally, referring to generalization as the degree the readers can relate the researcher's story to their own experiences or to the experiences of others they know. Richardson (2000b) writes about five criteria for evaluating any type of ethnographic research: substantialness of contribution, aesthetic merit, reflexivity, the impact of the narrative on the reader and the degree to which the narrative expresses 'embodied sense of lived-experience' (p. 254). Duncan

(2004) proposes applying the concepts of 'construct validity', external validity and reliability as key criteria for establishing the quality of her autoethnographic study. Starr (2010), however, argues that using the terms of validity, reliability and generalizability that are drawn from positivism 'generates a veil of ambiguity relating to conventional notions of methodological trustworthiness' (p. 5). She suggests, instead, to refer to Guba and Lincoln's (1989) five tenets of constructivist inquiry as essential in autoethnographic study: fairness, ontological authenticity, educative authenticity, catalytic authenticity and tactical authenticity. According to Guba and Lincoln (1989), 'fairness' is determined by the extent to which different constructions and their underlying value structures have been evaluated, taken into account and justified by the researcher; 'ontological authenticity' refers to the extent to which individual constructions have become more mature, better elaborated and better informed throughout the research; 'educative authenticity' relates to the extent to which the researcher and the participants have become more perceptive and considerate of the constructions of others; 'catalytic authenticity' is determined by 'the extent to which action is stimulated and facilitated by the evaluation process' (Guba and Lincoln, 1989, p. 249); and finally, 'tactical authenticity' is associated with the extent to which individuals are empowered to take the action that the evaluation implies or proposes. Richardson (1997) adds to this list of potential ways of addressing validity of autoethnographic research by offering a view of validity not as a rigid and fixed object but rather as 'the crystal, which combines symmetry and substance with an infinite variety of shapes, substances, transmutations, multidimensionalities and angles of approach' (p. 82). Richardson and St. Pierre (2005) apply the same principle to the issues of triangulation, suggesting that in autoethnographic research 'we do not triangulate – we crystallize' (p. 963).

Drawing on the metaphor of a crystal in the context of Symbiotic Autoethnography, I suggest replacing the long-established notion of validity with a transgressive multifaceted form of 'symbiotic cogency', which is determined by the extent to which the researcher engages in the interplay between meanings, representations and researcher's own critical reflexive thinking about the cultural phenomenon under study in symbiosis with the level of empathetic connection with the reader evoked by the researcher's narrative.

This approach aims to subvert traditional distilled and sanitized measures of research validity, prioritizing, instead, 'a deepened, complex, thoroughly partial understanding of the topic' (Richardson, 1997, p. 92). Yet, it does not present itself as an 'anti-criteria' approach, as, for example, argued by Szwabowski (2019), who suggests to 'forget all criteria' as it can 'kill the spirit of autoethnography'

(p. 476). In contrast, symbiotic cogency involves researchers' deeper reflexive and reflective submergence into multiple layers of meaning, through which 'we can see both "wave" (light wave/human currents) and "particle" (light as "chunks" of energy/elements of truth, feeling, connection, processes of the research that "flow" together' (Guba and Lincoln, 2005, p. 208). In this sense, arbitrating Symbiotic Autoethnography as 'valid' depends on the researcher's ability to convey, as cogently as possible, the 'waves' and 'particles' of their lived-body experiences as 'narrative truths' (Ellis, Adams and Bochner, 2010) that would receive a 'high degree of empathic resonance' (Allen-Collinson and Hockey, 2008, p. 213) from the reader. Thus, symbiotic cogency is not about accuracy, reliability or generalizability but about presenting a convincing account of how multidimensional research elements connect to each other and to the reader within the autoethnographic narrative. As emphasized by Plummer (2001b), 'what matters is the way in which the story enables the reader to enter the subjective world of the teller – to see the world from her or his point of view, even if this world does not "match reality"' (p. 401). Holman Jones (2005) echoes this point of view, arguing that the main aim of autoethnographic research is to produce analytical, accessible texts that can change us and the world we live in for the better rather than being preoccupied with accuracy. With this in mind, symbiotic cogency does not mean that it is necessary for all readers to find autoethnographic narrative to be accurate compared to their own lived experiences; it is only necessary that they agree that the researcher's narrative is cogent and the interpretative analysis of the latter is consistent with the evidence presented in the research. Such cogency promises to create a more compelling connection to the reader as the Other, whilst also attempting to disrupt the 'researcher/reader' dichotomy. Such position resonates with Derrida's (1985) ideas on what makes autobiographical data meaningful. According to Derrida it is 'the ear of the other' that 'signs the autos' of autobiography by interpreting the author's messages:

> It is rather paradoxical to think of an autobiography whose signature is entrusted to the other. Every text answers to this structure. It is the structure of textuality in general. A text is signed only much later by the other. And this testamentary structure doesn't befall a text as if by accident but constructs it. (Derrida, 1985, p. 51)

Yet, in the case of symbiotic cogency, it is not just about the Other signing 'the autos' but, equally, about the Other signing 'the -ethnos' and 'the -graphies' of autoethnography by responding to both the researcher's interpretation as well as representation of the cultural phenomena under study. As discussed in Chapter 4, one of the features of Symbiotic Autoethnography is concerned with the role of autoethnographic research in stimulating meaningful social change in the context of specific political conditions and discourse. Based on this supposition, symbiotic cogency of 'the -ethno' is also about the level of researcher's aspirations of illuminating issues of inequality, oppression and imbalances of power. As highlighted by Pasque and Salazar Pérez (2015), the main objective of any critical qualitative inquiry is to address historical, economic and sociopolitical issues of oppression and disparities across such dimensions as 'race, gender, class, sexual orientation, dis/ability and the intersectionality of diverse identities' (p. 140). These various dimensions of cultural phenomena depend, ultimately, on different autoethnographic contexts; however, what symbiotic cogency seeks to do is not to create another measurement of validity or 'the container into which the data must be poured' (Lather, 1986b, p. 267) but to open up new spaces for researcher's reflexivity that are not constrained by clear-cut benchmarks but rather derive instinctively from 'how stories work' (Ellis and Bochner, 2006, p. 438). The focus of reflexivity here is on researcher's interpretative, political and dialogical investments into their autoethnographic performance.

Another essential aspect of symbiotic cogency is its dynamic nature – it is not considered to be a static prescription but a continuous fluid process, where researchers' reflexive thinking changes throughout their temporal autoethnographic writing. Starr (2010) also writes about the importance of conscientiously documenting the researcher's reflexive engagement with the changes that arise as a result of continually evolving methodological constructions, as 'such changes are paramount to successful autoethnography' (p. 4). Symbiotic cogency takes this argument one step further, as it also involves researchers documenting their reflexive deliberations about the temporal changes in their views on and emotional responses to the cultural phenomenon under study. In this sense, symbiotic cogency is about finding your 'own validity', as St. Pierre (1997, p. 181) puts it, writing about her 'painful search for validity':

> I find my own validity when I write and cry and then write some more. As the bones of my soul break ground for my intellect, I push through into spaces of understanding I did not particularly want to occupy. Why do the tears come? My posture as academic researcher and writer is jolted and deflated and displaced by connections and thoughts and folds erased from awareness until they are worded. ... The outside folds inside and I am formed anew. This is

deconstruction at its finest, most caustic and abyssal – my own displacement and irruption into difference – self-formation. (p. 114)

This emotional account signifies a new direction in the debates related to the notion of validity in general, opening additional opportunities for researchers to outline and justify their own unique insights into what makes their autoethnographic research 'valid'. In the context of a symbiotic approach, the notion of symbiotic cogency is just one of the ways of theorizing about the legitimacy and value of an autoethnographic study, whilst acknowledging the impossibility of any autoethnographic narrative to be considered a precise match to 'reality'. As observed by Gergen (2000), there is no means of privileging any particular account on the grounds of its factual accuracy, since 'the intelligibility of our accounts of the world derives not from the world itself, but from our immersion within a tradition of cultural practices' (p. 1026). And in the case of a symbiotic approach, it is exactly that 'immersion' in cultural phenomenon that enables autoethnographers to engage more deeply in the continuous interplay between meanings, representations and their own reflexive temporal thinking in symbiosis with their empathetic connection with the reader. Subsequently, documenting these reflexive accounts in their autoethnographic performance will enhance symbiotic cogency of their autoethnographic study. In summary, to be symbiotically cogent, autoethnographers are expected to perform at both the microlevel of their personal thoughts, feelings and experiences simultaneously with the macrolevel of sociopolitical inquiry that avoids closure, whilst contributing to ongoing debates on the issues of social justice and structures of power.

To conclude this part of the discussion, I would like to lean on Herrmann's (2021) argument that brings us back to the origins of autoethnographic research as a 'triad of auto-, ethno-, and -graphy as the three main criteria for a work to be considered autoethnographic' (p. 1). Whilst rejecting positivist notions of validity and reliability, a symbiotic approach embraces already existing criteria of autoethnographic research in amalgamation with symbiotic cogency as additional means of making judgements about the value of symbiotic autoethnography.

Autoethnographic Ethics in Symbiosis

Introduction

The focus of this chapter is on the ethical dilemmas associated with 'doing' Symbiotic Autoethnography. Here I present an argument that autoethnography requires a more synergetic approach to ethics, which has a central focus on the importance of de-stabilizing privileged positions of researchers in relation to the Other as well as the dangers of appropriating 'the lives of others into consumption' (Lather, 2001). A symbiotic approach to the issues of ethics is discussed in this chapter alongside suggested practical strategies to help autoethnographic researchers address key ethical challenges.

Autoethnographic ethics in symbiosis

Ethical considerations present continuous concern for autoethnographers, as well as other researchers across various fields, permeating every aspect of their research studies from the moment of conception through to their completion and beyond. As in the case of a symbiotic approach in general, in this chapter I am not intending to provide a recipe that would resolve all ethical quandaries in all autoethnographic contexts. Neither am I intending to delve into a detailed discussion about the philosophy of ethics, as this will shift the focus on the book well outside its intended scope. In view of that, I will start with acknowledging that ethical issues are multifaceted, dissimilar and closely concomitant with specific research situations; thus, it is impossible to suggest a set of criteria that would categorize autoethnographers' decisions into right and wrong, as this process, in itself, would present a further ethical dilemma. As argued by Lambek (2012),

Sometimes the course of action is obvious but more often it is ambiguous, as one is confronted with novel circumstances and criteria, or even the ostensible absence of criteria and pulled between different sets and kinds of obligations and commitments. It is a mistake – an ethical blind spot – to expect there is always an obvious, single, right, virtuous judgement to make or a correct path to follow in every situation. (p. 143)

Furthermore, autoethnographic ethics in Symbiotic Autoethnography cannot be separated from specific historical, sociopolitical and cultural contexts, in which the research takes place. Since the concept of ethics is, by and large, concerned with questions related to human systems of beliefs on what is 'right' or 'wrong', it is unquestionable that these beliefs along with concomitant codes of ethics are shaped by specific historical conditions, cultural practices, social norms, religious influences and various societal power structures. This profusion of variations and constant shifts in human systems of beliefs make associated ethics codes ambiguous and fuzzy, resulting in difficulties for researchers and particularly, for autoethnographers, in making judgements about the ethicality of their research practices. As confirmed by Goodwin et al. (2003), the ethical dilemmas inextricably bound to specific sociocultural and political environments are so diverse that they are often difficult to anticipate and 'have the power to derail even the most reasonable-sounding general guidelines' (p. 568).

In light of one of the foci of Symbiotic Autoethnography on political aspects of autoethnographic research, researchers' considerations of ethics are expected to go beyond a standard set of procedures, raising broader questions about how issues of equity, power imbalances and social justice have been pursued and addressed in the context of their autoethnography. One of the goals of researchers' critical engagement with these issues is also a possibility of drawing attention to certain constraints of the 'Westernized' approach to research ethics. In this sense, foregrounding questions of autoethnographic ethics in wider sociopolitical and cultural research environments may support the advancement of international debates on research ethics through problematizing Western ethics as containing universal principles that are applicable to all contexts.

In Figure 5 I have attempted to represent all aspects of autoethnographic ethics as construed in the context of Symbiotic Autoethnography. In the next few pages, I will discuss in more detail each of the identified features.

Despite the ambiguity of ethics criteria in the field of autoethnographic research, autoethnographers, like any qualitative researchers conducting studies that involve humans, are required to meet the guidelines of research ethics

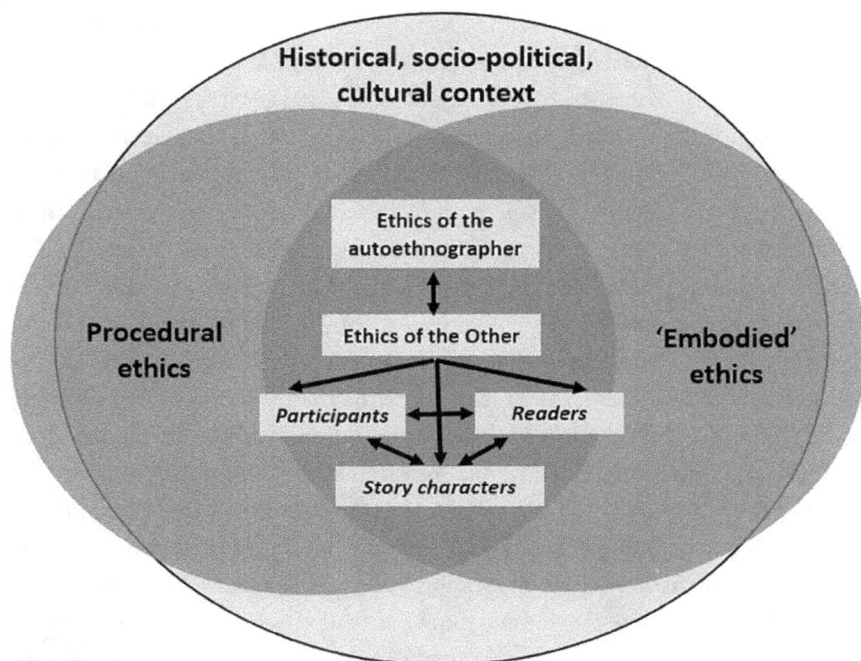

Figure 5 Autoethnographic ethics in Symbiotic Autoethnography.

committees associated with particular institutions, countries and cultures. The general role of these committees, the names of which differ from country to country, is to review researchers' applications for ethics approval and ensure that research processes are duly attended to. Guillemin and Gillam (2004) categorize these formal processes as 'procedural ethics' that involve researchers' engagement with issues, such as participants' informed consent, the right to withdraw, confidentiality, deception and protecting participants from harm. Chiumento, Rahman and Frith (2020) suggest that procedural ethical guidelines can be broadly characterized as adopting a principalist approach founded upon a 'common morality' claimed to be universally applicable across disciplines. And though principalism is packaged as a universal approach to addressing ethical issues in research, the authors argue that the ideas of universal applicability have aided the development of bureaucratic procedural research governance enforced by research ethics committees. Research ethics committees use a different set of criteria and function differently in different countries; however, they share the same aim of guiding researchers towards ethical research practices, which are anticipated to protect both the participants and the researchers. Though there is a general consensus on the usefulness of research ethics committees, a number of researchers (Hammersley, 2009; McNeill, 2014; Reid et al., 2018; Friesen, Yusof and Sheehan, 2019; Bell and Wynn, 2021) express their concerns about the processes that these committees deploy. As explained by Tutenel, Ramaekers and Heylighen (2019), research ethics committees tend to draw upon a biomedical model that is inappropriate for social research and, thus, many researchers 'accuse them of methodological myopia, ethical surveillance, control and imperialism' (p. 642). Reid et al. (2018) also add that 'ethical approval procedures are often viewed as a "hurdle" to be surmounted and arguably overshadow full consideration of the challenges of process ethics, the ethical tensions and dilemmas which arise throughout the practice of research' (p. 70). Denzin (2003) makes a specific point in relation to performance ethnography, arguing that institutional research ethics committees assume that one model of research fits all forms of inquiry, presuming a static, monolithic view of the human subject. He uses an example of an informed consent in the context of performance autoethnography, which falls outside this model, since participation there is purely voluntary and hence, there is no need for subjects to sign forms indicating that their consent is 'informed': 'the activities that make up the research are participatory; that is, they are performative, collaborative and action and praxis based' (Denzin, 2003, p. 249).

In contrast to 'procedural ethics', Guillemin and Gillam (2004) suggest another dimension of ethics – 'ethics in practice', which pertain to the day-to-day ethical issues arising throughout the research process and which are not usually addressed in research ethics committee applications or are anticipated when applying for approval. Engaging with only procedural ethics or 'ethics in practice', is not, according to Guillemin and Gillam (2004), sufficient for the research to be ethical: procedural ethics serve a valuable function in forcing researchers to consider and reflect on the fundamental guiding principles that govern research integrity, whilst 'ethics in practice' offer a valuable discursive tool to allow researchers better understand the ethically important moments in their research practices. Hence, the distinction between these two aspects does not imply that the researchers switch their engagement from one to another. Instead, it rather suggests that procedural ethics form the basis of 'ethics in practice', intentionally instilling a commitment to ethical practice going beyond the tick box exercise demanded by institutions' policies towards an orientation to research practice in a substantive and engaged way (Fletcher, 2021).

This position gains firm traction in the context of a symbiotic approach to ethics, as one of the key assumptions of the latter is based on a symbiotic interconnection between procedural framing of ethics, or what Guillemin and Gillam (2004) refer to as 'procedural ethics' and the 'embodied ethics', which, in the context of Symbiotic Autoethnography, is understood as a fusion of situated, situational, relational and reflexive ethical judgements that autoethnographers face throughout their research process. Spry (2011b) supports that autoethnography, as a written text and as a moral imperative, is reliant on the researcher's embodied craft, where 'the body is the actor, agent and text at once' (p. 507). Whereas procedural research ethics is broadly concerned with the adherence of research to institutional codes of research practices, 'embodied' ethics in a symbiotic approach is specifically concerned with the intersection between various formal aspects of research ethics and 'embodied' discernments of the autoethnographer and the Other (i.e. participants, story characters, readers). Thus, autoethnographic ethics in Symbiotic Autoethnography is both broader (including in its domain 'embodied' ethics) and narrower (excluding from its domain non-autoethnographic research) than procedural ethics. In this sense, a symbiotic approach to ethics extends previous theoretical deliberations on the subject, proposing that there should be a symbiotic connection between procedural ethics and the above-mentioned aspects of 'embodied' ethics to enable autoethnographers to effectively embrace all relevant ethical considerations according to the sociocultural and political context in which their study takes place. Let us have a closer look at each of the facets of 'embodied' ethics, starting with situated ethics.

Situated ethics

In Symbiotic Autoethnography, the complexities related to autoethnographic ethics cut across all of its seven features, highlighting, once again, the impossibility of offering a criteria-based set of guidelines for resolving all ethical issues in all sociocultural contexts. Instead, one of the key tenets of a symbiotic approach to ethics is based on the acknowledgement of the uniqueness of every ethical dilemma, calling for individual approach and 'situated' ethical considerations for all those involved in research. In the context of 'embodied ethics', situated ethics are understood as autoethnographers' ethical decisions associated with and drawn from particular spatio-temporal localities 'situated' in the context of cultural phenomenon under study. The principles of situated ethics have been widely accepted in the field of autoethnographic research, where both theorists and researchers (Tolich, 2010; Adams, Holman Jones and Ellis, 2013; Lapadat, 2017; Henriksen and Schliehe, 2020; Edwards, 2021) acknowledge that it is not the kind of ethics that can be easily tailored to the requirements of research ethics committees. As explained by Hall (2014),

> it is based on relationships and its focus is collective knowledge sharing and creation that actively works as a decolonizing and transformative process for all participants, including the researcher. Situated ethics equips the researcher with a flexible approach and to respond to most situations during fieldwork in an ethical, collaborative and respectful manner. (p. 332)

Indeed, since situated ethics lack a single vantage point from which any standard ethics criteria could be applied, autoethnographers are faced with the difficulties of bridging the gap between situated and procedural ethics. As supported by Simons and Usher (2000), situated ethical principles are local and have different significances, depending on various research situations; thus, making ethical decisions in these situated contexts involves 'a process of creating, maintaining and justifying an ethical integrity that is more dependent on sensitivity to politics and people than it is on ethical principles and codes' (p. 11). Several authors (Simons and Usher, 2000; Jackson, 2013; Spenser, 2016; Cremin et al., 2021) suggest ways of using situated ethics in practice, by highlighting the importance of researcher reflexivity in justifying in situ decisions with consideration of autoethnographic sensitivity to the issues of power dynamics and positionality. Danaher and Danaher (2008), for example, suggest three fundamental processes in the application of situated ethics: 'unfreezing' the elements of research ethics to highlight their fluidity and unpredictability; unsettling the common assumptions about the research ethics in relation to specific projects; and interrogating the contexts in which these project-specific ethics are practised. The authors note that these processes should be seen as interdependent rather than linear and consecutive and so, they are separated into three aspects only for analytical purposes:

> For example, unfreezing might relate to identifying aspects of relationships with research participants that might otherwise assume their homogeneity and might thereby essentialise them, keeping their subjectivities 'frozen'. … Unsettling might include reflecting on the strategies of homogenisation and essentialisation at a broader level, looking for instance at other groups subject to those strategies and at why those strategies endure. Interrogating might include looking carefully at documentation such as consent forms and interview schedules for evidence of resilient assumptions that the participants in the particular study will automatically exhibit certain kinds of behaviours because of their assumed homogeneous characteristics. (Danaher and Danaher, 2008, p. 62)

In the context of a symbiotic approach, possible ways of addressing situated ethics derive from the 'embodied' nature of our autoethnographic stories. Spry (2001) writes about the autoethnographic texts emerging from the researchers' bodily standpoints as they recognize and interpret the residue traces of culture inscribed upon them. These 'embodied' interactions of autoethnographers with specific cultural and sociopolitical contexts, essentially, shape their ethical considerations, requiring researchers' amplified attention to the ways these contexts influence the processes of writing, discerning the data and interpretative analysis. Reflecting explicitly on these aspects within the documentation accompanying procedural ethics would help autoethnographers to create a stronger nexus between the requirements of research ethics committees and the researchers' 'embodied' situated ethics. For example, in the ethics application for my autoethnographic research project about educational leadership in Soviet and neoliberal contexts, I made explicit references to the potential influences of my 'embodied' Soviet experiences on the research processes and my interactions with the participants. At the same time, to strengthen the links to procedural ethics, I also aligned my ethical consideration with the relevant ethical standards, which, in my case, were associated with the British Ethical Research Association (BERA, 2018) guidelines, emphasizing the point that certain guidelines 'may not be appropriate to all circumstances; in particular, different cultural contexts are likely to require *situated* (my emphasis) judgments' (p. 1). Furthermore, I also included in my ethics application my deliberations on the temporality of autoethnographic writing and, thus, the spatio-temporal nature of ethical decisions made 'in the moment of writing'. Indeed, even though the focus of 'embodied' situated ethics is on the continuity of the reflexive process, which requires autoethnographers to question continuously the ethicality of their actions, the moment of writing captures these ethical decision in the moment of stillness in that particular space and time. This means, in agreement with Roulet et al. (2017), that the ethical decisions, which were considered appropriate at the moment of writing, might be perceived as wrong at a later point in time.

Thus, situated ethics as part of embodied ethics in Symbiotic Autoethnography offers a conception of ethics, which recognizes not only the influences of sociocultural contexts on the researcher's ethical decisions but also draws attention to the 'embodied' spatio-temporal practices of ethics as varied and nuanced experiences that account for the position from which the autoethnographer speaks at that moment in time. Autoethnographers' acute awareness of these issues would help them to produce research that is ethically sound as well as providing more convincing evidence for research committees on how their autoethnographic study anticipates meeting the requirements of procedural ethics. Yet, it is important to emphasize that a symbiotic approach to situated ethics offers only one of the possibilities of addressing related ethical concerns and so, it is essential that we continue these debates and view situated ethics as a subject open to interpretations by various philosophies, cultures and world views.

Situational ethics

Situational ethics is considered to be another aspect of 'embodied' ethics in the context of a symbiotic approach. The concept seems to be often used interchangeably with situated ethics and yet, these two concepts are quite different. As previously discussed, situated ethics deals with ethical issues related to specific physical (or in the case of a symbiotic approach – physical and spatio-temporal) contexts. In contrast, situational ethics, as the name suggests, deal with ethical issues arising from different research situations, where commonly accepted ethical standards are considered less important than the outcome of a particular situation. Some of the most popular examples of situational ethics are related to such scenarios as euthanasia, abortion, conjoined twins, murder, to name just a few. The idea of situational ethics is not new. It was originally proposed by Fletcher ([1966] 1997), who tried to find a middle ground between moral absolutism, which maintained that any ethical dilemmas could be resolved by applying fixed universal moral principles, and moral relativism, which rejected the existence of any fixed moral principles. Fletcher based his situation ethics on the Christian ideas of brotherly love, suggesting that loving ends justify any means: 'the situationist follows a moral law or violates it according to love's need' (p. 26). Fletcher's thinking gave rise to broader understanding of situational ethics as an approach that evaluates ethics of any action with consideration of specific circumstances rather than judging it according to universal criteria. It is a dynamic process, since it is not 'transcendental and clearly defined in advance for everyone in every situation' but rather 'explodes anew in every circumstance, demands a specific re-inscription and hounds praxis unmercifully' (St. Pierre, 1997, p. 176).

A number of authors interpret the concept of situational ethics in different ways. For example, Robertson et al. (2002), when referring to the term 'situational ethics', are 'describing the numerous situational factors associated with an ethical dilemma. An ethical dilemma is a situation when an individual can see two sides to an issue, with no clear moral right or wrong that dominates a plausible decision'

(p. 328). Reid et al. (2018) suggest that situational ethics involve ethical issues 'arising specific to context' (p. 70). Adams (2008) writes about narrative ethics, suggesting that 'every situation is different, and a preformed set of principles runs the risk of doing violence to a story and its author' (p. 179). In relation to autoethnographic research, situational ethics resonates with Ellis's (2007) interpretation of 'ethics in practice', which, according to her, is 'the kind that deal with the unpredictable, often subtle, yet ethically important moments that come up in the field. ... For example, what if someone discloses something harmful, asks for help, or voices discomfort with a question or her or his own response?' (p. 4). In many ways, this position is similar to Guillemin and Gillam's (2004) concept of 'ethically important moments' in doing research, which the authors define as 'the difficult, often subtle and usually unpredictable situations that arise in the practice of doing research' (p. 262). Though not without criticism based mainly on the point that situational ethics contradicts the fundamental universal values of ethics and morality, elements of situational ethics seem to be perceived in autoethnographic circles as useful tools for probing ethical situations that can be far removed from the binary choices of procedural ethics (Ellis, 2007; Sieber and Tolich, 2013; Edwards, 2021).

In the context of a symbiotic approach, situational ethics are considered to be an integral part of 'embodied' ethics. The core of ethical decisions in any autoethnographic study is surrounded by ethical ambiguity, where the researchers find themselves torn between two or more sides of an argument related to specific research situations. Similar to 'embodied' situated ethics, situational research ethics goes against the grain of criteria-based approaches that rely on universalizing ethical norms without taking into consideration researchers' embodied ethical agency. And yet, as confirmed by Kupers (2015), neglecting the embodied nature of ethics leads to its impoverished status, which loses its capacity for flexibility, as it becomes blind to empathetic and caring relations experienced through the body. Drawing on these reflections, I suggest that situational ethics as part of 'embodied' ethical praxis is understood as a dynamic and symbiotic interconnection between the researcher's bodily responses to different ethical situations and sociocultural circumstances in which the situations take place. In this sense, situational ethics cannot be separated from situated ethics, since any ethical dilemma is embedded in a specific sociocultural context. Thus, a symbiotic approach to ethics aims to bring together 'the immediacy of embodied experience with a multiplicity of cultural meaning in which we are always and inevitably immersed' (Csordas, 1999, p. 143).

Nonetheless, the idea of embodiment gains more importance in situational ethics, as autoethnographers' ethical decisions in different unpredicted situations are determined by their intuitive conscious ethics that are intertwined with all their corporeal feelings and senses. For example, when I was carrying out an online interview with one of my participants, her parents overheard our discussion and decided to join the conversation. I was aware at that point that it was against the procedural requirement to gain a written informed consent from all participants prior to the interview; however, using my intuitive situational ethics, I continued the interview, as I found it inappropriate to ask the participant's parents to leave. Instead, I asked the participant 'on the spot' whether she was comfortable with the interview to be carried on. As a result, I was provided with new valuable insights into the issues of Soviet leadership, since the parents appeared to have had more experience of the phenomenon than the participant herself. At a later stage, I shared my transcripts with both the participant and her parents; however, should I have followed procedural ethics at the time of the interview, that valuable data would have been lost. I took full responsibility for the ethical soundness of my choice based purely on my 'gut feeling', as I believed that it was an ethically right decision in that particular situation. Beu, Buckley and Harvey (2003) confirm that 'the integrity of a researcher's behaviour depends on the decision that he or she makes in a situation with ethical implications. Making an ethical decision is a complex process that involves taking into consideration causes and outcomes that are often not black and white' (p. 102). Thus, in situational ethics, autoethnographers' 'embodied reflexivity' becomes paramount, as finding a balance between the requirements of procedural ethics and 'embodied' ethics of particular situations requires a genuinely reflexive approach.

The importance of autoethnographers' reflexivity, as discussed in Chapter 4, has been highlighted in literature across different disciplines by a number of authors (Ellis and Bochner, 2000; McIlveen, 2008; Grant et al., 2013; Lapadat, 2017; Koopman, Watling and LaDonna, 2020; Poulos, 2021). And whilst the need for reflexivity permeates all aspects of autoethnographic research, when it comes to situational ethics, the researcher's embodied reflexivity becomes the ethical pivot around which all spontaneous ethical decisions are centred in relation to the situations that fall outside the rules of procedural ethics. In the attempt to bridge the gap between procedural and situational ethics, autoethnographers might want to make it explicit in their ethics application that they are aware of potential unpredictability of ethical situations. At the same time, it is worth acknowledging the need for heighted levels of reflexivity in dealing with these situations as well as the researcher's ability and preparedness to conduct research with integrity, that is, exercising intellectual honesty, fairness, transparency and high sensitivity to the issues of social justice, power imbalance and conflicts of interests.

Relational ethics

Autoethnographic modes of inquiry, aimed at moving away from the idea of one objective truth towards subjective 'narrative truth', resulted in more incongruences between 'embodied' and procedural ethics. These ethical intricacies are embraced by the notion of relational ethics and are, generally, related to engaging with and representing the Other in autoethnographic research. Ellis (2007) explains that the issue of relational ethics, as defined by the ethics of writings about personal experiences that involve intimate others, is not associated with 'definitive rules or universal principles that can tell you precisely what to do in every situation or relationship you may encounter, other than the vague and generic "do no harm"' (p. 6). Indeed, unlike most qualitative research, where participants' identities are anonymized, autoethnographers, typically, use their own name in publishing the research, which makes it difficult and, sometimes, impossible to protect the anonymity of others mentioned in the story (Ellis, 2007; Delamont, 2009; Tolich, 2010; Lapadat, 2017; Edwards, 2021). Roth (2009) also confirms that even the most narcissistic piece of writing that we might imagine already implies the Other. Similarly, Morse (2002) challenges autoethnographers by claiming that the autoethnographic narratives always contain information about others who are, by association, recognizable, even if their names have been changed, which violates their anonymity: 'if these "others" do not know about the article, it still violates their rights, for they have not given their permission and they do not have the right of withdrawal or refusal the informed consent provides' (p. 1159). Wall (2008) also expresses her concerns about the ethics of representing others 'who are unable to represent themselves in writing', whereas Delamont (2009) contributes to the debate by claiming that 'autoethnography is almost impossible to write and publish ethically' (p. 59), since it is normally impossible for other actors to be disguised or protected in autoethnography: 'readers will always wish to read autoethnography as an authentic and consequently "true" account of the writer's life and therefore the other actors will be, whatever disclaimers, or statements about fictions are included, identifiable and identified' (Delamont 2009). In response to these claims, Edwards (2021) suggests that autoethnographers

> need to find a range of acceptable ways to ensure that persons referred to in autoethnography should be advised and where possible their recall as to what happened should be sought for clarification. … There is a delicate balancing act involved in getting this right and what may seem to be advisable in one situation might not be appropriate in another. The challenges arising from the tension between the relational ethic and the ethic of the self in autoethnography are real and ongoing. (p. 5)

Such dense theoretical antagonism towards the possibilities of conducting an autoethnographic study ethically has, naturally, affected my thinking behind a symbiotic approach to autoethnographic ethics. In the next few pages, I aim to outline how relational ethics fits with Symbiotic Autoethnography as well as suggest a couple of practical strategies to help autoethnographers deal with emerging issues. Though these strategies are not exclusively associated with Symbiotic Autoethnography and are commonly used across various autoethnographic studies, they remain pertinent to 'embodied' autoethnographic ethics as part of an overall symbiotic approach.

In the context of 'embodied' ethics, relational ethics are symbiotically connected to situated and situational ethics, as autoethnographers' relations with the Other are always influenced by the dynamics of the researcher's spatio-temporal bodily responses to different ethical situations taking place in specific sociocultural circumstances. Indeed, our relations with the characters from our autoethnographic stories and with our participants are always 'embodied' in the sense that they are always shaped by and within our bodies that carry sensory and emotive experiences brought about through our encounters with the Other. Though practising relational ethics presents multiple challenges, it also enables autoethnographers to create new meanings that emerge in the process of their symbiotic interactions with the Other. Yet, in 'embodied' relational ethics, researchers' ethical decisions are not informed only by their bodily intuitive reactions to ethical situations but also capture wider social implications of these decisions, adding another link to the symbiotic connection between auto-, ethno- and -graphy. Through such symbiosis the notion of relational ethics goes beyond the 'researcher-the Other' dichotomy, bringing into focus sociocultural dimensions of these relations. As Larkin, de Casterle and Schotsmans (2008) suggest, encapsulating the breadth of relations in a wider environment 'moves ethical decisions from the individual as isolated to the individual as interconnected and intertwined in meaningful relationships with others' (p. 235), creating a 'relational space', where due consideration is given to personal and global implications of ethical decision making. Siddique (2016) also adds that 'relational ethics can offer the liminal space to question reality, to cross borders and find authenticity' (p. 414). Thus, in a symbiotic approach, relational ethics are understood as an integral part of 'embodied' ethics with a focus on autoethnographers' heightened reflexive attention to the ways the Other is represented in their narratives in relation to both the researcher and the sociocultural dimensions of the study. Autoethnographers, who practise relational ethics symbiotically, are in a privileged position to determine the ethical salience of their encounters with the Other in various circumstances. This means that representing the Other in a particular way should be substantiated with consideration of a symbiotic connection between the researcher's own integrity and specific sociocultural contexts. This connection is dynamic, multifaceted and embedded in the autoethnographer's emotive response to specific ethical situations, where the welfare of the Other becomes paramount in informing consequent ethical decisions. It symbiotically combines the researcher's obligations to the self and the Other in diverse networks of relationships, whilst also necessitating researchers' continuous reflexive interrogation of the everchanging sociocultural circumstances that surround ethical judgements. As argued by Tamminen et al. (2021), such relationships and associated ethical decisions may evolve over time and thus, we have to consider the temporal nature of relational ethics through 'maintaining mutual respect; and acknowledging the diverse social and historical contexts of lived experiences and the emotional, physical and social spaces in which ethical decision making occurs' (p. 8).

So, what practical steps can autoethnographers take in the process of justifying concomitant ethical choices in Symbiotic Autoethnography in relation to representing the Other? Since some of the issues of representing the Other as the characters from the researchers' stories, their participants and the researchers' multiple Selves have already been discussed in Chapter 4, in this part of my discussion I will focus explicitly on some practical ways of addressing the most challenging aspect of relational ethics, that is, writing about the characters of our stories. This is particularly important for bringing closer procedural and 'embodied' ethical practices, as when it comes to offering researchers advice on how to deal with specific ethical issues, the practical guidance here is, largely, limited. This opinion is echoed by a number of authors in the field of autoethnographic research (Bochner, 2000; Ellis, 2007; Roth, 2009; Dauphinee,

2010; Tolich, 2010; Sikes, 2015; Lapadat, 2017; Andrew, 2017; Grant, 2020) and, particularly, in relation to the requirement of an informed consent.

Indeed, whilst procedural ethics seem to be more or less straightforward, even though the completion of the ethics application can be quite laborious, when it comes to practical situations that go beyond the tick box exercise, autoethnographers are often faced with the dilemmas that cannot be resolved through references to an informed consent. Here the specificity of procedural ethics clashes with the autoethnographers' aspiration to produce a subjective account through the lens of their own lived experiences, where gaining an informed consent from those they write about proves impossible. This issue, of course, is less problematic when researchers work with the data acquired through their relations with participants, where the participants' stories represented by the researcher go through a process known as 'member checking', 'participant verification' or 'respondent validation' that is expected to authenticate the participants' stories. Yet, as argued by Byrne (2017), how narrative researchers tell the stories of their participants is not unproblematic, since the notion of authenticity implies that a single 'true' representation is achievable.

Whilst the need to be concerned about the ethics of representing those we mention in our autoethnographies has been widely acknowledged by autoethnographers (Denzin, 2006; Ellis, 2007; Dauphinee, 2010; Sikes, 2015; Campbell, 2016; Edwards, 2021; Racine, 2021), alongside these acknowledgements, some (Morse, 2002; Atkinson, 2006; Delamont, 2009) also express their pessimistic views on the possibility of writing autoethnography ethically, suggesting that our autoethnographic stories inevitably involve people who were a part of the author's written or performed experience and that those people might not have given explicit permission for their story to be included in our work. Delamont (2009) goes as far as asserting that

> it is normally impossible for other actors to be disguised or protected in autoethnography. Readers will always wish to read autoethnography as an authentic and consequently 'true' account of the writer's life and therefore the other actors will be, whatever disclaimers, or statements about fictions are included, identifiable and identified. (p. 59)

Naturally, these accusations of unethicality create a serious challenge for autoethnographers in terms of dealing with the issues of relational ethics. In the context of a symbiotic approach, one way forward is seen in the implicit acknowledgement of the researcher's 'embodied' subjective position in their autoethnographic story as an attempt to 'capture the continuous, lived flow of historically situated, phenomenal experiences, with all the ambiguity, variability, malleability and even uniqueness that such experience implies' (Plummer, 2001, p. 37). Even though we implicate other people in our stories, our narratives represent not one single 'truth' in its traditional sense but our embodied feelings, emotional reactions and subjective opinions captured in the moment of writing. From this perspective, our narratives represent *our* 'narrative truths' that might not be, necessarily, perceived in the same way by other people, including the characters of our stories. Moreover, autoethnographers themselves might not even perceive these relations and events in the same way at different times and in different circumstances, as our autoethnographic experiences are spatio-temporal in nature. Similar to Turner (2013), we might write about our childhood, describing our relationship with our parents and yet, these descriptions are unlikely to be the same as our parents would remember them. As Turner (2013) goes further to explain,

> Perhaps a little more controversially, if I am to reveal a person's identity alongside their words, it is still my experience of their words, filtered through my own selves. Furthermore, if I were to write about my reflections on others' words to or about me, asking permission from the originators of these words might be a moot point. I would argue that my experience is my construction of events. Within a constructed ontology, there ceases to be 'factual' accounts which can be identified as the 'true' version of events, there are just different constructions of an event, or moment in history. (p. 220)

Writing about the Other in an 'embodied' way problematizes the position of the autoethnographer as 'the knower', spotlighting instead the ambiguity and partiality of their interpretations, whilst questioning the possibility of 'knowing the Other'. As highlighted by a French philosopher Levinas (1969), renowned for his work on the ethics of the Other, the relation with the Other 'is the relation with its absence, an absence on the plane of knowledge – the unknown' (p. 277). Freistadt (2011), for example, uses phenomenological approach to argue that expecting to have absolute clarity in our experiences of the Other is absurd, since we are always in the position of viewing the world from our embodied perspective and thus, we cannot and should not expect to achieve an account of experience that completely corresponds with another person's. Furthermore, as discussed in Chapter 4, our embodied experiences, including our encounters with the Other, remain omnipresent across spatio-temporal dimensions of our autoethnographic journeys. This means that, as in the case with situated ethics, our ethical decisions related to the ways we represent characters of our stories involve temporal 'longitudinal efforts', or as Feristadt (2011) explains, 'although we might not understand another person at one moment, we can, overtime, gain a partial understanding of them by sharing in their experiences' (p. 33).

Acknowledging explicitly the subjectivity and temporality of representing the Other would allow autoethnographers not only to minimize the gap between procedural and 'embodied' ethics but also reduce the tensions associated with, what Lather (2001) calls, 'appropriating the lives of others' (p. 484). In practice, this endeavour would require autoethnographers' heightened attention to, what Ellis (2017) refers to as, 'relational ethics of care' (p. 431), which involves researchers' continuous mindful reflexive thinking about their role, motives and feelings during writing about the Other. In this sense, relational ethics of care provide another symbiotic connection between the autoethnographer and the Other, as it creates a relational space, where the story of the Other merges with the researcher's embodied responses to related ethical situations. As noted by Rhodes and Carlsen (2018), the adoption of relationally reflexive research practice enables researchers to question their prejudices, the limits to their thinking and the culturally situated nature of their relationships, whilst decentring authority from the researcher to the interrelations between the researcher and the Other.

Autoethnographers can use a number of strategies to help them engage in 'relational ethics of care' in a meaningful and conscious way. These strategies are not unique to a symbiotic approach, however, but are relevant and applicable in the context of symbiotically embodied ethics. Gergen (2000), for example, suggests that the debates about ethical issues related to research and representation have resulted in an effulgent range of methodological innovations, such as reflexivity, multiple voicing, literary representation and performance. Doloriert and Sambrook (2009) suggest using the notion of 'mindful slippage' (Medford, 2006, p. 853), arguing that it could be adapted for minimizing harm from the autoethnographer's self-disclosure through deliberate acknowledgement of the 'slippage between Truth (or our experience of reality) and truthfulness because sometimes it seems appropriate – even necessary – to abbreviate, edit, or otherwise modify our life stories in our writing' (Medford, 2006).

Writing autoethnography in third person can be seen as one of the ways of addressing such 'slippage'. Wyatt (2006), for example, proposes that there are three ethical angles on writing in the third person: creating distance for others (including readers), establishing distance within the researchers themselves and striving to write in a tentative and authentic way, avoiding to sound certain about the feelings and events, allowing readers to make their own judgement, allowing 'space for otherness' (p. 815). Denzin (in Ellis et al., 2008) admits that he used third-person writing to disguise his, essentially autoethnographic, works – *The Alcoholic Self and The Recovering Alcoholic* – as traditional ethnographies, as he struggled with how to write about himself in that space.

Writing in third person as one of the ways of addressing ethical issues related to representing characters from our stories bears a strong connection to fictionalization of narratives, or what Clough (2002) refers to as 'storying methodology' in his attempt to address crisis of representation through fictional writing as a process of inquiry. Clough (2002) argues that fictionalized narratives should be judged not by positivist standards of validity and reliability but by emotive force, authenticity and integrity to the people they portray, offering 'a version of the truth as the researcher sees it' (p. 18). Earlier on, Booth ([1961] 1983) offered a useful point, highlighting that the effectiveness of fictionalization needs to be assessed in relation to the larger purposes of the author's work and thus, in some cases, the narrators might choose to overlook some negative qualities to generate sympathy and 'a parallel emotional response' (p. 249) between the character and the reader, even when used in the representation of ethically deficient personalities. Richardson and St. Pierre (2005) suggest that, when autoethnographers decide to write about another person and to protect their identity, they change their name, gender and the circumstances around the event they describe, they will create 'a kind of 'factional' story' (p. 961). Similarly, Sikes (2015) notes that skilful writers craft evocative accounts, drawing the reader in, sometimes using fiction and other literary conceits too; however, writers need to be aware of how they use that 'narrative power', 'since depictions can be personally and even socially damaging to individuals and to their family members, friends and colleagues' (p. 1). Hence, even though this approach to autoethnographic writing enables researchers to write about the Other with reduced risks of revealing any specific details of their times, locations and identities, it is important to use their judgements in an embodied symbiosis with situational ethics. As noted by Byrne (2017), the researcher 'leaves her mark on the data but does so in a much more explicit and transparent way through the production of fictive forms of representation' (p. 46). Edwards (2021) agrees that writing the account as fiction or disguising the others extensively can be used as an alternate options for finding satisfactory ethical bounds. Autoethnographers use fictionalization in many different ways, which can be facilitated by employing different autoethnographic genres, such as poetry, unconventional textual formats, dance, music and other creative approaches. Yet, as Edwards (Edwards 2021) suggests,

> there is a delicate balancing act involved in getting this right and what may seem to be advisable in one situation might not be appropriate in another. The challenges arising from the tension between the relational ethic and the ethic of the self in autoethnography are real and ongoing. (p. 5)

Other ways of dealing with relational ethics of care include using pseudonyms, creating composite characters and engaging in a polyvocal narration. Polyvocality has already been discussed in Chapter 4 as one of the essential features of Symbiotic Autoethnography. Yet, it is worth mentioning here that, in the context of embodied relational ethics, polyvocality creates another opportunity for autoethnographers to address the issues of representing the characters of their stories. Withdrawing the power of a single 'omniscient narrator' (Visweswaran, 1994, p. 75) by intertwining it with the voices of participants and characters from the story will help autoethnographers to obscure identities without affecting the purpose of the narrative. In addition, researchers might also want to emphasize the polyvocality of the researcher's Self (see Chapter 4 for more detailed discussion of the Other as researchers' multiple Selves) through adding another layer of polyvocality to their autoethnographic studies. Gergen (2000), however, warns us that, whilst polyvocality provides a potentially rich array of perspectives, multiple voicing is not without its complexities. According to Gergen (2000), one of the most difficult questions is how the researchers should treat their voices within the chorus of voices of the Other. Similarly, Wall (2008) questions whether it is possible for researchers to overcome the feeling of guilt for 'making use of another person's life, of borrowing another person's identity, to tell my own story?' (p. 49). Addressing these questions would, of course, depend on autoethnographers' personal positioning in relation to the context of their research and the nature of the cultural phenomenon under study. To conclude this part of the discussion, I lean here on Byrne (2017), who advises us to leave opportunities for multiple interpretations open, since 'allowing for the interpretation of others, for other "truths", means relinquishing some control but not all responsibility' (p. 46).

Indeed, the responsibility for the ethical integrity of any research study always remains with the researcher. Ellis (2007) elaborates that such responsibility requires autoethnographers to act from their hearts and minds, to acknowledge their 'interpersonal bonds to others and initiate and maintain conversations' (p. 4). Specifically, dealing with the responsibilities of addressing situated, situational and relational ethics simultaneously could be particularly challenging. As previously mentioned, a symbiotic approach does not and cannot offer solutions to all ethical situations and neither can it suggest a set of unique guidelines that would be universally applicable. I would like, however, to emphasize once again that, in the context of Symbiotic Autoethnography, it is essential for autoethnographers to engage reflexively and symbiotically with all three facets of embodied ethics, whilst also acknowledging their position explicitly in response to the requirements of procedural ethics.

Addressing ethical issues in autoethnography is, perhaps, one of the most challenging aspect of autoethnographic research process and though we try to avoid as much as possible using what Bergin and Westwood (2003) refer to as 'violent' (p. 212) textual strategies that inscribe and privilege a particular chosen meaning, we have to recognize that our attempts cannot claim 'the innocence of success' (Pillow, 2003, p. 192). So, all we can do is to continue to approach the voices of the Other in our stories in a sensitive, ethically vigilant and appreciative way, whilst continuously questioning the ethical integrity of our decisions. This type of reflexivity pushes us towards a deeper exploration of these problematic, unfamiliar and uncomfortable dilemmas of representation and, at the same time, permits us 'to be surely unsure' (Guttorm, 2012, p. 600) and that it is 'important/significant/even reasonable to write from this partial, nomadic place, where I am and where I travel' (Guttorm, 2012). The feelings of doubt will always continue to permeate our autoethnographic journeys, revealing 'the fractures, sutures and seams of self interacting with others in the context of researching lived experience' (Spry, 2001, p. 712). And the same doubt of uncertainty will always remain present in our attempts to match the richness of our own voice and the voices of the Other to the boundaries of language possibilities, making a perpetual question of representation hover over us: 'How do I do representation knowing that I can never quite get it right?' (Pillow, 2003, p. 176). Nevertheless, asking these kind of questions helps autoethnographers to appreciate the immensity of ethical issues related to representing our own voices in symbiosis with the voices of the Other. We can expect that the exploration of ethical solutions associated with this symbiosis will continue to stimulate further debates and yield new insights and solutions.

Final Thoughts

In my concluding thoughts I would like to lean on Bateson's ([1972] 2000) argument that 'an explorer can never know what he is exploring until it has been explored' (p. xxiv). Indeed, throughout this writing escapade, I moved multiple times between 'knowing' and 'not knowing', with every new step, fine-tuning my ideas to the chorus of uncertainties and disorientations of my thinking trajectory. As a result, this book represents the concept of Symbiotic Autoethnography not as a systematic methodological framework but as an acquiescent and ambiguous space, occupied by the intimacy of my own multiple Selves connecting with the wisdoms of the Other, who carved their edges into my thoughts and deliberations, augmenting them into a deceptive illusion of practicality. In my writing, I searched for the meaning 'betwixt and between' theoretical assumptions and speculative spaces, looking for the traces of any tangible solutions within the intangibility of these illusions of closure, which continued to refuse any promise of significance or certainty. Similarly to Trahar (2009), holding on to this 'not knowing' was uncomfortable, but maintaining the position of the agnostic enabled me to keep moving forward. In this movement I managed to reconcile the process of writing with the feeling of continuous doubt of whether I can ever express the uncertainties of my thinking through 'the words of language, which bear the stamp of impressions, as counterfeit coin' (Horkheimer and Adorno, [1944] 2002, p. 2).

And so, this book is the product of my doubts, discomforts and exploratory attempts aimed at proposing a new symbiotic approach that goes beyond the commonly accepted boundaries of qualitative inquiry. Utilizing key features of a symbiotic approach in my own autoethnographic study helped me to recognize the process of 'doing autoethnography' as an 'embodied' experience of constant movement between my multiple Selves and the Other, between times and spaces, between real and illusory and between clear and ambiguous. Yet, I accept that the troubling interrogations of impermanence and multiplicity of the researcher's Selves always remain restrained by our incapacity to reach the depth of our subjective transcendental consciousness, and thus, this book can offer only a partial entry into the ways of exploring our autoethnographic experiences. As noted by Sparkes and Smith (2009), any criteria in qualitative research should be viewed as lists of characteristic features that are open to continuous reinterpretation, as times, conditions and the research purposes change; thus, 'researchers need to adopt the role of connoisseur in order to pass judgment on different kinds of study in a fair and ethical manner' (p. 491). This, I invite readers to become such connoisseurs in making judgements about the suitability of my ideas to their own research.

As Lewis (2011) points out, every story comes to an end and in that ending it is possible to see things heretofore unnoticed; and it is important 'because we desire a closure that completes the story in such a way that there is a sense of an ending that realizes something' (p. 506). I would like to end this book with a reflection on the impact of my engagement with Symbiotic Autoethnography on myself as a researcher and as a person. Writing this book allowed me a freedom to put myself in a position of a philosopher, whose writing, as suggested by Lyotard (1984), is not governed by pre-established rules and 'cannot be judged according to a determining judgement, by applying familiar categories to the text or to the work' (p. 81). Allowing myself this freedom of thinking made me a better researcher, who has been liberated from conventional methodological restraints, who is open to new ideas, receptive to the diversity of opinions and sources of evidence, whilst also being aware of the interplay of powers that affect all our perceptions and beliefs. And last, but not least, it has made me a better person, who is eager to engage in, what Kross and Grossmann (2012) call, 'wise reasoning' (p. 43), which involves recognizing the limits of one's own knowledge and developing a prosocial orientation that promotes the common good. Some time ago I remember reading Loren Eiseley's book *The Star Thrower*. The story went something like this: an old man, walking along a shore covered with thousands of washed-up dying starfish, noticed a boy, who was throwing them back into the ocean. The man said to the boy that there were miles and miles of beach covered with starfish and that he would never make a difference. As the boy threw a starfish back into the ocean, he said to the old man, 'I've just made a difference to that one.' Though at this point it remains uncertain whether this book is going to make a difference to other researchers, one thing is already certain – it has made a difference to me. Yet, I hope that this book can spur 'the power of feelings' (Dirkx, 2001, p. 63) in the readers that would prompt new investigations and new research stories to emerge, the stories that have no endings but new questions to explore and new trajectories to follow. Indeed, despite all our sincerities and efforts to find a certainty and a final terminus in our research endeavours, our research stories always remain unfinished, as research is essentially a non-dogmatic venture that builds upon the premises of continuous re-evaluation and unrelenting enduring inquiry.

References

Abrahao, M. H. (2012), Autobiographical research: Memory, time and narratives in the first person. *European Journal for Research on the Education and Learning of Adults*, 3(1): 29–41.

Adams, T. E. (2006), Seeking father: Relationally reframing a troubled love story. *Qualitative Enquiry*, 12(4): 704–23.

Adams, T. E. (2008), A review of narrative ethics. *Qualitative Inquiry*, 14(2): 175–94.

Adams, T. E., Ellis, C. and Holman Jones, S. (2017), Autoethnography. In J. Matthes, C. S. Davis and R. F. Potter (eds), *The International Encyclopedia of Communication Research Methods*, 1–11. New York: Wiley.

Adams, T. E., and Herrmann, A. (2020), Expanding our autoethnographic future. *Journal of Autoethnography*, 1(1): 1–8.

Adams, T. E., Holman Jones, S. and Ellis, C. (2013), Conclusion: Where stories take us. In S. Holman Jones, T. E. Adams and C. Ellis (eds), *Handbook of Autoethnography*, 669–77. Walnut Creek, CA: Left Coast Press.

Adams, T. E., Holman Jones, S. and Ellis, C. (2015), *Autoethnography*. Oxford: Oxford University Press.

Adams, T. E., Holman Jones, S. and Ellis, C. (2021), *Handbook of Autoethnography* (2nd edn). Oxon: Routledge.

Adkins, L. (2009), Sociological futures: From clock time to event time. *Sociological Research Online*, 14(4): 88–92.

Adler, P. A., and Adler, P. (1987), *Membership Roles in Field Research*. Newbury Park, CA: Sage.

Aiston, S. J., and Fo, C. K. (2021), The silence/ing of academic women. *Gender and Education*, 33(2): 138–55.

Alabdulhadi, A., Schyns, B. and Staudigl, L. F. (2017), Implicit leadership theory. In E. A. Curtis and J. G. Cullen (eds), *Leadership and Change for the Health Professional*, 20–36. London: Open University Press.

Alerby, E., and Bergmark, U. (2012), What can an image tell? Challenges and benefits of using visual art as a research method to voice lived experiences of students and teachers. *Journal of Arts and Humanities*, 1(1): 95–103.

Alexander, B. K. (2014), Bodies yearning on the borders of becoming: A performative reflection on three embodied axes of social difference. *Qualitative Inquiry*, 20(10): 1169–78.

Alexander, B. K. (2020), 'I thought I knew you': A performative reflection on knowing the other in autoethnography. *Journal of Autoethnography*, 1(2): 190–7.

Alexander, B. K., Moreira, C. and Kumar, H. S. (2015), Memory, mourning and miracles: A triple-autoethnographic performance script. *International Review of Qualitative Inquiry*, 8 (1): 229–55.

Alexander, B. K., Stephenson-Celadilla, A. E., Alhayek, K., Twishime, P. I., Sutton, T., Ojeda, C. H. and Moreira, C. (2019), 'I'm sorry my hair is blocking your smile': A performative assemblage and intercultural dialogue on the politics of hair and place. *International Review of Qualitative Research*, 12 (4): 339–62.

Allan, E. J., and Iverson, S. (2009), *Reconstructing Policy in Higher Education: Feminist Poststructural Perspectives*. Oxon: Routledge.

Allen, L. (2021), The smell of lockdown: Smellwalks as sensuous methodology. *Qualitative Research*. Available online: https://doi.org/10.1177/14687941211007663 (accessed 30 July 2021).

Allen-Collinson, J., and Hockey, J. (2008), Autoethnography as 'valid' methodology? A Study of disrupted identity narratives. *International Journal of Interdisciplinary Social Sciences*, 3(6): 209–17.

Allen-Collinson, J. (2012), Autoethnography: Situating personal sporting narratives in socio-cultural contexts. In K. Young and M. Atkinson (eds), *Qualitative Research on Sport and Physical Culture: Research in the Sociology of Sport*, 191–212. Bingley: Emerald Press.

Allen-Collinson, J., Vaittinen, A., Jennings, G. and Owton, H. (2018), Exploring lived heat, 'temperature work' and embodiment: Novel auto/ethnographic insights from physical cultures. *Journal of Contemporary Ethnography*, 47(3): 283–305.

Altheide, D. L., and Johnson, J. M. (1994), Criteria for assessing interpretive validity in qualitative research. In N. K. Denzin and Y. S. Lincoln (eds), *Handbook of Qualitative Research*, 485–99. London: Sage.

Altheide, D. L., and Johnson, J. M. (2011), Reflections on interpretive adequacy in qualitative research. In N. K. Denzin and Y. S. Lincoln (eds), *The SAGE Handbook of Qualitative Research*, 581–94. London: Sage.

Alvesson, M., and Skoldberg, K. (2017), *Reflexive Methodology* (3rd edn). London: Sage.

Amann, R. (2003), A sovietological view of modern Britain. *Political Quarterly*, 74(4): 468–80.

Amsler, M., and Shore, C. (2017), Responsibilisation and leadership in the neoliberal university: A New Zealand perspective. *Discourse Studies in the Cultural Politics of Education*, 38(1): 123–37.

Anderson, G. L. (1989), Critical ethnography in education: Origins, current status and new directions. *Review of Educational Research*, 59(3): 249–70.

Anderson, L. (2006), Analytic autoethnography. *Journal of Contemporary Ethnography*, 35(4): 373–95.

Anderson, L., and Glass-Coffin, B. (2013), I learn by going: Autoethnographic modes of enquiry. In S. H. Jones, T. E. Adams and C. Ellis (eds), *Handbook of Autoethnography*, 57–83. Walnut Creek, CA: Left Coast Press.

Andrew, S. (2017), *Searching for an Autoethnographic Ethic*. Oxon: Routledge.

Aoki, T. T. ([1996] 2005), Imaginaries of 'east and west': Slippery curricular signifiers in education. In W. F. Pinar and R. L. Irwin (eds), *Curriculum in a New Key: The Collected Works of Ted T. Aoki*, 313–19, Mahwah: Lawrence Erlbaum.

Atay, A. (2020), What is cyber or digital autoethnography? *International Review of Qualitative Research*, 13(3): 267–79.

Atkinson, P. (1997), Narrative turn or blind alley? *Qualitative Health Research*, 7(3): 325–44.

Atkinson, P. (2006), Rescuing autoethnography. *Journal of Contemporary Ethnography*, 35(4): 400–4.

Atkinson, P. (2015), Rescuing interactionism from qualitative research. *Symbolic Interaction*, 38(1): 467–74.

Axelrod, R. B., and Cooper, C. R. (2018), *The St. Martin's Guide to Writing* (12th edn). Boston: Bedford/St. Martins.

Babcock, B. A. (1987), Reflexivity. In M. Eliade (ed.), *Encyclopedia of Religion*, 234–8. New York: Macmillan.

Bakhtin, M. (1981), *The Dialogic Imagination: Four Papers*. Austin: University of Texas Press.

Bakhtin, M. (1984), *Problems of Dostoevsky's Poetics*. Minneapolis: University of Minnesota Press.

Ball, P. (2017), *The Strange Link between the Human Mind and Quantum Physics*. Available online: http://www.bbc.com/earth/story/20170215–the–strange–link–between–the–human–mind–and–quantum–physics (accessed 2 July 2021).

Barad, K. (2007), *Meeting the Universe Halfway: Quantum Physics and the Entanglement of Matter and Meaning*. Durham, NC: Duke University Press.

Barad, K. (2018), Troubling time/s and ecologies of nothingness: Re-turning, re-membering and facing the incalculable. *New Formations: A Journal of Culture/ Theory/Politics*, 92(1): 56–86.

Barbalet, J. M. (1999), *Emotion, Social Theory and Social Structure: A Macro-sociological Approach*. Cambridge: Cambridge University Press.

Bateson, G. ([1972] 2000), *Steps to an Ecology of Mind: Collected Essays in Anthropology, Psychiatry, Evolution and Epistemology*. Chicago: University of Chicago Press.

Bazeley, P., and Kemp, L. (2012), Mosaics, triangles and DNA: Metaphors for integrated analysis in mixed methods research. *Journal of Mixed Methods Research*, 6(1): 55–72.

Beattie, L. (2018a), From 'clientilism' to transformational leadership? An autoethnographic journey from Soviet Georgia to the UK. *Journal of Organizational Ethnography*, 7(3): 330–44.

Beattie, L. (2018b), 'We're all mad here …' Soviet leadership and its impact on education through the looking glass of Raymond Williams's cultural materialism. *International Journal of Educational Development*, 62: 1–8.

Beattie, L. (2020), Educational leadership: Producing docile bodies? A Foucauldian perspective on higher education. *Higher Education Quarterly*, 74: 98–110.

Behar, R. (1996), *The Vulnerable Observer: Anthropology That Breaks Your Heart.* Boston: Beacon Press.

Bell, D. ([1978] 1996), *The Cultural Contradictions of Capitalism.* New York: Basic Books.

Bell, K., and Wynn, L. (2021), Research ethics committees, ethnographers and imaginations of risk. *Ethnography.* Available online: https://doi.org/10.1177/14661 38120983862 (accessed 3 August 2021).

Benedek, A., and Veszelszki, A. (eds) (2016), *In the Beginning Was the Image: The Omnipresence of Pictures: Time, Truth, Tradition.* Frankfurt am Main: Peter Lang AG.

Benzecry, C. E., and Baiocchi, G. (2017), What is political about political ethnography? On the context of discovery and the normalization of an emergent subfield. *Theory and Society*, 46: 229–47.

Bergfeld, M. (2018), 'Do you believe in life after work?' The university and college union strike in Britain. *Transfer: European Review of Labour and Research*, 24(2): 233–6.

Bergin, J., and Westwood, R. (2003), The necessities of violence. *Culture and Organisation*, 9(4): 211–23.

Bericat, E. (2016), The sociology of emotions: Four decades of progress. *Current Sociology*, 64(3): 491–513.

Bettelheim, B. ([1975] 1991), *The Uses of Enchantment: The Meaning and Importance of Fairy Tales.* London: Penguin Books.

Bettez, S.C. (2015), Navigating the complexity of qualitative research in postmodern contexts: Assemblage, critical reflexivity and communion as guides. *International Journal of Qualitative Studies in Education*, 28(8): 932–54.

Beu, D. S., Buckley, M. R. and Harvey, M. G. (2003), Ethical decision-making: A multidimensional construct. *Business Ethics: A European Review*, 12: 88–107.

Bhabha, H. (1983), The other question. In P. Mongia (ed.), *Contemporary Postcolonial Theory*, 37–53. London: Arnold.

Bhabha, H. K. (1994), *The Location of Culture.* New York: Routledge.

Bhattacharya, K. (2020), Autohistoria-teoría: Merging self, culture, community, spirit and theory. *Journal of Autoethnography*, 1(2): 198–202.

Bhattacharya, K. (2021), Becoming a warrior monk: First, second and third shifts in academia. *Journal of Autoethnography*, 2(1): 123–7.

Bishop, M. (2021), 'Don't tell me what to do' encountering colonialism in the academy and pushing back with Indigenous autoethnography. *International Journal of Qualitative Studies in Education*, 34(5): 367–78.

Bleiker, R. (2019), Visual autoethnography and international security: Insights from the Korean DMZ. *European Journal of International Security*, 4(3): 274–99.

Blockmans, I. G. E., De Schauwer, E., Van Hove, G. and Enzlin, P. (2020), Retouching and revisiting the strangers within: An exploration journey on the waves of meaning and matter in dance. *Qualitative Inquiry*, 26(7): 733–42.

Boas, F. (1894), Human faculty as determined by race. *Proceedings of the American Association for the Advancement of Science*, 43: 4–29.

Boas, F. (1904), Some traits of primitive culture. *Journal of American Folklore*, 17(1): 243–54.

Boas, F. (1940), *Race, Language and Culture*. New York: Macmillan.

Bochner, A. P. (2000). Criteria against ourselves. *Qualitative Inquiry*, 6(2): 266–72.

Bochner, A. P. (2020), Autoethnography as a way of life: Listening to tinnitus teach. *Journal of Autoethnography*, 1(1): 81–92.

Bochner, A. P., and Adams, T. E. (2020), Autoethnography as applied communication research. In H. D. O'Hair, M. J. O'Hair, E. B. Hester and S. Geegan (eds), *The Handbook of Applied Communication Research*, 707–29. Hoboken: Wiley.

Bochner, A. P., and Ellis, C. (1996), Talking over ethnography. In C. Ellis and A. P. Bochner (eds), *Composing Ethnography: Alternative Forms of Qualitative Writing*, 13–45. Walnut Creek, CA: Alta Mira Press.

Bochner, A. P., and Ellis, C. (2016), *Evocative Autoethnography. Writing Lives and Telling Stories*. New York: Routledge.

Bochner, A. P. and Riggs, N. A. (2014). Practicing narrative inquiry. In P. Leavy (ed.), *The Oxford Handbook of Qualitative Research*, 195–222. Oxford: Oxford University Press.

Boler, M. (ed.) (2004), *Democratic Dialogue in Education: Troubling Speech, Disturbing Silence*. New York: Peter Lang.

Booth, W. C. ([1961] 1983), *The Rhetoric of Fiction*. Chicago: University of Chicago Press.

Bourdieu, P., and Wacquant, L. (1992), *An Invitation to Reflexive Sociology*. Chicago: University of Chicago Press.

Boyd, D. (2008), Autoethnography as a tool for transformative learning about white privilege. *Journal of Transformative Education*, 6(3): 212–25.

Boylorn, R. M., and Orbe, M. P. (2020), *Critical Autoethnography: Intersecting Cultural Identities in Everyday Life*. New York: Routledge.

Boylorn, R. M. and Orbe, M. P. (2021), Becoming: A critical autoethnography on critical autoethnography. *Journal of Autoethnography*, 2(1): 5–12.

Braidotti, R. (2006). *Transpositions: On Nomadic Ethics*. Cambridge: Polity Press.

Brandist, C. (2016), The risks of Soviet-style managerialism in UK universities. *Times Higher Education*, 5 May. Available online: https://www.timeshighereducation.com/comment/the-risks-of-soviet-style-managerialism-in-united-kingdom-universities (accessed 23 February 2021).

Brinkmann, S. (2014), Doing without data. *Qualitative Inquiry*, 20(6): 720–5.

British Educational Research Association (BERA) (2018), *Ethical Guidelines for Educational Research* (4th edn). London: BERA.

Brown-Vincent, L. D. (2019), Seeing it for wearing it: Autoethnography as black feminist methodology. *Taboo: The Journal of Culture and Education*, 18(1). Available online: https://doi.org/10.31390/taboo.18.1.08

Bruner, J. (1987), Life as narrative, *Social Research*, 54(1): 11–32.

Bullough, R., and Pinnegar, S. (2001), Guidelines for quality in autobiographical forms of self-study research. *Educational Researcher*, 30(3): 13–21.

Bunzl, M. (2006), Foreword: Syntheses of a critical anthropology. In J. Fabian (ed.), *Time and the Other: How Anthropology Makes Its Object*, vii–xxxiii. New York: Columbia University Press.

Burke, M. (2019), Childhood Trauma and its effects throughout the lifespan: An autoethnographic reflection of trauma. *Journal of Psychology at Truett McConnell University*, 1(6): 54–60.

Burnier, D. (2006), Encounters with the self in social science research: A political scientist looks at autoethnography. *Journal of Contemporary Ethnography*, 35(4): 410–18.

Butler, J. (1997), *The Psychic Life of Power: Theories in Subjection*. Stanford, CA: Stanford University Press.

Butler, J. (2005), *Giving an Account of Oneself*. New York: Fordham University Press.

Butler, N., and Dunne, S. (2012), Duelling with dualisms: Descartes, Foucault and the history of organizational limits. *Management and Organizational History*, 7(1): 31–44.

Byrne, G. (2017), Narrative inquiry and the problem of representation: 'Giving voice', making meaning. *International Journal of Research and Method in Education*, 40(1): 36–52.

Campbell, E. (2016), Exploring autoethnography as a method and methodology in legal education research. *Asian Journal of Legal Education*, 3(1): 95–105.

Capan, Z. G. (2018), Eurocentrism and the construction of the 'non-West'. Available online: https://www.e-ir.info/2018/06/19/eurocentrism-and-the-construction-of-the-non-west/ (accessed 12 March 2021).

Castree, N. (2009), The spatio-temporality of capitalism. *Time and Society*, 18(1): 26–61.

Chadwick, R. (2021), Theorizing voice: Toward working otherwise with voices. *Qualitative Research*, 21(1): 76–101.

Chakrabarti, S. (2012), Moving beyond Edward Said: Homi Bhabha and the problem of postcolonial representation. International Studies. *Interdisciplinary Political and Cultural Journal*, 14(1): 5–21.

Chang, H. (2008), *Autoethnography as Method*. Walnut Creek, CA: Left Coast Press.

Chang, H. (2016), Autoethnography in health research: Growing pains? *Qualitative Health Research*, 26(4): 443–51.

Chang, H., Nqunjiri, F. W. and Hernandez, K. C. (2013), *Collaborative Autoethnography*. Walnut Creek, CA: Left Coast Press.

Chang, H., and Bilgen, W. (2020), Autoethnography in leadership studies: Past, present and future. *Journal of Autoethnography*, 1(1): 93–8.

Chawla, D. (2021), Diversity work as second shift. *Journal of Autoethnography*, 2(1): 103–5.

Chew, K. A. B., Greendeer, N. H. and Keliiaa, C. (2015), Claiming space: An autoethnographic study of indigenous graduate students engaged in language reclamation. *International Journal of Multicultural Education*, 17(2): 73–91.

Chiumento, A., Rahman, A. and Frith, L. (2020), Writing to template: Researchers' negotiation of procedural research ethics. *Social Science and Medicine*, 255. Available online: https://doi.org/10.1016/j.socscimed.2020.112980 (accessed 30 June 2020).

Clandinin, D. J., and Connelly, F. M. (2000), *Narrative Inquiry: Experience and Story in Qualitative Research*. San Francisco, CA: Jossey-Bass.

Clarke, S. P., and Wright, C. (2020), Tactical authenticity in the production of autoethnographic mad narratives. *Social Theory Health*, 18: 169–83.

Clayton, K. A. (2013), Looking beneath the surface: A critical reflection on ethical issues and reflexivity in a practitioner inquiry. *Reflective Practice*, 14(4): 506–18.

Clifford, J. (1988), On ethnographic authority. In J. Clifford (ed.), *The Predicament of Culture: Twentieth Century Ethnography, Literature and Art*, 21–54. Cambridge, MA: Harvard University Press.

Clough, P. (1999), 'Crisis of Schooling' and the 'Crisis of Representation': The story of Rob. *Qualitative Inquiry*, 5(3): 428–48.

Clough, P. (2002), *Narratives and Fictions in Educational Research*. Buckingham: Open University Press.

Clough, P. T. (2000), Comments on setting criteria for experimental writing. *Qualitative Inquiry*, 6(2): 278–91.

Clough, P., and Nutbrown, C. E. (2012), *Justifying Enquiry: A Students' Guide to Methodology*. London: Sage.

Collins, R. (1988), *Theoretical Sociology*. San Diego, CA: Harcourt Brace Jovanovich.

Connelly, M. F., and Clandinin, D. J. (1990), Stories of experience and narrative inquiry. *Educational Researcher*, 19(5): 2–14.

Conquergood, D. (1991), Rethinking ethnography: Towards a critical cultural politics. *Communication Monographs*, 58(2):179–94.

Cowling, S., and Cray, W. D. (2017), How to be omnipresent. *American Philosophical Quarterly*, 54(3): 223–34.

Cremin, H., Aryoubi, H., Hajir, B., Kurian, N. and Salem, H. (2021), Post-abyssal ethics in education research in settings of conflict and crisis: Stories from the field. *British Educational Research Journal*. Available online: https://doi.org/10.1002/berj.3712 (accessed 31 March 2021).

Cresser, J. D. (2009), *Quantum Physics Notes*. Macquarie Park: Macquarie University.

Crotty, M. (1998), *The Foundation of Social Research: Meaning and Perspectives in the Research Process*. London: Sage.

Csordas, T. J. (1994), *Embodiment and Experience: The Existential Ground of Culture and Self*. Cambridge: Cambridge University Press.

Csordas, T. J. (1999), Embodiment and cultural phenomenology. In G. Weiss and H. F. Haber (eds), *Perspectives on Embodiment: The Intersections of Nature and Culture*, 43–164. New York: Routledge.

Danaher, M., and Danaher, P. A. (2008), Situated ethics in investigating nongovernment organisations and showgrounds: Issues in researching Japanese environmental politics and Australian Traveller education. *International Journal of Pedagogies and Learning*, 4(1): 58–70.

Darwin, C. ([1872]1965), *The Expression of the Emotions in Man and Animals*. Chicago: University of Chicago Press.

Dauphinee, E. (2010), The ethics of autoethnography. *Review of International Studies*, 36(3): 799–818.

Dawson, P. (2014), Temporal practices: Time and ethnographic research in changing organizations. *Journal of Organizational Ethnography*, 3(2): 130–51.

de Freitas, E. and Paton, J. (2009), (De)facing the self: Poststructural disruptions of the autoethnographic text. *Qualitative Inquiry*, 15(3): 483–98.

Delamont, S. (2007), Arguments against autoethnography. *Qualitative Researcher*, 4: 2–4.

Delamont, S. (2009), The only honest thing: Autoethnography, reflexivity and small crises in fieldwork. *Ethnography and Education*, 4(1): 51–63.

Deleuze, G. and Guattari, F. (1987), *A Thousand Plateaus: Capitalism and Schizophrenia*. Minneapolis: University of Minnesota Press.

Denejkina, A. (2017), Exo-Autoethnography: An introduction. *Forum Qualitative Sozialforschung/Forum: Qualitative Social Research*, 18(3). Available online: https://doi.org/10.17169/fqs–18.3.2754 (accessed 12 September 2020).

Denzin, N. K. (1984), *On understanding Emotion*. San Francisco, CA: Jossey–Bass.

Denzin, N. K. (1989), *Interpretive Biography*. Newbury Park: Sage.

Denzin, N. K. (1997), *Interpretive Ethnography: Ethnographic Practices for the 21st Century*. Thousand Oaks, CA: Sage.

Denzin, N. K. (2003), *Performance Ethnography: Critical Pedagogy and the Politics of Culture*. London: Sage.

Denzin, N. K. (2006). Analytic autoethnography, or déjà vu all over again. *Journal of Contemporary Ethnography*, 35: 419–28.

Denzin, N.K. (2014), *Interpretive Autoethnography* (2nd edn). London: Sage.

Denzin, N. K. (2015), What is critical qualitative inquiry? In G. S. Cannella, M. Salazar Pérez and A. Pasque (eds), *Critical Qualitative Inquiry: Foundations and Futures*, 31–50. Walnut Creek, CA: Left Coast Press.

Denzin, N. (2018), *Performance Autoethnography*. London: Routledge.

Denzin, N. K., and Lincoln, Y. S. (2000), The seventh moment: Out of the past. In N. K. Denzin and Y. S. Lincoln (eds), *The Handbook of Qualitative Research* (2nd edn), 1047–965. Thousand Oaks, CA: Sage.

Denzin, N. K., and Lincoln, Y. S. (2005), Introduction: The discipline and practice of qualitative research. In N. K. Denzin and Y. S. Lincoln (eds), *The Sage Handbook of Qualitative Research* (3rd edn), 1–32. Thousand Oaks, CA: Sage.

Denzin, N. K., and Lincoln, Y. S. (2008), Introduction: The discipline and practice of qualitative research. In N. K. Denzin and Y. S. Lincoln (eds), *Handbook of Qualitative Research*, vol. 3, The Landscape of Qualitative Research, 1–43. Thousand Oaks, CA: Sage.

Derrida, J., Domingo, W., Hulbert, J., Ron, M. and M.-R. L. (1975), The purveyor of truth. *Yale French Studies*, (52): 31–113.

Derrida, J. (1976), *Of Grammatology*. Spivak, G. C. (trans.), Baltimore, MD: Johns Hopkins University Press.

Derrida, J. (1985), *The Ear of the Other: Otobiography, Transference, Translation: Texts and Discussions with Jacques Derrida*. New York: Schocken Books.

Dervin, F. (2015), Discourses of othering. In J. Tracy (ed.), *The International Encyclopedia of Language and Social Interaction*, 1–9. New York: John Wiley.

Dervin F., and Machart R. (2015), Introduction: Omnipresent culture, omnipotent cultures. In F. Dervin and R. Machart (eds), *Cultural Essentialism in Intercultural Relations: Frontiers of Globalization Series*, 1–14. London: Palgrave Macmillan.

Dewey, J. ([1934] 2005), *Art as Experience*. New York: Perigee.

Dillet, B. (2017), What is poststructuralism? *Political Studies Review*, 15(4): 516–27.

Dimijian, G. G. (2000), Evolving together: The biology of symbiosis, part 1. *Baylor University Medical Center Proceedings*, 13(3): 217–26.

Dirkx, J. M. (2001), The power of feelings: Emotion, imagination and the construction of meaning in adult learning. *New Directions for Adult and Continuing Education*, 89: 63–72.

Diversi, M., and Moreira, C. (2016), Performing betweener autoethnographies against persistent us/them essentializing: Leaning on a Freirean pedagogy of hope. *Qualitative Inquiry*, 22(7): 581–7.

Dixon, T. (2012), 'Emotion': The History of a keyword in crisis. *Emotion Review*, 4(4): 338–44.

Doloriert, C., and Sambrook, S. (2009), Ethical confessions of the 'I' of autoethnography: The student's dilemma. *Qualitative Research in Organizations and Management: An International Journal*, 4(1): 27–45.

Doloriert, C., and Sambrook, S. (2011), Accommodating an autoethnographic PhD: The tale of the thesis, the viva voce and the traditional business school. *Journal of Contemporary Ethnography*, 40(5): 582–615.

Doloriert, C., and Sambrook, S. (2012), Organisational autoethnography. *Journal of Organizational Ethnography*, 1(1): 83–95.

Dowling, M. (2006), Approaches to reflexivity in qualitative research. *Nurse Researcher*, 13(3): 7–21.

Duncan, M. (2004), Autoethnography: Critical appreciation of an emerging art. *International Journal of Qualitative Methods*, 3(4): 28–39.

Dunn, T. R., and Myers, B. W. (2020), Contemporary autoethnography is digital autoethnography: A proposal for maintaining methodological relevance in changing times. *Journal of Autoethnography*, 1(1): 43–59.

Durham, A., McFerguson, M., Sanders, S. and Woodruffe, A. (2020), The future of autoethnography is Black. *Journal of Autoethnography*, 1(3): 289–96.

Dwyer, S. C., and Buckle, J. L. (2009), The space between: On being an insider–outsider in qualitative research. *International Journal of Qualitative Methods*, 8(1): 54–63.

Dye, J. F., Schatz, I. M., Rosenberg, B. A. and Coleman, S. T. (2000), Constant comparison method: A kaleidoscope of data. *Qualitative Report*, 4(1): 1–10.

Edwards, J. (2021), Ethical autoethnography: Is it possible? *International Journal of Qualitative Methods*. Available online: https://doi.org/10.1177/1609406921995306 (accessed 10 July 2021).

Eguchi, S. (2020), A transnational queer of color vision: Toward the 'future' of autoethnography. *Journal of Autoethnography*, 1(3): 309–14.

Eisler, R. (2004), Pragmatopia: Revisioning human possibilities. *Tikkun*, 19(6): 44–6.

Elie, S. D. (2013), From ethnography to mesography: A praxis of inquiry for a postexotic anthropology. *Qualitative Inquiry*, 19(3): 219–31.

Ellingson, L. L. (2017), *Embodiment in Qualitative Research*. London, UK: Routledge.

Ellingson, L. L., and Ellis, C. (2008), Autoethnography as constructionist project. In J. A. Holsteinand and J. F. Gubrium (eds), *Handbook of Constructionist Research*, 445–65. New York: Guilford.

Ellis, C. (1997), Evocative autoethnography: Writing emotionally about our lives. In W. G. Tierney and Y. S. Lincoln (eds), *Representation and the Text: Re-framing the Narrative Voice*, 115–42. Albany: State University of New York Press.

Ellis, C. (2004), *The Ethnographic I: A Methodological Novel about Autoethnography*. Walnut Creek, CA: AltaMira Press.

Ellis, C. (2007), Telling secrets, revealing lives: Relational ethics in research with intimate others. *Qualitative Inquiry*, 13(1): 3–29.

Ellis, C. (2013a), Carrying torch for autoethnography. In S. Holman Jones, T. E. Adams and C. Ellis (eds), *Handbook of Autoethnography*, 9–12. Walnut Creek, CA: Left Coast Press.

Ellis, C. (2013b), Crossing the rabbit hole: Autoethnographic life review. *Qualitative Inquiry*, 19(1): 35–45.

Ellis, C. (2017), Compassionate research: Interviewing and storytelling from a relational ethics of care. In I. Goodson, P. Sikes and M. Andrews (eds), *The Routledge International Handbook on Narrative and Life History*, 431–45. New York: Routledge.

Ellis, C. (2020), *Revision: Autoethnographic Reflections on Life and Work*. New York: Routledge.

Ellis, C., Adams, T. E. and Bochner, A. (2010), Autoethnography: An overview. *Forum: Qualitative Social Research*, 12(1): 273–90.

Ellis, C., and Bochner, A. (1996), *Composing Ethnography: Alternative Forms of Qualitative Writing*. Walnut Creek, CA: AltaMira.

Ellis, C., and Bochner, A. (2000), Auto-ethnography, personal narrative, reflexivity. In K. Denzin and Y. Lincoln (eds), *The Handbook of Qualitative Research* (2nd edn), 733–67. Thousand Oaks, CA: Sage.

Ellis, C., and Bochner, A. (2006), Analyzing analytic auto-ethnography: An autopsy. *Journal of Contemporary Ethnography*, 35(4): 429–49.

Ellis, C., and Bochner, A. (2016), *Evocative Autoethnography. Writing Lives and Telling Stories*. New York: Routledge.

Ellis, C., and Bochner, A. (2017), Foreword. In S. L. Pensoneau-Conway, T. E. Adams and D. M. Bolen (eds), *Doing Autoethnography*, vii–ix. Rotterdam: Sense.

Ellis, C., Bochner, A., Denzin, N., Lincoln, Y., Morse, J., Pelias, R. and Richardson, L. (2008), Talking and thinking about qualitative research. *Qualitative Inquiry*, 14(2): 254–84.

Ellis, C., and Calafell, B. M. (2020), Toward praxis: Interrogating social justice within autoethnography. *Journal of Autoethnography*, 1(2): 203–7.

Etherington, K. (2004), Research methods: Reflexivities – roots, meanings, dilemmas, *Counselling and Psychotherapy Research*, 4(2): 46–7.

Etherington, K. (2007a), Ethical research in reflexive relationships. *Qualitative Inquiry*, 13(5): 599–616.

Etherington, K. (2007b), *Trauma, Drug Misuse and Transforming Identities: A Life Story Approach*. London: Jessica Kingsley.

Ettorre, E. (2017), Feminist autoethnography, gender and drug use: 'Feeling about' empathy while 'storying the I'. *Contemporary Drug Problems*, 44(4): 356–74.

Ettorre, E. (2019), *Autoethnography as Feminist Method*. New York: Routledge.

Fabian, J. ([1983] 2006), *Time and The Other: How Anthropology Makes Its Object*. New York: Columbia University Press.

Faulkner, S. L. (2017), Poetry is politics: An autoethnographic poetry manifesto. *International Review of Qualitative Research*, 10(1): 89–96.

Ferdinand, R. (2022), *An Autoethnography of African American Motherhood: Things I Tell My Daughter (Writing Lives: Ethnographic Narratives*. New York: Routledge.

Fitz, J. (1999), Reflections on the field of educational management studies. *Educational Management and Administration*, 27(3): 313–21.

Fletcher, E. (2021), Navigating procedural ethics and ethics in practice in outdoor studies: an example from sail training. *Journal of Adventure Education and Outdoor Learning*. Available online: https://www.tandfonline.com/doi/abs/10.1080/14729 679.2021.1902826?journalCode=raol20 (accessed 10 April 2021).

Fletcher, J. ([1966] 1997), *Situation Ethics: The New Morality*. Louisville, KY: Westminster John Knox Press.

Fontana, A., and Frey, J. H. (1998), Interviewing: The art of science. In N. K. Denzin and Y. S. Lincoln (eds), *Collecting and Interpreting Qualitative Materials*, 47–78. Thousand Oaks, CA: Sage.

Foucault, M. (1972a), Two lectures. In C. Gordon (ed.), *Power/knowledge: Selected Interviews and Other Writings, 1972–1977*, 79–108. New York: Pantheon Books.

Foucault, M. (1972b), *The Archaeology of Knowledge and the Discourse on Language*. New York: Pantheon Books.

Foucault, M. (1977), Truth and power. In C. Gordon (ed.), *Power/Knowledge: Selected Interviews and Other Writings, 1972–1977*, 109–34. New York: Pantheon Books.

Foucault, M. (1978), *The History of Sexuality. Volume I: An Introduction*. New York: Pantheon Books.

188 *References*

Foucault, M. (1986), Technologies of the self. In L. H. Martin, H. Gutmanand and
P. H. Hutton (eds), *Technologies of the Self. A Seminar with Michel Foucault*, 16–49.
London: Tavistock.
Foucault, M. (1991), *Discipline and Punish. The Birth of the Prison*. New York:
Vintage Books.
Foucault, M. (1993), About the beginning of the hermeneutics of the self: Two lectures
at Dartmouth. *Political Theory*, 21(2): 198–227.
Fox, E. (2018), Perspectives from affective science on understanding the nature of
emotion. *Brain and Neuroscience Advances*, 2: 1–8.
Freeman, J. (2015), Trying not to lie and failing: Autoethnography, memory,
malleability. *Qualitative Report*, 20(6): 918–29.
Freistadt, J. (2011), Understanding others' experience: Phenomenology and/beyond
violence. *Journal of Theoretical and Philosophical Criminology Special Edition*, 1: 1–42.
Fricker, M. (2007), *Epistemic Injustice: Power and the Ethics of Knowing*. Oxford: Oxford
University Press.
Friesen, P., Yusof, A. N. M. and Sheehan, M. (2019), Should the decisions of
institutional review boards be consistent? *Ethics and Human Research*, 41: 2–14.
Gabriel, M. (2015), *Why the World Does Not Exist*. Cambridge: Polity Press.
Gale, K. (2020), Writing in immanence: A creative-relational doing? *Departures in
Critical Qualitative Research*, 9(2): 92–102.
Gale, K., and Wyatt, J. (2019), Autoethnography and activism: Movement, intensity and
potential. *Qualitative Inquiry*, 25(6): 566–8.
Gannon, S. (2013), Sketching subjectivities. In S. Holman Jones, T. E. Adams and
C. Ellis (eds), *Handbook of Autoethnography*, 228–43. Walnut Creek, CA: Left
Coast Press.
Gannon, S. (2017), Autoethnography. *Oxford Research Encyclopedia of Education*.
Available online: https://oxfordre.com/education/view/10.1093/acrefore/9780190264
093.001.0001/acrefore-9780190264093-e-71 (accessed 15 April 2020).
Garratt, D. (2014), Psychoanalytic-autoethnography: Troubling natural bodybuilding.
Qualitative Inquiry, 21(4): 343–53.
Geertz, C. (1973), *The Interpretation of Cultures*. New York: Basic Books.
Geertz, C. (1983), 'From the native's point of view': On the nature of anthropological
understanding. In C. Geertz, *Local Knowledge: Further Essays in Interpretive
Anthropology*, 55–72. New York: Basic Books.
Gergen, K. J. (1991), *The Saturated Self*. New York: Basic Books.
Gergen, K.J. (2000), Qualitative inquiry: tensions and transformations. In N. K. Denzin
and Y. S. Lincoln (eds), *The Handbook Of Qualitative Research* (2nd edn), 1025–46.
Thousand Oaks, CA: Sage.
Giddens, A. (1990), *The Consequences of Modernity*. Cambridge: Polity Press.
Gill, M., Gill, D. and Roulet, T. (2018), Constructing trustworthy historical
narratives: Criteria, principles and techniques. *British Journal of Management*,
29(1): 191–205.

Gillies, D. (2011), Agile bodies: A new imperative in neoliberal governance. *Journal of Education Policy*, 26(2): 207–23.

Gillies, D. (2013), *Educational Leadership and Michel Foucault*. Abington: Routledge.

Goldschmidt, W. (1977), Anthropology and the coming crisis: An autoethnographic appraisal. *American Anthropologist*, 79: 293–308.

Goodall, H. L. (2005), Narrative inheritance: A nuclear family with toxic secrets. *Qualitative Inquiry*, 11: 492–513.

Goodall, H. L. (2006), *A Need to Know: The Clandestine History of a CIA Family*. Walnut Creek, CA: Left Coast Press.

Goode, J. (2019), *Clever Girls: Autoethnographies of Class, Gender and Ethnicity*. Loughborough: Palgrave Macmillan.

Goodson, I. F. (2014), Defining the Self through autobiographical memory. In I. F. Goodson and S. Gill (eds), *Critical Narrative as Pedagogy*, 123–46. London: Bloomsbury.

Goodwin, D., Pope, C., Mort, M. and Smith, A. (2003), Ethics and ethnography: An experiential account. *Qualitative Health Research*, 13(4): 567–77.

Graci, M. E., and Fivush, R. (2017), Narrative meaning making, attachment and psychological growth and stress. *Journal of Social and Personal Relationships*, 34(4): 486–509.

Grant, A. (2010), Autoethnographic ethics and rewriting the fragmented self. *Journal of Psychiatric and Mental Health Nursing*, 17: 111–16.

Grant, A. (2018), Voice, ethics and the best of autoethnographic intentions (or Writers, readers and the spaces in–between). In L. Turner, N. P. Short, A. Grant and T. E. Adams (eds), *International Perspectives on Autoethnographic Research and Practice*, 107–22. London: Routledge.

Grant, A. (2019), Dare to be a wolf: Embracing autoethnography in nurse educational research. *Nurse Education Today*, 82(1): 88–92.

Grant, A. (2020), Autoethnography. In K. Aranda (ed.), *Critical Qualitative Research in Healthcare: Exploring the Philosophies, Politics and Practices*, 159–76. London: Routledge.

Grant, A., Short, N. P. and Turner, L. (2013), Introduction: Storying life and lives. In N. P. Short, L. Turner and A. Grant (eds), *Contemporary British Auto-ethnography*. Studies in Professional Life and Work, 1–16. Rotterdam: Sense.

Grant, A., and Young, S. (2022) Troubling tolichism in several voices: Resisting epistemic violence in creative analytical and critical autoethnographic practice. *Journal of Autoethnography* (in press).

Grant, A. J., and Zeeman, L. (2012), Whose story is it? An autoethnography concerning narrative identity. *Qualitative Report*, 17(36): 1–12.

Gray, J. H., and Densten, I. L. (2007), How leaders woo followers in the romance of leadership. *Applied Psychology: An International Review*, 56(4): 558–81.

Grbich, C. F. (2004), *New Approaches in Social Research*. London: Sage.

Greenough, C. (2017), Queering fieldwork in religion: Exploring life-stories with non-normative Christians. *Fieldwork in Religion*, 12(1): 8–26.

Griffin, R. (2012), I AM an angry Black woman: Black feminist autoethnography, voice and resistance. *Women's Studies in Communication*, 35: 138–57.

Griffin, S. N., and Griffin, N. (2019), A millennial methodology? Autoethnographic research in do-it-yourself (DIY) punk and activist communities. *Forum Qualitative Sozialforschung/Forum: Qualitative Social Research*, 20(3). Available online: https://www.qualitative-research.net/index.php/fqs/article/view/3206 (accessed 10 May 2021).

Grosz, E. (1989), *Sexual Subversions. Three French Feminists*. St. Leonards: Allen and Unwin.

Grosz, E. (2001), *Architecture from the Outside: Essays on Virtual and Real Space*. Cambridge, MA: MIT Press.

Guba, E. G., and Lincoln, Y. S. (1989), *Fourth Generation Evaluation*. Newbury Park: Sage.

Guba, E. G., and Lincoln, Y. S. (2005), Paradigmatic controversies, contradictions and emerging confluences. In N. K. Denzin and Y. S. Lincoln, *The Sage Handbook of Qualitative Research* (3rd edn), 191–216. Thousand Oaks, CA: Sage.

Guillemin, M., and Gillam, L. (2004), Ethics, reflexivity and 'ethically important moments' in research. *Qualitative Inquiry*, 10(2): 261–80.

Guttorm, H. E. (2012), Becoming-(a)-paper, or an article undone: (Post-)knowing and writing (again), nomadic and so messy. *Qualitative Inquiry*, 18(7): 595–605.

Hall, L. (2014), Developing an ethics of relational responsibility: Locating the researcher within the research and allowing connection, encounter and collective concern to shape the intercultural research space. *Ethics and Education*, 9(3): 329–39.

Hamann, J., and Suckert, L. (2018), Temporality in discourse: Methodological challenges and a suggestion for a quantified qualitative approach. *Forum Qualitative Sozialforschung/Forum: Qualitative Social Research*, 19(2). Available online: https://www.qualitative-research.net/index.php/fqs/article/view/2954/4215 (accessed 11 February 2021).

Hamilton, M. L., and Pinnegar, S. (1998), Conclusion: The value and the promise of self-study. In M. L. Hamilton (ed.), *Reconceptualizing Teaching Practice: Self-Study in Teacher Education*, 235–46. London: Falmer Press.

Hamilton, M. L., and Pinnegar, S. (2014), Self-study of teacher education practices as a pedagogy for teacher educator professional development. In C. J. Craig and L. Orland-Barak (eds), *International Teacher Education: Promising Pedagogies*, 137–52. Bingley: Emerald.

Hamilton, M. L., Smith, L. and Worthington, K. (2008), Fitting the methodology with the research: An exploration of narrative, self-study and auto-ethnography. *Studying Teacher Education*, 4(1): 17–28.

Hammersley, M. (2008), *Questioning Qualitative Inquiry: Critical Essays*. London: Sage.

Hammersley, M. (2009), Against the ethicists: On the evils of ethical regulation. *International Journal of Social Research Methodology*, 12(3): 211–25.

Hammersley, M., and Atkinson, P. (2007), *Ethnography. Principles in Practice* (3rd edn). New York: Routledge.

Hamood, T. (2016), An autoethnographic account of a PhD student's journey towards establishing a research identity and understanding issues surrounding validity in educational research. *Bridge: Journal of Educational Research-Informed Practice,* 3(1): 41–60.

Harris, A., and Holman Jones, S. (2019), Activist affect. *Qualitative Inquiry,* 25(6): 563–5.

Hayano, D. (1979), Auto-ethnography: Paradigms, problems and prospects. *Human Organization,* 38(1): 99–103.

Hayes, C., and Fulton, J. A. (2015), Autoethnography as a method of facilitating critical reflexivity for professional doctorate students. *Journal of Learning Development in Higher Education,* 8. Available online: https://journal.aldinhe.ac.uk/index.php/jldhe/article/view/237 (accessed 16 October 2020).

Hays, D. G., and McKibben, W. B. (2021), Promoting rigorous research: Generalizability and qualitative research. *Journal of Counseling and Development,* 99: 178–88.

Heath, M., Darkwah, A., Beoku-Betts, J. and Purkayastha, B. (eds) (2022), *Global Feminist Autoethnographies During COVID-19: Displacements and Disruptions (Routledge Advances in Feminist Studies and Intersectionality).* New York: Routledge.

Heidegger, M. (1962), *Being Arid Time.* Translated by John Macquarie and Edward Robinson. Oxford: Blackwell.

Heider, F. (1958), *The Psychology of Interpersonal Relations.* New York: Wiley.

Heider, K. G. (1975), What do people do? Dani auto-ethnography. *Journal of Anthropological Research,* 31(1): 3–17.

Henn, M., Weinstein, M. and Foard, N. (2014), *A Critical Introduction to Social Research* (2nd edn). London: Sage.

Henriksen, A. K., and Schliehe, A. (2020), Ethnography of young people in confinement: On subjectivity, positionality and situated ethics in closed space. *Qualitative Research,* 20(6): 837–53.

Hermans, H. J. M. (2001), The dialogical self: Toward a theory of personal and cultural positioning. *Culture and Psychology,* 7(3): 243–81.

Herrmann, A. F. (2020). *The Routledge International Handbook of Organizational Autoethnography.* New York: Routledge

Herrmann, A. (2021). The future of autoethnographic criteria. *International Review of Qualitative Research,* 0(0): 1–11.

Heywood, R. G. (2020), Autoethnography for extraterrestrials. *Journal of Autoethnography,* 1(2): 175–85.

Hirsch, E., and Stewart, C. (2005), Introduction: Ethnographies of historicity. *History and Anthropology,* 16(3): 261–74.

Hochschild, A. R. (1979), Emotion work, feeling rules and social structure. *American Journal of Sociology,* 85(3): 551–75.

Hokkanen, S. (2017), Analyzing personal embodied experiences: Autoethnography, feelings and fieldwork. *Translation and Interpreting,* 9: 24–35.

Holman Jones, S. (2005), Autoethnography: Making the personal political. In
N. K. Denzin and Y. S. Lincoln (eds), *The Sage Handbook of Qualitative Research*
(3rd edn), 763–91. Thousand Oaks, CA: Sage.

Holman Jones, S. (2007), Autoethnography. In G. Ritzer (ed.), *The Blackwell
Encyclopedia of Sociology*, 230–2. New York: Wiley.

Holman Jones, S. (2016), Living bodies of thought: The 'critical' in critical
autoethnography. *Qualitative Inquiry*, 22(4): 228–37.

Holt, N. L. (2003), Representation, legitimation and autoethnography: An
autoethnographic writing story. *International Journal of Qualitative Methods*,
2(1): 18–28.

Hordvik, M., MacPhail, A. and Ronglan, L. T. (2020), Developing a pedagogy of teacher
education using self-study: A rhizomatic examination of negotiating learning and
practice. *Teaching and Teacher Education*, 88. Available online: https://www.scienc
edirect.com/science/article/pii/S0742051X19304299 (accessed 17 March 2021).

Horkheimer, M., and Adorno, T. ([1944] 2002), *Dialectic of Enlightenment: Philosophical
Fragments*. Stanford, CA: Stanford University Press.

Hospers, J. ([1956] 1997), *An Introduction to Philosophical Analysis* (4th edn). London:
Routledge.

Houston, J. (2007), Indigenous autoethnography: Formulating our knowledge, our way.
Australian Journal of Indigenous Education, 36(1): 45–50.

Howe, K. R. (2001), Qualitative educational research: The philosophical issues. In
V. Richardson (ed.), *Handbook of Research on Teaching* (4th edn), 201–8.
Washington, DC: American Educational Research Association.

Hughes, S. (2020), My skin is unqualified: An autoethnography of black scholar-
activism for predominantly white education. *International Journal of Qualitative
Studies in Education*, 33(2): 151–65.

Hughes, S., and Pennington, J. (2017), Histories and applications of autoethnography as
critical social research. In S. Hughes and J. Pennington (eds), *Autoethnography*, 1–3.
Thousand Oaks, CA: Sage.

Hunter, A. (2020), Snapshots of selfhood: Curating academic identity through visual
autoethnography. *International Journal for Academic Development*, 25(4): 310–23.

Husserl, E. (1991), *On the Phenomenology of the Consciousness of Internal Time*.
Dordrecht: Kluwer.

Inman, R. (2017), Omnipresence and the location of the immaterial. *Oxford Studies in
Philosophy of Religion*, 8: 167–206.

Iosefo, F., Holman Jones, S. and Harris, A. (2021), *Wayfinding and Critical
Autoethnography*. New York: Routledge.

Jackson M. (2013), *The Wherewithal of Life: Ethics, Migration and the Question of Well-
Being*. Berkeley: University of California Press.

James, W. (1890), *The Principles of Psychology* (vol. 1), New York: Henry Holt.

Jameson, F. (1991), *Postmodernism or the Cultural Logic of Late Capitalism*. Durham,
NC: Duke University Press.

Johnson, R. (2018), *Embodied Social Justice*. London: Routledge.

Johnson, P., and Duberley, J. (2003), Reflexivity in Management Research. *Journal of Management Studies*, 40: 1279–303.

Johnson, A., and LeMaster, B. (eds) (2020), *Gender Futurity, Intersectional Autoethnography*. New York: Routledge.

Johnston, D., and Strong, T. (2008), Reconciling voices in writing an autoethnographic thesis. *International Journal of Qualitative Methods*, 1: 47–61.

Karnieli–Miller, O., Strier, R. and Pessach, L. (2009), Power relations in qualitative research. *Qualitative Health Research*, 19(2): 279–89.

Keefer, J. M. (2010), Autoethnographer communities of practice. In L. Dirckinck-Holmfeld, V. Hodgson, L. Jones, M. de Laat and T. Ryberg (eds), *Proceedings of the 7th International Conference on Networked Learning*, 207–14. Available online: https://www.academia.edu/30564149/Autoethnographer_Communities_of_Practice (accessed 17 July 2020).

Keightley, E. (2010), Remembering research: Memory and methodology in the social sciences. *International Journal of Social Research Methodology*, 13(1): 55–70.

Kelley, A. (2014), Layers of consciousness: An autoethnographic study of the comprehensive exam process. *International Journal of Doctoral Studies*, 9: 347–60.

Kensinger, E. A., and Murray, B. D. (2012), Emotional memory. In N. M. Seel (ed.), *Encyclopedia of the Sciences of Learning*, 1128–31. Boston: Springer.

Kleres, J. (2011), Emotions and narrative analysis: A methodological approach. *Journal for the Theory of Social Behaviour*, 41: 182–202.

Klevan, T., and Grant, A. (2020), Performing wild time: Workshopping friendship as critical authoethnographic paraversity method. *Critical Education*, 11(1): 1–18.

Knight, D. (2014), Mushrooms, knowledge exchange and polytemporality in Kalloni, Greek Macedonia. *Food, Culture and Society*, 17(2): 183–201.

Koopman, W. J., Watling, C. J. and LaDonna, K. A. (2020), Autoethnography as a strategy for engaging in reflexivity. *Global Qualitative Nursing Research*. Available online: https://journals.sagepub.com/doi/full/10.1177/2333393620970508 (accessed 1 August 2021).

Kracen, A. C., and Baird, K. (2018), Exploring influence and autoethnography: A dialogue between two counselling psychologists. *European Journal of Counselling Psychology*, 6(1): 162–73.

Kristeva, J. (1982), *Powers of Horror: An Essay on Abjection*. New York: Columbia University Press.

Kross, E., and Grossmann, I. (2012), Boosting wisdom: Distance from the self enhances wise reasoning, attitudes and behavior. *Journal of Experimental Psychology: General*, 141(1): 43–48.

Kupers, W. (2015), Embodied responsive ethical practice the contribution of Merleau-Ponty for a corporeal ethics in organizations. *Electronic Journal of Business Ethics and Organization Studies*, 20 (1): 30–45.

LaBoskey, V. K. (2004), The methodology of self-study and its theoretical underpinnings. In J. J. Loughran, M. L. Hamilton, V. K. LaBoskey and T. Russell (eds), *International Handbook of Self-Study of Teaching Practices*, 817–69. Dordrecht: Kluwer Academic.

Lambek, M. (2012), Ethics out of the ordinary. In R. Fardon, O. Harris, T. Marchand, C. Shore, V. Strang, R. Wilson and M. Nuttall (eds), *The Sage Handbook of Social Anthropology*, vol. 2, 140–52. Thousand Oaks, CA: Sage.

Langellier, K. (1998), Voiceless bodies, bodiless voices: The future of personal narrative performance. In S. J. Dailey (ed.), *The Future of Performance Studies: Visions and Revisions*, 207–13. Annandale: National Communication Association.

Lapadat, J. C. (2017), Ethics in autoethnography and collaborative autoethnography. *Qualitative Inquiry*, 23(8): 589–560.

Larkin, P. J., de Casterle, B. D. and Schotsmans, P. (2008), A relational ethical dialogue with research ethics committees. *Nursing Ethics*, 15(2): 234–42.

Lather, P. (1986a), Issues of validity in openly ideological research: Between a rock and a soft place. *Interchange*, 17(4): 63–84.

Lather, P. (1986b), Research as praxis. *Harvard Educational Review*, 56: 257–77.

Lather, P. (1993), Validity after poststructuralism. *Sociological Quarterly*, 34(4): 673–93.

Lather, P. (1996), Troubling clarity: The politics of accessible language. *Harvard Educational Review*, 66(3): 525–45.

Lather, P. (1997), Drawing the line at angels: Working the ruins of feminist ethnography. *International Journal of Qualitative Studies in Education*, 10(3): 285–304.

Lather, P. (1998), Critical pedagogy and its complicities: A praxis of stuck places. *Educational Theory*, 48(4): 487–97.

Lather, P. (2001), Postmodernism, post-structuralism and post (critical) ethnography: Of ruins, aporias and angels. In P. Atkinson, A. Coffey, S. Delamont, J. Lofland and L. Lofland (eds), *Handbook of Ethnography*, 477–92. London: Sage.

Lather, P. (2006), Paradigm proliferation as a good thing to think with: Teaching research in education as a wild profusion. *International Journal of Qualitative Studies in Education*, 19(1): 35–57.

Lavie, S., and Swedenburg, T. (1996), Between and among the boundaries of culture: Bridging text and lived experience in the third timespace. *Cultural Studies*, 10(1): 154–79.

Leavy, P. (2015), *Method Meets Art: Arts-Based Research Practice* (2nd edn). New York: Guilford Press.

Le Blanc, A. M. (2017), Disruptive meaning-making: Qualitative data analysis software and postmodern pastiche. *Qualitative Inquiry*, 23(10): 789–98.

Le Roux, C. S. (2017), Exploring rigour in autoethnographic research. International *Journal of Social Research Methodology*, 20(2): 195–207.

Lee, J. (1999), The utility of a strategic postmodernism. *Sociological Perspectives*, 42(4): 739–53.

Leigh, J., and Brown, N. (2021), *Embodied Inquiry: Research Methods*. London: Bloomsbury.

Levi-Strauss, C. (1962), *The Savage Mind*. London: Weidenfeld and Nicolson.

Levinas, E. (1969), *Totality and Infinity: An Essay on Exteriority*. Pittsburgh: Duquesne University Press.

Lewis, P. L. (2011), Storytelling as research/research as storytelling. *Qualitative Inquiry*, 17(6): 505–10.

Lincoln, Y. S., and Guba, E. G. (1985), *Naturalistic Inquiry*. Beverly Hills: Sage.

Lofland, J. (1995), Analytic ethnography: Features, failings and futures. *Journal of Contemporary Ethnography*, 24(1): 30–67.

Long, S., and Manley, J. (eds) (2019), *Social Dreaming: Philosophy, Research, Theory and Practice*. London: Routledge.

Lord, R. G., Foti, R. J. and Philips, J. S. (1982), A theory of leadership categorization. In J. G. Hunt, U. Sekaranand and C. Schriesheim (eds), *Leadership: Beyond Establishment Views*, 104–21. Carbondale: Southern Illinois University Press.

Low, K. E. Y. (2015), The sensuous city: Sensory methodologies in urban ethnographic research. *Ethnography*, 16(3): 295–312.

Low, S. (2017), *Spatializing Culture*. London: Routledge.

Lucas G. (2005), *The Archeology of Time*. London: Routledge.

Lyotard, J. F. (1984), *The Postmodern Condition*. Minneapolis: University of Minnesota Press.

Macbeth, D. (2001), On 'Reflexivity' in qualitative research: Two readings and a third. *Qualitative Inquiry*, 7(1): 35–68.

Mackinlay, E. (2022). *Writing Feminist Autoethnography: In Love With Theory, Words, and the Language of Women Writers*. New York: Routledge.

MacLure, M. (2003), *Discourse in Educational and Social Research*. Maidenhead: Open University Press.

Madison, D. S. (2006), The dialogic performative in critical ethnography. *Text and Performance Quarterly*, 26(4): 320–4.

Madison, D. S. (2010), *Acts of Activism: Human Rights as Radical Performance*. Cambridge: Cambridge University Press.

Madison, D. S. (2012), *Critical Ethnography: Method, Ethics and Performance* (2nd edn). Los Angeles: Sage.

Maitlis, S., and Christianson, M. (2014), Sensemaking in organizations: Taking stock and moving forward. *Academy of Management Annals*, 8: 57–125.

Malinowski, B. (1967), *A Diary in the Strict Sense of the Term*. New York: Harcourt, Brace and World.

Manning, J., and Adams, T. (2015), Popular cultural studies and autoethnography: An essay on method. *Popular Culture Studies Journal*, 3: 187–211.

Marcus, G. (1995), Ethnography in/of the world system: The emergence of multi-sited ethnography. *Annual Review of Anthropology*, 24: 95–117.

Marowitz, C. (1991), *Recycling Shakespeare*. London: Applause Theatre Book.

Masi, M. (2019), *Quantum Physics: An Overview of a Weird World: A Primer on the Conceptual Foundations of Quantum Physics*. Scotts Valley: CreateSpace.

Martin, J. P., and Garza, C. (2020), Centering the marginalized student's voice through autoethnography: Implications for engineering education research. *Studies in Engineering Education*, 1(1): 1–19.

Marx, S., Pennington, J. and Chang, H. (2017), Critical autoethnography in pursuit of educational equity: Introduction to the IJME Special Issue. *International Journal of Multicultural Education*, 19(1): 1–6.

Massey, D. B. (2005), *For Space*. London: Sage.

Matus, C. (2019), Poststructural temporalities in school ethnography. *Oxford Research Encyclopedia of Education*. Available online: https://oxfordre.com/education/view/10.1093/acrefore/9780190264093.001.0001/acrefore–9780190264093–e–339 (accessed 28 July 2020).

Maydell, E. (2010), Methodological and analytical dilemmas in autoethnographic research. *Journal of Research Practice*, 6(1): 1–13.

Maxwell, J. A. (2006), Literature reviews of and for educational research: A commentary on Boote and Beile's 'Scholars Before Researchers'. *Educational Researcher*, 35(9): 28–31.

Mazzei, L. (1997), Inhabited silences in feminist poststructural inquiry. *Paper presented at the Annual Meeting of the American Education Research Association*, Chicago. Available online: https://files.eric.ed.gov/fulltext/ED411217.pdf (accessed 12 May 2020).

Mazzei, L. (2003), Inhabited silences: In pursuit of a muffled subtext. *Qualitative Inquiry*, 9(3): 355–68.

Mazzei, L. A. (2004), Silent listenings: Deconstructive practices in discourse-based research. *Educational Researcher*, 33(2): 26–34.

Mazzei, L. A. (2007), Toward a problematic of silence in action research. *Educational Action Research*, 15(4): 631–42.

Mazur, J. (2020), *The Clock Mirage: Our Myth of Measured Time*. Yale: Yale University Press.

McGuire, J. E., and Slowik, E. (2012), Newton's ontology of omnipresence and infinite space. *Oxford Studies in Early Modern Philosophy*, 6: 279–308.

McIlveen, P. (2008), Autoethnography as a method for reflexive research and practice in vocational psychology. *Australian Journal of Career Development*, 17(2): 13–20.

McKenna, T., and Woods, D. (2012), An indigenous conversation: Artful ethnography: A pre-colonised collaborative research method? *Creative Approaches to Research*, 5(3): 75–88.

Mclaren, P. (1992), Collisions with otherness: 'traveling' theory, post-colonial criticism and the politics of ethnographic practice the mission of the wounded ethnographer. *International Journal of Qualitative Studies in Education*, 5(1): 77–92.

McMillan, C., and Ramirez, H. E. (2016), Autoethnography as therapy for trauma. *Women and Therapy*, 39(3): 432–58.

McNeill, P. M. (2014), Research ethics review and the bureaucracy. *Monash Bioethics Review*, 21: 72–3.

Mead, G. H. (1934), *Mind, Self and Society*. Chicago: University of Chicago Press.

Medford, K. (2006), Caught with a fake ID: Ethical questions about slippage in autoethnography. *Qualitative Inquiry*, 12(5): 853–64.

Meindl, J. R., Ehrlich, S. B. and Dukerich, J. M. (1985), The romance of leadership. *Administrative Science Quarterly*, 30(1): 78–102.

Merleau-Ponty, M. (1962), *Phenomenology of Perception*. Atlantic Highlands: Humanities Press.

Merton, R. K. (1948), The self-fulfilling prophecy. *Antioch Review*, 8(2): 193–210.

Mezirow, J. (1991), *Transformative Dimensions in Adult Learning*. San Francisco, CA: Jossey-Bass.

Miles, M. B., and Huberman, A. M. (1994), *Qualitative Data Analysis: An Expanded Sourcebook*. Thousand Oak, CA: Sage.

Miller, C. (2002), Foreword. In P. Sipiora and J. S. Baumlin (eds), *Rhetoric and Kairos: Essays in History, Theory and Praxis*, xi–xiii. New York: State University of New York Press.

Miller, G. T. (1994). *Living in the Environment* (9th edn). Belmont: Wadsworth.

Miller, J. M. (2008), Otherness. In L. M. Given (ed.), *The SAGE Encyclopedia of Qualitative Research Methods*, 587–98. Thousand Oaks, CA: Sage.

Mills, C. W. (1959), *The Sociological Imagination*. New York: Oxford University Press.

Mizzi, R. (2010), Unraveling researcher subjectivity through multivocality in autoethnography. *Journal of Research Practice*, 6(1): 1–13.

Moen, T. (2006), Reflections on the narrative research approach. *International Journal of Qualitative Methods*, 1: 56–69.

Mooney, R. L. (1957), The researcher himself. In *Research for Curriculum Improvement: 1957 Yearbook*, 154–86. Washington, DC: Association for Supervision and Curriculum Development.

Moors, A. (2017), On autoethnography. *Ethnography*, 18(3): 387–9.

Morrison, B. (2015), Too much information? The writers who feel the need to reveal all. *Guardian*, 27 November 2015. Available online: https://www.theguardian.com/books/2015/nov/27/confessional–writing–memoirs–biography–writers–feel–need–reveal–all (accessed 20 August 2020).

Morse, J. M. (2002), Writing my own experience. *Qualitative Health Research*, 12: 1159–60.

Morse, J. M. (2018), Reframing rigor in qualitative inquiry. In N. K. Denzin and Y. S. Lincoln (eds), *The Sage Handbook of Qualitative Inquiry* (5th edn), 796–817. Thousand Oaks, CA: Sage.

Muncey, T. (2010), *Creating Autoethnographies*. Los Angeles: Sage.

Munn, N. (1992), The cultural anthropology of time: A critical essay. *Annual Review of Anthropology*, 21: 93–123.

Murphy, P. D., and Kraidy, M. M. (2003), International communication, ethnography and the challenge of globalization. *Communication Theory*, 13(3): 304–23.

Nash, R. J. (2004), *Liberating Scholarly Writing: The Power of Personal Narrative.* New York: Teachers College Press.

Natoli, J. (2001), *Postmodern Journeys: Film and Culture.* Albany: State University of New York Press.

Neufeld, M. (1993), Reflexivity and international relations theory. *Millennium: Journal of International Studies*, 22(1): 53–76.

Nielsen, H. B. (2017), Temporality in methods. In H. B. Nielsen (ed.), *Feeling Gender: A Generational and Psychosocial Approach*, 45–64. London: Palgrave Macmillan.

Nietzsche, F. (1910), *Human, All Too Human.* Edinburgh: Morrison and Gibb.

Norris, J. (2008), Collage. In L. M. Given (ed.), *The SAGE Encyclopedia of Qualitative Research Methods*, 94–7. Thousand Oaks, CA: Sage.

Oatley, K., and Jenkins, J. M. (1992), Human emotions: Function and dysfunction. *Annual Review of Psychology*, 43: 55–85.

O'Donoghue, T. (2007), *Planning Your ualitative Research Project: An Introduction to Interpretivist Research in Education.* Abington: Routledge.

O'Hara, S. (2018), Autoethnography: The science of writing your lived experience. *Health Environments Research and Design Journal*, 11(4): 14–17.

Onwuegbuzie, A. J., and Frels, R. (2016), *Seven Steps to a Comprehensive Literature Review: A Multimodal and Cultural Approach.* London: Sage.

Orelus, P. W. (2020), What It Means Being Black in the Ivy Halls of White America. In P. W. Orelus, *Living in the Shadows: A Biographical Account of Racial, Class and Gender Inequities in the Americas*, 67–87. Leiden: Brill Sense.

O'Reilly, K. (2009), Reflexivity. In K. O'Reilly (ed.), *Key Concepts in Ethnography*, 187–93. London: Sage.

Osei, K. (2019), Fashioning my garden of solace: A black feminist autoethnography. *Fashion Theory*, 23(6): 733–46.

Palmer, H. (2014), *Deleuze and Futurism: A Manifesto For Nonsense.* London: Bloomsbury.

Parkes, A. (2015), Reflexivity as autoethnography in indigenous research. In L. Bryant (ed.), *Critical and Creative Research Methodologies in Social Work*, 93–108. London: Routledge.

Parker, I. (2020), *Psychology Through Critical Auto-Ethnography: Academic Discipline, Professional Practice and Reflexive History.* Oxon: Routledge.

Parr, M. (2011), Venturing into the unknown of ethnography: Reflexive questions to love and cautionary ethics to live by. *Reflective Practice: International and Multidisciplinary Perspectives*, 12: 803–15.

Parry, K. W., and Boyle, M. (2009), Organizational autoethnography. In D. Buchanan and A. Bryman (eds), *Sage Handbook of Organizational Research Methods*, 690–702. London: Sage.

Pasque, P. A., and Salazar Pérez, M. (2015), Centering critical inquiry: Methodologies that facilitate critical qualitative research. In G. S. Cannella, M. Salazar Perez and P. A. Pasque (eds), *Critical Qualitative Inquiry: Foundations and Futures*, 139–70. Walnut Creek, CA: Left Coast Press.

Patton, M. Q. (2015), *Qualitative Research and Evaluation Methods* (4th edn). Thousand Oaks, CA: Sage.

Pelias, R. J. (2004), *A Methodology of the Heart: Evoking Academic and Daily Life.* Oxford: AltaMira Press.

Pelias, R. J. (2005), Performative writing as scholarship: An apology, an argument, an anecdote. *Cultural Studies ↔ Critical Methodologies*, 5(4): 415–24.

Pelias, R. J. (2019), *The Creative Qualitative Researcher: Writing That Makes Readers Want to Read.* Oxon: Routledge.

Pels, D. (2000), Reflexivity: One step up. *Theory, Culture and Society*, 17(3): 1–25.

Peters, J. E. (2020), *A Feminist Post-transsexual Autoethnography: Challenging Normative Gender Coercion.* New York: Routledge.

Pham, Minh-Ha T. (2011), Blog ambition: Fashion, feelings and the political economy of the digital raced body. *Camera Obscura: Feminism, Culture and Media Studies*, 26: 1–37.

Piacenti, D. J., Rivas, L. B. and Garrett, J. (2014), Facebook ethnography: The poststructural ontology of transnational (im)migration research. *International Journal of Qualitative Methods*, 13: 224–36.

Pillow, W. S. (2003), Confession, catharsis, or cure? Rethinking the uses of reflexivity as methodological power in qualitative research. *International Journal of Qualitative Studies in Education*, 16: 175–96.

Pillow, W. S. (2006), Teen pregnancy and education: Politics of knowledge, research and practice. *Educational Policy*, 20(1): 59–84.

Pillow, W. S. (2019), Epistemic witnessing: Theoretical responsibilities, decolonial attitude and lenticular futures. *International Journal of Qualitative Studies in Education*, 32(2): 118–35.

Pillow, W. S. (2020) Erotic power futures/relations that matter. *Departures in Critical Qualitative Research*, 1 May 2020, 9 (2): 40–52.

Pineau, E. (2012), Haunted by ghosts: Collaborating with absent others. *International Review of Qualitative Research*, 5(4): 459–65.

Plummer, K. (2001a), *Documents of Life 2: An Invitation to a Critical Humanism.* London: Sage.

Plummer, K. (2001b), The call of life stories in ethnographic research. In P. Atkinson, A. Coffey, S. Delamont, J. Lofland and L. Lofland (eds), *Handbook of Ethnography*, 395–406. Thousand Oaks, CA: Sage.

Polanyi, M. ([1958] 2005), *Personal Knowledge: Towards a Post-Critical Philosophy.* London: Routledge.

Polanyi, M. (1966), *The Tacit Dimension.* Garden City, NY: Doubleday.

Pole, C., and Morrison, M. (2003), *Ethnography for Education.* Berkshire: McGraw-Hill Education.

Polkinghorne, D. (1988), *Narrative Knowing and the Human Sciences.* Albany: State University of New York Press.

Polkinghorne, D. (1997), Reporting qualitative research as practice. In W. G. Tierney and Y. S. Lincoln (eds), *Representation and the Text*. Albany: State University of New York Press.

Popper, K. (1957), *The Poverty of Historicism*. London: Routledge.

Poulos, C. N. (2009), *Accidental Ethnography: An Inquiry Into Family Secrecy*. Walnut Creek, CA: Left Coast Press.

Poulos, C. N. (2020), The perils and the promises of autoethnography: Raising our voices in troubled times. *Journal of Autoethnography*, 1(2): 208–11.

Poulos, C. N. (2021), *Essentials of Autoethnography (Essentials of Qualitative Methods)*. Washington, DC: American Psychological Association.

Powell, J. A. (1996), The multiple self: Exploring between and beyond modernity and postmodernity. *Minnesota Law Review*, 81: 1481–520.

Powis, B. (2019), Soundscape elicitation and visually impaired cricket: Using auditory methodology in sport and physical activity research. *Qualitative Research in Sport, Exercise and Health*, 11(1): 35–45.

Prince, C. (2021). Experiments in methodology: Sensory and poetic threads of inquiry, resistance, and transformation. *Qualitative Inquiry*, 28(1): 94–107.

Puar, J. (2007), *Terrorist Assemblages: Homonationalism in Queer Times*. Durham, NC: Duke University Press.

Punch, K., and Oancea, A. (2014), *Research Methods in Education* (2nd edn). London: Sage.

Quantz, R. A., and O'Connor, T. W. (1988), Writing critical ethnography: Dialogue, multivoicedness and carnival texts. *Educational Theory*, 38: 95–109.

Racine, C. A. (2021), *Beyond Clinical Dehumanisation toward the Other in Community Mental Health Care: Levinas, Wonder and Autoethnography*. Oxon: Routledge.

Ramalho-de-Oliveira, D. (2020), Overview and prospect of autoethnography in pharmacy education and practice. *American Journal of Pharmaceutical Education*, 84(1): 7127.

Ravitch, S. M., and Riggan, M. (2017), *Reason and Rigor: How Conceptual Frameworks Guide Research*. Los Angeles: Sage.

Reed-Danahay, D. E. (1997), *Auto/Ethnography. Rewriting the Self and the Social*. Oxford: Berg.

Reed-Danahay, D. (2001) Ethnography. In M. Jolly (ed.), *Encyclopedia of Life Writing*. London: Fitzroy Dearborn.

Reid, A. M., Brown, J. M., Smith, J. M., Cope, A. C. and Jamieson, S. (2018), Ethical dilemmas and reflexivity in qualitative research. *Perspectives on Medical Education*, 7(2): 69–75.

Rhodes, C., and Carlsen, A. (2018), The teaching of the other: Ethical vulnerability and generous reciprocity in the research process. *Human Relations*, 71(10): 1295–318.

Richardson, L. (1997), *Fields of Play: Constructing an Academic Life*. New Brunswick: Rutgers University Press.

Richardson, L. (2000a), Writing: a method of inquiry. In N. K. Denzin and Y. S. Lincoln (eds), *Handbook of Qualitative Research* (2nd edn), 923–48. Thousand Oaks, CA: Sage.

Richardson, L. (2000b), Evaluating ethnography. *Qualitative Inquiry*, 6(2): 253–5.

Richardson, L. (2000c), New writing practices in qualitative research. *Sociology of Sport Journal*, 17(1): 5–20.

Richardson, L., and St Pierre, E. A. (2005), Writing: A method of inquiry. In N. K. Denzin and Y. S. Lincoln (eds), *Handbook of Qualitative Research* (3rd edn), 959–78. Thousand Oaks, CA: Sage.

Riessman, K. (2008), *Narrative Methods for the Human Sciences*. Thousand Oaks, CA: Sage.

Ringel, F. (2016), Beyond temporality: Notes on the anthropology of time from a shrinking field site. *Anthropological Theory*, 16(4): 390–412.

Robertson, C. J., Crittenden, W. F., Brady, M. K. James and J. Hoffman, J. J. (2002), Situational ethics across borders: A multicultural examination. *Journal of Business Ethics*, 38: 327–38.

Roessner, A., and Teresa, C. (2020), Always already hailed: Negotiating memory and identity at the Newseum. *Journal of Autoethnography*, 1(2): 156–74.

Ronai, C. R. (1995), Multiple reflections of child sex abuse: An argument for a layered account. *Journal of Contemporary Ethnography*, 23(4): 395–426.

Rorty, R. (1989), *Contingency, Irony and Solidarity*. Cambridge: Cambridge University Press.

Roth, W. (2009), Auto/ethnography and the question of ethics. *Forum Qualitative Sozialforschung/Forum: Qualitative Social Research*, 10(1): 1–10.

Roulet, T. J., Gill, M. J., Stenger, S. and Gill, D. J. (2017), Reconsidering the value of covert research: The role of ambiguous consent in participant observation. *Organizational Research Methods*, 20(3): 487–517.

Roulston, K. (2018), Qualitative interviewing and epistemics. *Qualitative Research*, 18(3): 322–41.

Roy, R., and Uekusa, S. (2020), Collaborative autoethnography: "Self-reflection" as a timely alternative research approach during the global pandemic. *Qualitative Research Journal*, 20(4): 383–92.

Said, E. ([1978] 1995), *Orientalism*. New Delhi: Penguin.

Saldana, J. (2021), *The Coding Manual for Qualitative Researchers* (4th edn). Los Angeles: Sage.

Salvo, J. (2019), *Reading Autoethnography*. New York: Routledge.

Samaras, A. P. (2011), *Self-study Teacher Research: Improving Your Practice Through Collaborative Inquiry*. Los Angeles: Sage.

Sambrook, S. and Herrmann, A. F. (2018), Organisational autoethnography: Possibilities, politics and pitfalls. *Journal of Organizational Ethnography*, 7(3): 222–34.

Sambrook, S. A., Jones, N. and Doloriert, C. (2014), Employee engagement and autoethnography: Being and studying self. *Journal of Workplace Learning*, 26(3/4): 172–87.

Sandelowski, M. (1995), Sample size in qualitative research. *Research in Nursing and Health*, 18: 179–83.

Sartre, J. P. ([1938] 2000), *Nausea*. London: Penguin Classics.

Scheurich, J. (1997), *Research Method in the Postmodern*. London: Routledge.

Scheller, V. K. (2020), Understanding, seeing and representing time in tempography. *Forum Qualitative Sozialforschung/Forum: Qualitative Social Research*, 21(2). Available online: https://www.qualitative–research.net/index.php/fqs/article/view/3481/4587 (accessed 28 July 2020).

Schmid, J. (2019), Autoethnography: Locating the self as standpoint in post-apartheid South Africa. In S. Laher, A. Fynn and S. Kramer (eds), *Transforming Research Methods in the Social Sciences: Case Studies from South Africa*, 265–79. Johannesburg: Wits University Press.

Schmidt, B. E., and Leonardi, J. (2020) (eds), *Spirituality and Wellbeing: Interdisciplinary Approaches to the Study of Religious Experience and Health*. Sheffield: Equinox.

Schulz Y. (2012), Time representations in social science. *Dialogues in Clinical Neuroscience*, 14(4): 441–7.

Schutz, A. (1953), Common-sense and scientific interpretation of human action. *Philosophy and Phenomenological Research*, 14(1): 1–38.

Scott, R. L. (1993), Dialectical tensions of speaking and silence. *Quarterly Journal of Speech*, 79(1): 1–18.

Scott-Hoy, K. (2002), The visitor: juggling life in the grip of the text. In A. P. Bochner and C. Ellis (eds), *Ethnographically Speaking: Autoethnography, Literature and Aesthetics*, 274–94. Walnut Creek, CA: AltaMira Press.

Seidel, J. V. (1998), Qualitative data analysis. *The Ethnograph v5.0: A Users Guide*. Colorado Springs: Qualis Research.

Sharma, S. (2014), *In the Meantime: Temporality and Cultural Politics*. Durham, NC: Duke University Press.

Short, N. P. (2010), Multiple selves, multiple voices and autoethnography. *Linguistic and Communicative Performance Journal*, 3(2): 31–54.

Sibley, D. (1995), *Geographies of Exclusion: Society and Difference in the West*. London: Routledge.

Siddique, S. (2016), Bhaji on the beach: Relational ethics in practice. In Q. Marak (ed.), *Doing Autoethnography*, 401–25. New Delhi: Serials.

Sidhu, R. (2018), A post-colonial autoethnography of transnational adoption. *British Journal of Social Work*, 48(8): 2176–94.

Sieber, J., and Tolich, M. (2013), *Planning Ethically Responsible Research*. Thousand Oaks, CA: Sage.

Sikes, P. (2015), *Ethical Considerations in Autoethnographic Research*. Available online: https://www.sheffield.ac.uk/polopoly_fs/1.586562!/file/SREGP–Autoethnography-2015.pdf (accessed 26 September 2020).

Silova, I., Rappleye, J. and You, Y. (2020) Beyond the western horizon in educational research: Toward a deeper dialogue about our interdependent futures. *ECNU Review of Education*, 3(1): 3–19.

Silverman, S. (2020), Comments on omissions and silences in ethnographic research. *Journal of Anthropological Research*, 76(1): 90–4.

Silverman, R. E. (2021), Autoethnography and memory/memorials of conflict and crisis. *Journal of Autoethnography*, 2(1): 75–7.

Simonova, O. (2019), Emotional culture as sociological concept: On emotional turn in understanding of modern society. *Culture e Studi del Sociale*, 4(2): 147–60.

Simons, H., and Usher, R. (2000), Introduction: Ethics in the practice of research. In H. Simons and R. Usher (eds), *Situated Ethics in Educational Research*, 1–11. London: Routledge/Falmer.

Snow, D. A., Morrill, C. and Anderson, L. (2003), Elaborating analytic ethnography: Linking fieldwork and theory. *Ethnography*, 4: 181–200.

Soja, W. (1996), *Thirdspace: Journeys to Los Angeles and Other Real-and-Imagined Places*. Oxford: Blackwell.

Sparkes, A. C. (2000), Autoethnography and narratives of self: Reflections on criteria in action. *Sociology of Sport Journal*, 17: 21–43.

Sparkes, A. C. (2002), Autoethnography: Self-indulgence or something more? In A. P. Bochner and C. Ellis (eds), *Ethnographically Speaking: Autoethnography, Literature and Aesthetic*, 209–32. Walnut Creek, CA: AltaMira Press.

Sparkes, A. C. (2013), Autoethnography at the will of the body: Reflections on a failure to produce on time. In N. P. Short, L. Turner and A. Grant (eds), *Contemporary British Autoethnography*, 203–11. Rotterdam: Sense.

Sparkes, A. C. (2020), Autoethnography: Accept, revise, reject? An evaluative self reflects. *Qualitative Research in Sport, Exercise and Health*, 12(2): 289–302.

Sparkes, A. C., and Smith, B. (2009), Judging the quality of qualitative inquiry: Criteriology and relativism in action. *Psychology of Sport and Exercise*, 10: 491–7.

Spencer, G. (2016), Schoolyard ethics: Getting close, blending in, keeping distance. In M. Tolich (ed.), *Qualitative Ethics in Practice*, 121–31. Walnut Creek, CA: Routledge.

Spivak, G. (1976), Translator's Preface. In J. Derrida (ed.), *Of Grammatology*, ix–xxxvii. Baltimore, MD: John Hopkins University Press.

Sprague, J. (2010), Seeing through science. In W. Luttrell (ed.), *Qualitative Educational Research: Readings in Reflexive Methodology and Transformative Practice*, 8–94. New York: Routledge.

Spry, T. (2001), Performing autoethnography: An embodied methodological praxis. *Qualitative Inquiry*, 7(6): 706–32.

Spry, T. (2011a), *Body, Paper, Stage: Writing and Performing Autoethnography*. Walnut Creek, CA: Left Coast Press.

Spry, T. (2011b), Performative autoethnography: Critical embodiment and possibilities. In N. K. Denzin and Y. S. Lincoln (eds), *The Sage Handbook of Qualitative Research* (4th edn), 497–512. Thousand Oaks, CA: Sage.

Spry, T. (2016), *Autoethnography and the Other: Unsettling Power through Utopian Performatives*. New York: Routledge.

Spry, T. (2018), Autoethnography and the Other: Performative embodiment and a bid for utopia. In N. K. Denzin and Y. S. Lincoln (eds), *The Sage Handbook of Qualitative Research* (5th edn), 627–49. Thousand Oaks, CA: Sage.

Stahlke Wall, S. (2016), Toward a moderate autoethnography. *International Journal of Qualitative Methods*. Available online: https://journals.sagepub.com/doi/full/10.1177/1609406916674966 (accessed 2 June 2020).

Stanley, P. and G. Vass (eds) (2018), *Questions of Culture in Autoethnography*. Abingdon: Routledge.

Stanley, P. (ed.) (2020), *Critical Autoethnography and Intercultural Learning: Emerging Voices*. Oxon: Routledge.

Starr, L. J. (2010), The use of autoethnography in educational research: Locating who we are in what we do. *Canadian Journal for New Scholars in Education*, 3(1): 1–9.

St. Pierre, E. A. (1997), Methodology in the fold and the irruption of transgressive data. *International Journal of Qualitative Studies in Education*, 10(2): 175–89.

St. Pierre, E. A. (2000), The call for intelligibility in postmodern educational research. *Educational Researcher*, 29(5): 25–8.

St. Pierre, E. A. (2008), Decentering voice in qualitative inquiry. *International Review of Qualitative Research*, 1(3): 319–36.

St. Pierre, E. A. (2009), Afterword: Decentering voice in qualitative inquiry. In A. Y. Jackson and L. A. Mazzei (eds), *Voice in Qualitative Inquiry*, 221–36. London: Routledge.

St. Pierre, E. A., and Jackson, A. Y. (2014), Qualitative data analysis after coding. *Qualitative Inquiry*, 20(6): 715–19.

Sternberg, R. J. (1985), Implicit theories of intelligence, creativity and wisdom. *Journal of Personality and Social Psychology*, 49: 607–27.

Subreenduth, S. and Rhee, J. (2010), A porous, morphing and circulatory mode of self-other: Decolonizing identity politics by engaging transnational reflexivity. *International Journal of Qualitative Studies in Education*, 23: 331–46.

Sughrua, W. M. (2019), A nomenclature for critical autoethnography in the arena of disciplinary atomization. *Cultural Studies ↔ Critical Methodologies*, 19(6): 429–65.

Szwabowski, O. (2019). Forget all criteria. *International Review of Qualitative Research*, 12(4): 476–81.

Taber, N. (2010), Institutional ethnography, autoethnography and narrative: An argument for incorporating multiple methodologies. *Qualitative Research*, 10(5): 5–25.

Taft-Kaufman, J. (2000), Critical claims, critical functions: Autoethnography and postscholarship. *American Communication Journal*, 4(1). Available online: http://acjournal.org/journal/vol4/iss1/special/taft.htm (accessed 12 October 2020).

Tamminen, K. A., Bundon, A., Smith, B., McDonough, M. H., Poucher, Z. A. and Atkinson, M. (2021), Considerations for making informed choices about engaging in open qualitative research, *Qualitative Research in Sport, Exercise and Health*. Available online: https://www.tandfonline.com/doi/full/10.1080/21596 76X.2021.1901138 (accessed 29 March 2021).

Tarnas, R. (1991), *The Passion of the Western Mind: Understanding The Ideas That Have Shaped Our World View*. New York: Ballantine Books.

Tedlock, D. (1983), *The Spoken Word and the Work of Interpretation*. Philadelphia: University of Pennsylvania Press.

Tedlock, B. (2013), Braiding evocative with analytic autoethnography. In S. Holman Jones, T. E. Adams and C. Ellis (eds), *Handbook of Autoethnography*, 358–62. Walnut Creek, CA: Left Coast Press.

Thomas, J. (1993), *Doing Critical Ethnography*. London: Sage.

Tillmann, L., Norsworthy, K. and Schoen, S. (2022). *Mindful Activism: Autoethnographies of Social Justice Communication for Campus and Community Transformation (Routledge Social Justice Communication Activism Series)*. New York: Routledge.

Tlostanova M. (2017), Postsocialist/Postcolonial Tempo-Localities. In M. Tlostanova, *Postcolonialism and Postsocialism in Fiction and Art*, 25–45. London: Palgrave Macmillan.

Tobin, J. (1989), Visual anthropology and multivocal ethnography: A dialogical approach to Japanese preschool class size. *Dialectical Anthropology*, 13: 173–87.

Tolich, M. (2010), A critique of current practice: Ten foundational guidelines for autoethnographers. *Qualitative Health Research*, 20(12): 1599–610.

Tolstoy, L. N. ([1869] 1960), *War and Peace* (in Russian), vols 1–2. Moscow: State Art Literature.

Tomaselli, K., Dyll, L. and Francis, M. (2008), 'Self' and 'other': Auto-reflexive and indigenous ethnography. In N. K. Denzin, Y. S. Lincoln and L. T. Smith (eds), *Handbook of Critical and Indigenous Methodologies*, 347–72. Thousand Oaks, CA: Sage.

Trahar, S. W. (2006), *Narrative Research on Learning: Comparative and International Perspectives*. Oxford: Symposium Books.

Trahar, S. W. (2009), Beyond the story itself: Narrative inquiry and autoethnography in intercultural research in higher education. *Forum Qualitative Sozialforschung/ Forum: Qualitative Social Research*, 10(1). Available online: http://nbn–resolving.de/ urn:nbn:de:0114–fqs0901308 (accessed 13 May 2020).

Trouillot, M. R. (1995), *Silencing the Past: Power and the Production of History*. Boston: Beacon Press.

Tuhiwai Smith, L. (1999), *Decolonizing Methodologies: Research and Indigenous People*. London: Zed Books.

Tullis, J. A. (2013), Self and others: Ethics in autoethnographic research. In S. Holman Jones, T. E. Adams and C. Ellis (eds), *Handbook of Autoethnography*, 244–61. Walnut Creek, CA: Left Coast Press.

Turner, B. S. (2009), The sociology of the body. In B. S. Turner (ed.), *The New Blackwell Companion to Social Theory*, 513–32. Oxford: Wiley-Blackwell.

Turner, L. (2013), The evocative autoethnographic I. In N. P. Short, L. Turner and A. Grant (eds), *Contemporary British Autoethnography*, 213–30. Rotterdam: Sense.

Tutenel, P., Ramaekers, S. and Heylighen, A. (2019), Conversations between procedural and situated ethics: Learning from video research with children in a cancer care ward. *Design Journal*, 22(1): 641–54.

Van Manen, M. (1990), *Researching Lived Experience: Human Science for an Action Sensitive Pedagogy*. Albany: State University of New York Press.

Van Maanen, J. (2011), *Tales from of the Field: On Writing Ethnography* (2nd edn). Chicago: University of Chicago Press.

Van Wolputte, S. (2004), Hang on to your self: Of bodies, embodiment and selves. *Annual Review of Anthropology*, 33: 251–69.

Varga, S., and Guignon, C. (2014), Authenticity. *Stanford Encyclopaedia of Philosophy*. Available online: https://plato.stanford.edu/entries/authenticity/ (accessed 12 March 2021).

Vasari, G., and Hemsoll, D. (2006), *The Life of Michelangelo*. London: Pallas Athene.

Vass, G. (2017), Getting inside the insider researcher: Does race-symmetry help or hinder research? *International Journal of Research and Method in Education*, 40(2): 137–53.

Visweswaran, K. (1994), *Fictions of Feminist Ethnography*. Minneapolis: University of Minnesota Press.

Vryan, K. D. (2006), Expanding analytic autoethnography and enhancing its potential. *Journal of Contemporary Ethnography*, 35(4): 405–9.

Walford, G. (2004), Finding the limits: Autoethnography and being an Oxford University proctor. *Qualitative Research*, 4: 403–17.

Walford, G. (2021), What is worthwhile auto-ethnography? Research in the age of the selfie. *Ethnography and Education*, 16(1): 31–43.

Walker, R. (1991), Making sense and losing meaning. In I. Goodson and R. Walker (eds), *Biography, Identity and Schooling: Episodes in Educational Research*, 107–13. Bristol: Falmer Press.

Wall, S. (2006), An autoethnography on learning about autoethnography. *International Journal of Qualitative Methods*, June 2006: 146–60.

Wall, S. (2008), Easier said than done: Writing an autoethnography. *International Journal of Qualitative Methods*, March 2008: 38–53.

Warren, W. P. (1935), Frames of reference in philosophy. *Philosophical Review*, 44(2): 182–8.

Weedon, C. (1987), *Feminist Practice and Poststructuralist Theory*. Oxford: Blackwell.

Werner, K. (2017), Autoethnography as a way of being (radiophonic). *International Review of Qualitative Research*, 10(1): 97–100.

Whitinui, P. (2014), Indigenous autoethnography: Exploring, engaging and experiencing 'self' as a native method of inquiry. *Journal of Contemporary Ethnography*, 43(4): 456–87.

Wiley, C. (2019), Autoethnography, autobiography and creative art as academic research in music studies: a fugal ethnodrama. *Action, Criticism and Theory for Music Education*, 18(2): 73–115.

Williams, E. L. (2021), Black girl abroad: An autoethnography of travel and the need to cite black women in anthropology. *Feminist Anthropology*, 2: 143–54.

Williams, S. J., and Bendelow, G. A. (1998), Emotions and 'sociological imperialism': A rejoinder to Craib. *Sociology*, 30: 145–53.

Winkler, I. (2018a), Identity work and emotions: A review. *International Journal of Management Reviews*, 20(1): 120–33.

Winkler, I. (2018b), Doing autoethnography: Facing challenges, taking choices, accepting responsibilities. *Qualitative Inquiry*, 24(4): 236–47.

Wyatt, J. (2006), Psychic distance, consent and other ethical issues: Reflections on the writing of 'a gentle going?' *Qualitative Inquiry*, 12(4): 813–18.

Wyatt, J. (2020), Encountering autoethnography: Of fragments and drawing blood. *Journal of Autoethnography*, 1(1): 60–3.

Yavas, G. (2015), 'Western-Centrism' as 'Particularism' in Neorealist Theory. *Kastamonu University Journal of Economics and Administrative Sciences Faculty*, 7: 64–74.

Zeeman, L., Poggenpoel, M., Myburgh, C. P. H. and Van der Linde, N. (2002), An introduction to a postmodern approach to educational research: Discourse analysis. *Education*, 123(1): 96–102.

Zeichner, K. (1995), Reflections of a teacher educator working for social change. In T. Russell and F. Korthagen (eds), *Teachers Who Teach Teachers*, 11–24. London: Routledge.

Zeichner, K. M. (1999), The new scholarship in teacher education. *Educational Researcher*, 28(9): 4–15.

Zimbardo, P. G., and, Boyd, J. N. (2008), *The Time Paradox: The New Psychology of Time That Will Change Your Life*. New York: Free Press.

Index